A HERO'S CURSE

KAJSA NORMAN

A Hero's Curse

The Perpetual Liberation of Venezuela

HURST & COMPANY, LONDON

First published in Swedish in 2015 by
Silc förlag as Den som tröttnar förlorar: Kampen om Venezuela.

First published in the United Kingdom in 2017 by
C. Hurst & Co. (Publishers) Ltd.,
41 Great Russell Street, London, WC1B 3PL

Printed in India

Distributed in the United States, Canada and Latin America by
Oxford University Press, 198 Madison Avenue, New York, NY 10016,
United States of America

A Cataloguing-in-Publication data record for this book
is available from the British Library.

ISBN: 9781849047951

This book is printed using paper from registered sustainable
and managed sources.

www.hurstpublishers.com

CONTENTS

"The hero of yesterday becomes the tyrant of tomorrow, unless he crucifies himself today."

Joseph Campbell, *The Hero With A Thousand Faces*

PROLOGUE

It is November 2013. A stray dog urinates on the empty dance floor of Flamboyant Beach Club, overlooking the Playa El Agua on the tropical Island of Margarita.

The beach used to be the main draw for large numbers of foreign tourists. Today, it is practically deserted. Granted, it's Monday and it's the end of November, a few days before the high season. But years ago, that didn't matter.

Two hungry beach vendors circle my friend Rita and I like sharks. They introduce themselves as Fernando and Angel.

"But people call me *el conquistador del Mercosur*, because of my success with the ladies. Where are you from?" asks Angel.

"Sweden"

"Aaaah, it's been a long time since I met Swedish ladies here," says Fernando, who has worked the beach as a vendor for thirteen years.

"Before, this place used to be packed, like the beaches of Europe. But about seven years ago tourists stopped coming. Now we only get the odd couple from Brazil or Colombia, and a few Russians."

We walk along the beach past the rows of deserted restaurants and small businesses barred shut. A concession stand owner tells me he didn't sell a single bottle of Coke this past weekend.

Although he just bought his little place six months ago, he is already contemplating selling. If he can.

It feels eerily abandoned. We pass one dilapidated structure after another; walls crumbling, plants growing inside houses, nature slowly moving in to reclaim its territory.

"What happened?" I ask Fernando.

He's quiet for a moment, fiddling with a long Rasta braid. Then he looks at me and answers simply:

"Politics."

* * *

In Caracas, endless rows of American-style SUVs stand still, stuck in the regular traffic jam that marks much of the day. In the shadows of shimmering skyscrapers, surgically enhanced women parade the streets shopping. It's the national pastime. It seems more reminiscent of Texas than a country in the midst of a socialist revolution.

I arrive in Venezuela at the outbreak of "the war" against the "bourgeoisie parasites." In a televised speech, President Nicolás Maduro orders the national guard to occupy the stores of the electronics chain Daka and lower their prices—by force.

"A small, modest air condition unit, 36,000 bolívares. Please! That's the bourgeoisie when they feel powerful. They abuse the poor and the people. They are selfish, petty egoists, thieves and anti-Christians. They take from the poor to enrich themselves ... I want to inform the people of Venezuela that the managers of this company have been detained by the national intelligence service and will be placed before the prosecution. And the owners of this company will have to pay for this robbery against the people. It's over. Enough abuse of the people!" Maduro thunders.

It is time to launch an "economic defensive" to win the war being waged against the people, he explains.

"Nothing should be left on the shelves!"

Mobs rush the stores, hauling away televisions and other appliances past the queues that snake around the block. Old ladies stumble under the weight of stacked microwaves, blenders, and air-conditioning units, sometimes taking two or three of the same item. People leaving the stores approach the queue offering their booty at hefty mark-ups. Meanwhile, those near the front of the queue try hawking their places to others arriving late. While socialism may be driving the bargains, in the masses here there is nothing but capitalism. Salvage capitalism.

In Valencia, dozens of looters are caught on video surveillance as they flee Daka electronics with their arms full of stolen television sets and appliances. Even soldiers join the fray, helping themselves to flat screens.

Within hours, most electronics stores are completely cleaned out. Soon, the whole country is "on sale." What started as an offensive against electronics stores spreads to a wide range of merchandise, including food, clothes, footwear, hardware, vehicles, and toys.

Some stores limit the number of items each customer can purchase. Others limit the number of customers allowed in the store at any one time. Some lower iron bars over their entrances, leaving only a gap at the bottom for people to crawl in.

In an effort to contain the chaos, Maduro takes to the airwaves to reassure people that it is not a sale but a permanent decrease in prices. But nothing appears to constrain the shoppers' madness. The queues persist. Everyone wants their turn, for they instinctively understand that once the goods are gone, these stores will never open again.

Maduro supporters claim that the merchants deserve their fate. Many have received US currency to purchase their imports at preferential, state-regulated rates. Therefore, by their logic, these are the people's goods.

Critics argue that regardless of the acquisition cost, the merchandise belongs to the storeowners. Forcing them to sell at prices they didn't set is the equivalent of theft. Meanwhile, inflation climbs to 54 percent, putting Venezuela in the top three worldwide, ahead of Syria. Toilet paper, milk, and other basic food items are nearly impossible to find. Venezuela now imports 70 percent of its food.

"Wait until you see people fighting over the last roll of toilet paper," I'm told.

I never do. When I manage to time a delivery of groceries at a Caracas Bicentenario store, the militia arrives to maintain the order. And they need to. When demand for essential goods exceeds supply in a country plagued by violence, things can quickly get out of hand. In 2013, Venezuela was branded the most dangerous country in Latin America, with its murder rate amongst the highest in the world.[1]

Yet the country has all the prerequisites for wealth. Venezuela is the world's fifth largest oil-exporting country and has the world's largest proven oil reserves (an estimated 296.5 billion barrels). For decades, Venezuelans have paid next to nothing for their gas. Consequently, traffic is virtually unnavigable. In this land of salvage entrepreneurs, those who live near Colombia or Brazil haul canisters of gas and subsidized food to the border where they can sell it for substantial profits.

As much as socialism may be the popular philosophy, capitalism is the popular practice. And almost everyone is fighting—either fighting to get ahead in a system built to encourage loyalty over merit, or fighting the system in its entirety.

This book is the story of Venezuela told through the experiences of five people, each fighting for their own vision of the country. There is Folco Riccio, the architect who dreams of social and economic development; María Corina Machado, the steel heiress turned politician, determined to leave her mark on history; Antonio Rivero, the general constantly challenging those in power; Juan Carlos Requesens, the student leader struggling to walk the line between violence and influence; and of course Hugo Chávez Frías, the father, the son, and the ghost, inspiring his loyal followers onward in their efforts to remain relevant.

The book is based on in-depth interviews with four of the protagonists, conducted between November 2013 and March 2015. A selection of their colleagues, friends, and relatives, as well as a number of subject-matter experts, provided additional background information.

The chapters about Hugo Chávez are based on the references listed in the bibliography, interviews with his former colleagues and friends, as well as his many televised broadcasts and speeches.

Each of the protagonists follows their own hero's journey, heeds their own call to purpose, and fights their own demons. Together, their life stories tell the tale of a beautiful, bountiful country torn apart by competing dreams and uncompromising dreamers.

1

ORIGINS

"There is at the head of this great continent a very powerful country, very rich, very warlike, and capable of anything."

Simón Bolívar

I

It is July 24, 1783. In an aristocratic home near Plaza de San Jacinto in central Caracas, a baby boy is born. His name is Simón Bolívar and he will go on to free Venezuela and its neighbors from Spanish colonialism, forever changing the destiny of the land and its people. Cities, states, plazas, streets, currencies, constitutions, revolutions, and entire countries will be named after him. In his name, much will be created, and much destroyed. His life and deeds, shrouded in romance, will inspire successive generations in their own quest for glory.

Bolívar's early life is marked by tragedy. He loses his father at the age of three and his mother at the age of nine. Entrusted to his uncle, whom he doesn't much care for, Bolívar is sent to Spain to complete his education at the age of sixteen. There he develops a close relationship with his tutor Simón Rodríguez who introduces him to the thoughts and ideas of Enlightenment philosophers such as Voltaire, Montesquieu, and Rousseau.

Witnessing the rise of Napoleon, Bolívar realizes one man can change the course of history. He too wants to leave his mark on his nation and the world. In 1805, during a visit to Rome, Bolívar makes his irrevocable decision to devote his life to the liberation of Venezuela. At the top of Monte Sacro, he grasps the hand of his friend Rodríguez, kneels, and swears to free his homeland: "I will not rest until I have rid it of every last one of those bastards!"[1]

* * *

Although the region that will become modern-day Venezuela is discovered by Christopher Columbus in 1498, Spain doesn't begin colonizing it until the second half of the sixteenth century. At first, the legend of El Dorado (Spanish for the golden one) is the main draw for European explorers and adventurers. This mysterious Indian ruler supposedly covers his naked body in gold dust and orders his subjects to throw jewels and golden objects into a lake during ceremonies and festivities. The gilded chief is never found, but tales of El Dorado amplify until the name comes to be associated with an entire empire made of gold. The quest for El Dorado, and other mythical cities of great fortune, accelerates the exploration and conquest of much of the Americas. But unlike the Aztec and Inca empires of modern-day Mexico and Peru, Venezuela's riches will remain undiscovered for four more centuries.

By 1600, the Spanish have developed twenty settlements across the Venezuelan Andes and Caribbean coast. In 1657, they inaugurate Caracas. Agriculture and stock-raising on the grassy *llanos* (plains) dominate the economy of the colony where the bulk of the manual labor is performed by indigenous and imported African slaves.

Royal Spanish bureaucrats rule colonial Venezuela, but white descendants of Europeans born in the Americas—known as Creoles—also have significant influence. Some, like Bolívar's family, are wealthy landowners, unlike the mestizos (persons of mixed European and Indian ancestry) and mulattoes (of European and African ancestry) who typically lack property and influence.

In his romantic masterpiece *Venezuela Heroica*, published in the late 1800s, Eduardo Blanco describes the atmosphere of the times:

> Like dust, people lived struck to the ground; there were no hurricanes to stir them up.
>
> Silence and quietude were our compulsory badges. Deprived of our rights, we did not exist for the world.
>
> Only the thunder that roared above our heads and the mysterious convulsions that shook the earth beneath our feet, troubled us in spite of the Spanish Crown, daring to act against the silence and sleepy rest of the Colony.[2]

* * *

The year 1808 marks the beginning of the Latin American independence movement. Despite the wealth and comfort they enjoy, Creoles are still considered second-class citizens, barred from the government's most powerful positions. When news of Napoleon's invasion of Spain reaches Spanish America, the colonies see their chance to forge change. Some of the Creoles simply want more rights and influence. They argue for a junta that would declare its continued loyalty to King Ferdinand. Others, like Bolívar, want true liberty, without compromise, declaring loyalty to no king. Meanwhile, the non-white majority fears either option. Without the supervision of Spain, they worry about increased brutality from the Creole landowners for whom they work. Despite their differences however, the factions agree on one thing: they will not be ruled by Napoleon.

On April 19, 1810, a junta takes control of Caracas. By the end of the year, the colonies of Buenos Aires, Bogotá, Quito, and Mexico all declare autonomous juntas, loyal to King Ferdinand. All, except for Lima, oust their Spanish garrisons. Hoping for military backing and international recognition, the junta of Caracas sends diplomatic missions to various countries.

Although Bolívar favored a clean break with Spain, he offers the new junta leaders his services. Still inexperienced and known for his uncompromising views, Bolívar is at first met with suspicion. But when he offers to bear the costs for the diplomatic mission to London, the leaders accept his services and give him the rank of colonel to increase his prestige. With former Caracas mayor Luis López Méndez and Andrés Bello as his chaperones, Bolívar sets off for England.

In London, the delegation meets with Britain's Foreign Minister Lord Wellesley. Bolívar has been instructed to profess loyalty to King Ferdinand VII and to make no mention of independence. But his passion overcomes him and he delivers a fervent speech for self-determination. Certainly, they could do a better job of ruling than Spain's war-torn offices or imprisoned king. The response is cold. England and Spain are allies against France, and Lord Wellesley is neither prepared to sanction nor sponsor the colony's desire for independence.

* * *

It is July of 1811 and the Caracas junta is in turmoil. Agents of the Spanish crown have infiltrated its ranks and now one of them has eloped with the War Department's plans. There is uproar. Why should Venezuelans continue to pledge loyalty to a king who sends spies to steal documents? Heated debates ensue and on the night of July 4, Bolívar delivers another impassioned speech, arguing that the time for total sovereignty has come: "Let us valiantly lay the cornerstone of South American liberty! To hesitate is to perish!"[3]

The following day, on July 5, 1811, the national assembly declares Venezuela independent.

The new republic, however, is far from egalitarian. Congress favors a federation of states that entrench old ruling factions and a constitution that ensures that all power remains in the hands of rich whites. Royalists and Spanish loyalists take advantage of the popular discontent that follows. Slaves who have been cheated of their promised freedom rise up and slaughter their Creole masters. Within a year of independence, Spain regains control.

Bolívar escapes to Cartagena in New Granada where the revolution is still alive, but in turmoil. A number of independent governments are at odds over how to win freedom and who should govern. The city of Cartagena has established its own constitution, opposing that of Bogotá and Tunja. Hoping to convince the Granadans that their struggle is intimately tied to Venezuela's, that all South Americans are linked by a common past and a common destiny, Bolívar decides to join the chaos. He is welcomed by Manuel Rodríguez Torices, president of Cartagena, who needs help, both against the Spaniards and against rivals within his own ranks. Suspicious of Bolívar, Torices' general, Pedro Labatut, assigns him to the remote outpost of Barrancabermeja on the banks of the Magdalena River. There, Bolívar begins to recruit tribesmen, runaway slaves, and unemployed peasants to swell his ranks. Blatantly ignoring the orders of General Labatut, he then launches a bold campaign to purge the area of all Spanish troops. He manages to surprise and overwhelm every Spanish fort and outpost along the 500-kilometer long stretch of river, gathering ammunition and equipment, as well as fresh recruits along the way. General Labatut tries to have him court-martialed for insubordination, but President Torices, grateful to Bolívar for having opened nearly 300 miles of the region's main shipping route and freeing the plains to its west, overrules him.[4]

Meanwhile, in Venezuela, the Spanish Commander General Juan Domingo de Monteverde unleashes a wave of terror by encouraging his officers to let their bloodlust reign free; the plains surrounding Caracas become the setting for killing, burning, looting, and torment. Soldiers wear human trophies as decorations and nail body parts to patriots' doors. Twelve thousand Creoles are brutally slaughtered. Then, General Monteverde decides to invade New Granada.[5]

President Torices asks Bolívar to join Colonel Manuel del Castillo in his march against the Spanish in Cúcuta, Colombia. Knowing his numbers to be vastly inferior to those of the Spaniards, Bolívar decides to send a messenger with a false letter claiming that Castillo and his forces are advancing from Pamplona. The messenger is captured, the letter confiscated, and the Spanish general takes the bait. He abandons the pass, enabling Bolívar to attack his rear and inflict crucial losses. Bolívar then joins Castillo and together they defeat the Spaniards at Cúcuta. Shortly thereafter, New Granada proclaims its independence from Spain. President Torices promotes Bolívar to brigadier general, awards him the title of honorary citizen, and grants Bolívar's fervent wish to march his men into Venezuela.

Eager to free his homeland, Bolívar has masked the true condition of his troops. His army is small and his soldiers malnourished and worn. They seem destined for certain defeat. But Bolívar's reputation precedes him, and by the time he arrives, the Spaniards have already fled the city. When Bolívar and his army descend the Andes and enter Mérida, he is greeted as a liberator.

On June 14, Bolívar's army frees the province of Trujillo. Again, he is able to trick the Spaniards into believing that his troops are much more numerous and fierce than they really are. The Spaniards flee.

On August 6, 1813, Bolívar enters Caracas. He is hailed as a hero and assumes dictatorial powers. Only eight months previously, he set out with fewer than 500 men. Now he has defeated the Spanish army. A great fan of Julius Caesar, he arranges for a similar entrance to the city as that of Caesar's to Rome. But instead of white horses, young, beautiful girls dressed in white meet him at the gates of Caracas.

While commanders of other Venezuelan cities insist on separate states, Bolívar is adamant that this new republic, later known as the second republic, should be ruled as one. Fragmentation caused the fall of the first republic, he argues. Venezuela should have only one head of state—himself. And it should unite with New Granada to create a nation that inspires respect. It is the first glimpse of his authoritarian streak.

But there is little time to develop his train of thought. Spain has not given up. And they now have the support of many black locals who continue to distrust the white-led revolution. The battles grow increasingly brutal. Rough-riding *llaneros* (the Venezuelan equivalent of cowboys) declare their loyalty to Spain and begin terrorizing the plains, eager to raid the rich and massacre Creoles. As their ranks are fed by a seemingly endless supply of discontented blacks, Indians, and mixed-raced, the revolution soon turns into a racial conflict; a civil war. Under the lead of the infamously sadistic Spaniard José Tomás Boves, forces loyal to Spain manage to retake Caracas and other cities in 1814, ending the second Venezuelan republic.

After a crushing defeat at Aragua, Bolívar is forced into exile. Contemplating his failure from the distant shores of Jamaica, he realizes he must win over the blacks.

By 1815, Spain has significantly reinforced its military presence in its rebellious colony. Failing to get assistance elsewhere, Bolívar turns to Haiti for help. Haiti has recently liberated itself from France and agrees to provide Bolívar with money and weapons, on the condition that he promises to end slavery. With a fleet supplied by Haiti, Bolívar sets sail once again for Venezuela.

In Carúpano on June 2, 1816, Bolívar declares absolute freedom for Spanish America's slaves. "I have come to decree, as law," he announces, "full liberty to all slaves who have trembled under the Spanish yoke for three centuries." He then pressures them to join his revolution. It is a calculated risk. Freeing the slaves could cost him the support of his fellow Creoles who depend on slave labor in their fields, but Bolívar is now convinced that the revolution faces certain defeat without the support of the blacks.

Bolívar also manages to recruit substantial numbers of British mercenaries. After the Battle of Waterloo, British soldiers are returning home to unemployment and poverty. Bolívar's London agent López Méndez enlists whole regiments of experienced war veterans who used to fight alongside Spain against the French.

In 1817, Bolívar sets up headquarters in the Orinoco River region and makes Angostura (now Ciudad Bolívar) his capital. He allies himself with the revolutionary forces of the plains, including one group led by José Antonio Páez and another group led by Francisco de Paula Santander.

Drafting strategies, writing persuasive letters and manifestos, he continues to work toward his vision of a united South America. "Unity, unity, unity must be our motto!" he reiterates time and time again. He also engages in numerous battles across the region. To keep the revolutionary spirit alive, he brings a printing press with him on all military campaigns and into battle. It is obviously an inconvenient burden to haul around and the Spaniards mock him for it, but Bolívar regards it as an essential weapon in the battle for hearts and minds.

In 1819, after years of small, indecisive victories and losses, Bolívar conceives of a daring, but brilliant move.

On May 23, Bolívar calls his officers to a council of war in the deserted little village of Setenta. There, he lets them in on his plan to take his army across the Andean mountain range at the hazardous pass of Pisba in order to surprise the enemy on the Granadan side.

The rain period has started, slowly turning rivers into seas, submerging valleys, and covering the Andes with ice, making the *cordillera* virtually impassable. It is such an audacious undertaking that, fearing desertions, Bolívar doesn't tell the troops until a few days into the march. More than 2,000 soldiers, accompanied by their women, children, and cattle, are more or less tricked into performing one of the most remarkable feats in military history. Weighted down by mud, forced to wade or swim through waist-high water, the expedition makes its way across flooded fields. Using cowhides and blankets, they do their best to keep weapons and equipment dry. The weak are soon sick, and the sick soon gone. Mosquitoes, sand flies, and flesh-eating fish assault them. Then comes the ascent up the 13,000 feet of unforgiving slopes across the Pisba passage itself. The air is thin and the constant rain punishing, growing chillier the higher they climb. A sheet of ice soon covers the rocky paths, making passing hazardous and difficult. The expedition leaves behind a trail of cadavers as a third of the soldiers and all of the horses perish to frost and starvation.

On July 6, those who have survived begin their descent down the other side of the mountain. They are weak and famished, but as the Spaniards have dismissed the passage of Pisba as an impossible route, there are no enemies waiting to fight them. They can rest, eat, and recruit fresh volunteers to reinforce their attack.

On August 7, 1819, after just two hours of fighting, the bulk of the Spanish army surrenders at the Battle of Boyacá. 200 dead Spaniards lay scattered in the open meadow when the rest decide to lay down their arms. More than 1,600 Spanish soldiers are taken prisoner that day. The road to Bogotá is now open.

Three days later, Bolívar enters the capital, bare-chested, galloping on his faithful white horse, Palomo, with his long wild hair flowing in the wind. The Spaniards, terrified by Bolívar's sudden appearance on this side of the *cordillera* and his vow of "war to the death," flee with little more than the clothes on their backs.

On September 18, the official victory celebration takes place. Again, the most beautiful young ladies of Bogotá come out dressed in all whites and covered in flowers. In a sweeping, seventy-five day motion, Bolívar has pulled off an improvised crossing of the most perilous part of the Andes, crushed an army, captured a capital, and conquered a country, paving the way for the final liberation of much of Spanish America.

Within the course of a few weeks, he establishes the basics of government: a supreme court, a system of governors and ministers, and a police force. Bolívar then appoints Santander as vice president, leaving him to take care of the mundane business of government while Bolívar starts to make his way back to Venezuela. En route, he enlists fresh troops, raises money for weapons, and greets the adoring crowds.

On December 11, 1819, Bolívar arrives back in Angostura. Three days later, he addresses the members of Congress, arguing for his lifelong dream: the union of Venezuela and New Granada, a new American nation that would stretch across the continent from sea to sea. The world will never recognize the independence of the former Spanish colonies unless they speak with one voice, he argues. On December 17, the new nation of Gran Colombia is created. Its territory includes modern-day Colombia, Panama, Venezuela, and Ecuador. Bolívar is named president, liberator, and military dictator. On paper, his dream of a united South America free from Spanish oppression has come true, but it will take another few years to expel all the Spanish forces from the region.

On June 24, 1821, the decisive battle for the freedom of Venezuela takes place on the Carabobo savanna west of Caracas. The night before the battle, torrential rains drench the plains and all the soldiers who camp on it. The British who fought against Napoleon say it is a good omen; the same happened before Waterloo. As the rain subsides, giving way to bright blue sky, Bolívar and his army of about 6,500 patriots, including 600

British volunteers, get ready to face the Spanish royalists, confident that they will prevail.

At the southern end of the Valencia valley, the plains of Carabobo are wedged between forests and hills. The Spanish royalists occupy the field and the hills that protect it. This means that Bolívar and his men have to fight their way on to the battlefield before being able to join the battle itself. The access points are narrow and heavily defended, and as they battle to enter, Bolívar's army is taking heavy losses.

His battalion "Apure" is forced to retreat and is about to disintegrate, when the British Legion comes to its rescue. In the words of Eduardo Blanco:

> That brilliant regiment, with beating drums and flags unfurled, enters the battle with the severe mien and the impassive temperament of its race; erect, calm, correct in its attitude and movements, it marches shoulder to shoulder to the accompaniment of fifes and drum heads, under frightening volleys of fire, without giving an inch or firing a shot, until they form their battle line and Ashdown, their standard bearer, plants the tricolor flag in front of the enemy battalions. The whole fury of the royalists pours then on the "Legión Británica," which becomes the center of the battle, the target of all the shots fired in that storm. ...
>
> Bullets hit and kill many of the heroic soldiers; its lines grow thinner; entire segments of their battle line fall down, and like a building that crumbles bit by bit, their rubble grows and piles up at the base of the foundation. Nevertheless, the English regiment, like an erupting volcano, spews torrents and mouthfuls of fire. ...
>
> With a front line of four hundred soldiers and only two men deep, "Apure," "Tiradores," and the "Legión Británica" advance simultaneously, with fixed bayonets, on the Spanish regiments commanded by La Torre: a brilliant charge, before whose thrust the royalists give in, lose their positions, and without much firing on our lines, retreat looking for support among the bulk of their cavalry.[6]

Blanco then recounts how the cavalries of both sides clash in a dense cloud of smoke and dust, engulfing the battling squadrons:

> Suddenly, amidst the restive expectation that grips both sides, the flying flame stops, and Páez, overcome by wonder, spies coming from the cloud of dust that hides the outcome of that violent clash, a rider bathed in his own blood, whom he recognizes at once as the Black man most vigorous among the *llaneros* of his guard, he whom the entire army honors with the nickname, *The First*.
>
> The horse ridden by that intrepid soldier gallops haphazardly to the spot where Páez stands; it drops from gallop to trot and then to walk, step by step, with the reins loose upon its vanquished neck, the head abated, and the nostrils flaring, brushing the ground that reddens on contact with it, shaking its heavy rider who appears to balance himself instinctively upon the saddle. ... The horse, incapable of taking one more step, folds its knees before falling; the rider opens wide his eyes that flame like red-hot embers, rises erect on the saddle, throws to the ground the powerful lance, breaks with both hands the bloody hussars jacket, and uncovering his chest on which two deep wounds spurt blood, exclaims stammering, "My General ... I come to say good-bye ... for I am dead!" And forthwith both rider and mount roll dead upon the rippled dust, just as the cloud dispels and lets us see our *llaneros*, victors, slashing with their lances the backs of the Spanish squadrons that flee in utter fright.[7]

Venezuela is free at last. In the autumn of that year, Bolívar is named president and Congress passes a new constitution. Bolívar thinks it's too weak to preserve unity, but leaves it in place as he has more important issues to attend to than politics.

"I need to give a third sister to the Battles of Boyacá and Carabobo," he says, and is off again. There are more nations to free.

Assisted by the brightest shining star among his officers, Antonio José de Sucre, Bolívar spends the following year battling to liberate Ecuador. On May 24, 1822, the decisive victory takes place at Pichincha. But no rest follows. The rising star of Argentinian José de San Martín, the liberating hero of the southern part of South America, keeps Bolívar going. After the successful independence of Argentina and Chile, San Martín sets out to liberate Peru, declaring its independence on July 28, 1821, but the Spanish forces still linger in the highlands. San Martín turns to Bolívar for assistance in finishing them off, but Bolívar is not about to serve under someone else's command. San Martín and Bolívar finally meet behind closed doors in Ecuador. After the meeting, San Martín unexpectedly resigns the command of his army and leaves the country, opting to back down rather than face the absurdity of going to war against another liberating army. Apparently, there could only be one Liberator and Bolívar is adamant that his army, not San Martín's, should free the mineral-rich land of Upper Peru.

Together with Sucre, Bolívar sets out to finish the liberation of Peru. On December 9, 1824, Sucre triumphs in the Battle of Ayacucho where the Spanish viceroy surrenders with his entire army. On December 31, Britain announces its recognition of Colombia. The following day, at a presidential dinner in Washington, a toast is given "to General Simón Bolívar, the George Washington of South America!"

In April 1825, Bolívar's army conquers the last remaining territory on the continent still under Spanish control. The inhabitants of the area, known as Upper Peru, name their new country Bolivia after their Liberator. They also vote to make Bolívar their president. Bolívar now rules over an area that exceeds the size of modern Europe. Over night, his Greater Colombia has acquired a million new citizens.

Bolívar drafts a constitution for the new nation of Bolivia, which he also hopes to implement in the rest of the region. The document acts as testimony to how time has changed his vision.

Mixed in with the republican and libertarian principles are obvious streaks of authoritarian rule. While most of the proposed constitution resembles its British and North American counterparts, it differs on a crucial issue: Bolívar wants a president appointed for life. And, to extend his powers even further, the president would be entitled to select a vice president to succeed him. The man who had once argued: "regular elections are essential to popular government, for nothing is more perilous than to permit one citizen to retain power for an extended period," is now arguing "we shall avoid elections, which always result in that great scourge of republics, anarchy ... the most imminent and terrible peril of popular government."[8]

Power can't simply be handed over to the ignorant masses, Bolívar maintains. Gran Colombia needs strong, authoritative leadership. It is a far cry from the ideals of Rousseau, Voltaire, and Montesquieu that first inspired Bolívar, but experience has convinced him that his people aren't ready for democracy.

Besides Bolivia, Peru also accepts Bolívar's constitution, albeit reluctantly. But this proof of his increased appetite for power also earns him more enemies. In July of 1826, Bolívar's staff in Lima foils a plot to assassinate him. Closer to home, more conflicts are brewing.

While traveling to Bogotá to deal with the regional turmoil, Bolívar learns how vastly unpopular his suggested constitution is among Granadans. It also becomes increasingly clear that many still oppose his dream of a united continent.

Provincial power players are not willing to give up their regional control in favor of a centralized government. The regional divisions encouraged by Spain during the colonial era still prevail and many yearn for independent nation-states. There is no joint purpose, no sense of loyalty or solidarity. Caudillos[9] still want to rule their own turfs and politicians are radicalized against one another.

While Bolívar is away leading the final campaigns, regional rivalries, particularly between Páez in Venezuela and Santander in New Granada, fester. In 1826, they erupt into civil war. Bolívar narrowly escapes another assassination attempt in 1827. Antonio José de Sucre, by now a general, fights hard to keep internal turmoil and regional rebellions at bay, but others among Bolívar's closest men revolt. His hard-won South American union is crumbling.

In 1830, in a last desperate attempt to keep the country together, Bolívar resigns as president of Gran Colombia. In his last address to the nation, he says:

> Colombians! Gather around the constitutional congress. It represents the wisdom of the nation, the legitimate hope of the people, and the final point of reunion of the patriots. Its sovereign decrees will determine our lives, the happiness of the Republic, and the glory of Colombia. If dire circumstances should cause you to abandon it, there will be no health for the country, and you will drown in the ocean of anarchy, leaving as your children's legacy nothing but crime, blood, and death.
>
> Fellow Countrymen! Hear my final plea as I end my political career; in the name of Colombia I ask you, beg you, to remain united, lest you become the assassins of the country and your own executioners.[10]

In the end, Bolívar is unable to prevent the collapse of the nation he has been instrumental in creating. Later that year, Gran Columbia is dissolved and replaced by the republics of Venezuela, New Granada (now Colombia and Panama), and Ecuador. His most trusted ally, General Sucre, whom Bolívar considers his direct successor, is assassinated. Bolívar is devastated. In a letter to the new president of Ecuador, General Juan José Flores, he writes: "Avenge Sucre's murder" and "then get out while you can." Bolívar then goes on to list his depressing conclusions after two decades of rule:

1. America is ungovernable;
2. He who serves a revolution ploughs the sea;
3. All one can do in America is leave it;

4. The country is bound to fall into unimaginable chaos, after which it will pass into the hands of an undistinguishable string of tyrants of every color;
5. Once we are devoured by all manner of crime and reduced to a frenzy of violence, no one—not even the Europeans—will want to subjugate us;
6. And, finally, if mankind could revert to its primitive state, it would be here in America, in her final hour.[11]

On December 17, 1830, Bolívar dies of tuberculosis, disillusioned and broke. He is buried in a borrowed shirt, in a simple ceremony paid for by a volunteer.

II

"The prosperity of Venezuela was the first thought of Bolívar, the first motive for his heroic deeds; we have omitted nothing we could possibly do in honoring his memory. It is not only the triumph of Bolívar that we celebrate: it is also the triumph of Venezuela. We have witnessed the arrival on our shores of the great Bolívar escorted by the warships of powerful nations mixing their flags with ours in honor of the Hero, in honor of Venezuela."[12]

It is November 1842, almost twelve years after Bolívar's death, and President Páez celebrates the successful repatriation of the Liberator's remains to his native Venezuela. In Caracas, a massive delegation of dignitaries honor the arrival of Bolívar's exhumed remains, save his heart, which Colombia has insisted on keeping interred in the Cathedral of Santa Marta. As the funeral procession moves through Caracas, citizens pour down from the hills to pay tribute to their dead Liberator.[13] Struggling to maintain control over a country plagued by constant civil unrest, Páez has undertaken to restore Bolívar's fallen honor. In death, Bolívar has ceased to be a rival, an object of jealousy, or a threat. No other leader has been able to measure up, and a unanimous recognition of the Liberator's achievements is spreading throughout South

America. In death, Bolívar's virtues are enhanced and his flaws forgotten. He is the epitome of Latin American greatness: a hero willing to risk everything for a dream, for liberty. Like a modern-day superhero, he even donned a cape that would famously flap against him as he came charging on his white horse. Known as the "iron ass," he was said to keep pace with anyone of his soldiers and outride even the fiercest of cowboys. Whether truth or myth doesn't really matter. In their quest for a strong leader, the people of South America turn Bolívar into the blueprint against which all future leaders will be judged. Famous writer and Cuban national hero José Martí predicts: "From son to son, for as long as America shall live, the echo of his name will resound in our manly hearts."[14]

* * *

Over time, the legend grows, and more politicians, regardless of their ideological conviction, begin to use Bolívar's legacy to augment their own.

In 1870, caudillo Antonio Guzmán Blanco seizes control of the government. While he manages to end civil war, stimulate economic development, and start the modernization of Venezuela, his dictatorial rule is marked by flagrant corruption and fierce anti-Catholicism. Though his leadership has little in common with that of Bolívar, Guzmán Blanco knows what positive impact Páez derived from associating himself with the Liberator's image. He sees an opportunity to legitimize his government by pledging to continue Bolívar's legacy. Consequently, he too decides to have Bolívar's remains exhumed. They are moved from the cathedral and placed in the newly completed National Pantheon.[15]

Guzmán Blanco emphasizes the need for a unitary nation-state, built around Bolívar's nationalistic ideals. He also creates Venezuela's modern currency—the bolívar—acquires Bolívar's family home in Caracas, and announces the publication of a thirty-two-volume history of the Liberator's career. In 1883, at the centenary of Bolívar's birth, he organizes extravagant celebrations, aiming to immortalize himself as much as the Liberator.[16]

On July 24, Bolívar's birthday, celebrations take place by the National Pantheon amid a sea of flowers. In his speech, Guzmán Blanco emphasizes that Venezuela has become precisely what Bolívar envisioned. "This Motherland, constituted, organized, and prosperous, celebrating his centenary, with even the inauguration of railways, clearly shows that we have already entered the horizons illuminated by the sun of true and great civilization."[17]

The following day, Guzmán Blanco inaugurates the new railroad between Caracas and its main port, La Guaira, in honor of the Liberator.[18]

It is the era of great European exhibitions. In London, Crystal Palace has been built to house the city's exhibition and soon Paris will flaunt its completed Eiffel Tower at the Exposition Universelle. Guzmán Blanco wants nothing less. He orders the construction of an impressive building in the neo-Gothic style (today part of Palacio de las Academias) to house a massive exhibition of the Liberator's personal belongings, while also showcasing the history of Venezuela's agricultural, industrial, and artistic achievements. Significant technological progress has taken place during his rule. The month-long exhibition, part of the centennial celebrations, is a brilliant way of allowing his own achievements to bask in the glory of the Liberator.[19,20] Although Bolívar would hardly have approved, the ploy works. Guzmán is able to hang on to power for eighteen years.[21]

Political instability and dictatorial rule continue to mark the next few decades as caudillos vie for power. Then, in 1914, the hidden treasure that explorers have sought for the past four hundred years reveals itself. Only it isn't gold, it's the thick, black fluid the Indians use to seal their canoes on Lake Maracaibo. Venezuela's dictator Juan Vicente Gómez bargains cunningly with Western nations interested in the oil.[22]

While the wealth remains concentrated in a small number of hands, mainly his friends and family, Vicente Gómez does manage to improve Venezuela's finances in the process. In 1930, on the centenary of Bolívar's death, he pays off the country's entire foreign debt as homage to the Liberator. He also assigns his Foreign Minister César Zumeta the task of recovering important documents chronicling Bolívar's life. They are added to a collection known as the Bolívar Archive, which includes documents from Bolívar's public life, as well as his letters, observations, and war decrees. In 1921, the archive becomes part of a newly inaugurated museum, located in Bolívar's birthplace in Caracas.[23]

Vicente Gómez invests in public works and a well-equipped army, while controlling the nation through force and terror. Elections are manipulated, political activity banned, and the press muzzled, but his efficient political order attracts foreign petroleum investors. By 1928, the country has become the world's leading exporter and second-largest producer of oil.[24] By the late 1930s, Standard Oil and Shell control 85 percent of Venezuela's total oil production.[25] This dominance is not unproblematic, and left-wing politicians, particularly members of the Communist Party, warn of conflict to come between foreign oil companies and the Venezuelan population.[26]

Already in 1937, directors of Standard Oil and its Venezuelan affiliate, Creole, observe that "a growing feeling of nationalism and its inevitable reaction of antagonism to foreigners [had] made it an imperative for any foreign company operating in Latin America to give more attention to industrial and public relations."[27]

Seeking to bridge the divide that separates them from the Venezuelan public, these corporate giants also turn to Bolívar. "From the standpoint of understanding Venezuela today," reads a Creole case study, "Bolívar's great military achievements are of less interest than the evolution of his political thinking ... his consistent emphasis throughout his life on the duties of a soldier-statesman to maintain order and to participate actively in the peaceful development of his country." Featuring pictures of Bolívar's birthplace and statue in the city center, the report recognizes the Liberator and his ideas as foundational to Venezuelan society.[28] Shell and Creole petroleum companies later go on to fund a significant indexation project of the Bolívar Archive, thereby forging their own ties with the Liberator.[29]

Though Gómez eventually dies an old man in 1935, many try to end his rule sooner. One of his opponents is the young Marxist student Rómulo Betancourt, leader of the student movement "Generation of 1928." Launching their movement, Betancourt and his fellow students march from Caracas' Central University to the Pantheon where Bolívar is buried. They place a band of flowers over his tomb while one of the leaders declares: "Your rebel voice can be heard again."[30]

The group goes on to mobilize opposition against Gómez, but their protests and conspiracies to overthrow the dictator fail. Betancourt goes into exile, but stays politically active, most prominently in Costa Rica where he becomes leader of the Communist Party at the age of twenty-two. Returning to Venezuela after the death of Gómez, Betancourt quickly rises to become a key left-wing leader and founds what will become the Acción Democrática (AD) political party.[31]

This time Betancourt and his allies are more successful in mobilizing the growing resentment toward the regime. In October 1945, a military coup topples the government and Betancourt takes on the role as temporary leader of a self-proclaimed "Revolutionary Junta." Betancourt introduces universal suffrage, and in 1947 Acción Democrática organizes the country's first democratic elections. The AD wins with more than 70 per cent of the vote, and novelist Rómulo Gallegos becomes president. The party introduces a number of economic reforms that are unpopular among conservatives. Only a year after being elected, their government is toppled by the same military junta that helped them achieve power. Venezuela has returned to the realm of dictators, and Betancourt is once again forced into exile. Chaos dominates the next few years as one president is assassinated and another overthrown.[32]

Of the many military contenders, Major Marcos Pérez Jiménez eventually comes out on top and assumes the presidency in 1952. He is ruthless—crushing political opposition and the labor movement, while censoring the press. Popular with the United States, Pérez Jiménez sympathizes with the American fight against communism. He also offers preferential tax rates and concessions to foreign oil companies. Social reform programs are scrapped so that more resources can be invested in modernizing Caracas and enriching a selected few. Finally, the public revolts and on January 23, 1958, a civilian–military alliance, fueled by popular uprisings in the *barrios*, rises to overthrow Pérez Jiménez. A temporary junta governs while exiled political leaders like Betancourt return to Venezuela to prepare for the upcoming elections.

Given the discouraging history of democracy in Venezuela, Betancourt and other political leaders of the time realize a drastic change of governance is needed. In the 132 years between Venezuela's final independence and the upcoming election, the country has spent less than ten years under civilian-led regimes.[33] What's the point of winning an election if one can expect to be immediately toppled by the losing side? As a result, the most influential political leaders decide to make a deal. Later that year, representatives of the three main political parties of Venezuela—Labor-leftist Acción Democrática, right-leaning Social Christian Copei, and left-leaning Unión Republicana Democrática (URD)—meet to reach an agreement to establish representative democracy. Known as the Pact of Punto Fijo (as the house of Copei-founder Rafael Caldera was called), the agreement calls for democratic elections and a coalition government that will include cabinet representation from all three parties.[34]

The parties agree on a basic common platform, which narrows the political spectrum. They commit to increased social spending and strong labor laws, but also promise to respect private property, and assure the elites that their businesses will be allowed to operate regardless of who wins. Part of the compromise includes purging all radical ideas, which explains why the Venezuelan Communist Party is not invited to join the pact.[35]

Rómulo Betancourt wins the 1958 election. Adhering to the Punto Fijo agreement, he creates an inclusive cabinet with members of the Copei and the URD, as well as some independents. However, he does not include any representatives of the extreme left.[36] In his inaugural address, on February 13, 1959, Betancourt quotes Simón Bolívar's famous Jamaica Letter, urging Venezuelans in the Liberator's name to observe "the practices of civil society."[37] But the radical fringes of both left and right, which Betancourt sought to exclude, will not give up without a fight.

In the past, Acción Democrática had portrayed itself as a leftist-revolutionary and anti-imperialist party. Following their victory, Fidel Castro is quick to declare his solidarity with Venezuela. Staying true to his new allies, President Betancourt announces that communism is not the right path for Venezuela. The communists were instrumental in the 1958 coup that brought the AD to power. While Betancourt and other leaders remained in exile, Venezuelan communists organized worker strikes and street demonstrations. Now, they feel excluded and deceived. The conflict also causes a rift within the AD itself, with its younger and more radical members breaking away to form the Movement of the Revolutionary Left (MIR).[38]

As many students protest, Betancourt orders the shutdown of all universities and high schools. But the students continue to mobilize, so Betancourt orders the military to occupy the campus of Universidad Central de Venezuela. Betancourt, who started as a student leader and used to promote the university as the site of "permanent conflict between the nation and those governing against its will," is now denouncing it as a "den of terrorists."[39]

Speaking at a government-organized rally, Betancourt turns to Bolívar to justify his use of military force. "I always wished that no one would suffer under my government. But then I remembered the bitter, desolate, experience of our republic. And I remembered Bolívar when he said: 'Absolute freedom invariably leads to absolute tyranny.'"[40]

Seeing their demonstrations and propaganda fail, the dissidents become increasingly convinced that they need a proper revolutionary plan. In order to acquire the necessary knowledge and experience to launch an effective guerrilla war, Venezuelan radical youth begin travelling to Cuba to receive training in rural and urban insurgency and guerilla warfare tactics. This causes President Betancourt to break diplomatic relations with the Castro government on November 11, 1961.[41]

Failing to mobilize the Venezuelan public, the insurgents begin robbing banks, burning warehouses, killing policemen, and conducting kidnappings.[42]

On May 4, 1962, a battalion of 450 marines revolts against the government at a naval base near Caracas. The attempted coup is easily crushed by government-loyal troops, but it leaves Betancourt worried. The revolt was backed by the communists. Any last hesitations the party might have harbored toward toppling a democratically elected government have obviously vanished. Betancourt and his cabinet arrest several members of the Communist Party and ban it.

Less than a month later, on June 3, a second coup attempt takes place at the Puerto Cabello naval base, west of Caracas. This revolt requires over 1,000 government troops and days of bloody fighting to subdue the 400 rebels, leaving thirty-five dead and over 100 wounded. A number of rebels from the uprising escape to the hills where guerilla-training camps have been established. Beyond young students, the guerillas are able to recruit an increasing number of prominent members. One of them is Fabricio Ojeda, the former head of the Patriotic Junta that overthrew the Pérez Jiménez dictatorship. After serving as a member of Congress for four years, Ojeda resigns, delivering a passionate resignation speech drawing on the country's liberating hero. Following "the lessons of Bolívar," the Venezuelan left wing has taken on the Liberator's "courage, nobility, and patriotism," he says. Ojeda intends do the same. While Betancourt suppresses the radical left in the name of the Liberator, Ojeda now conjures him in support of that same movement working to overthrow Betancourt.[43]

Betancourt also faces strong opposition from the right wing. In April 1960, military officials under the direction of Pérez Jiménez's former minister of defense attempt a failed military coup. In June, Betancourt barely survives an assassination attempt when a car bomb explodes. His chauffeur and a military colonel are killed, while Betancourt manages to escape with second-degree burns.[44]

Another failed attempt at a military coup takes place in June 1961. The rebellion gains local civilian support, but is violently crushed by government loyal troops who kill seventeen citizens in the process. At an independence day rally following the second coup attempt, Betancourt once again invokes Bolívar, linking his own political project to the one Bolívar embarked on a century before: "These enemies to our rule of law are determined to justify that maxim of Bolívar in the Angostura Discourse: It is more difficult to maintain the balance of liberty than to endure the weight of tyranny."[45]

By July 1962, Rómulo Betancourt has withstood four coup attempts, one assassination plot, strikes and riots in the cities, and guerrilla warfare in the countryside. And the troubles are far from over as the leftist insurgency intensifies their urban terrorism efforts.[46]

In 1963, the Communist Party and MIR join forces with disenchanted members of the military to form Armed Forces of National Liberation (FALN) and the National Liberation Front (FLN). Together, they turn 1963 into one of the most violent years in the modern history of Venezuela. The FALN coordinates the different guerrilla groups operating throughout the country, while the FLN provides political leadership. The goal is to destabilize the government, derail the upcoming elections of December 1963, and create the conditions for a coup. Through terrorism, sabotage, arson, robbery, and bombings, the insurgents aim to make Venezuela ungovernable. In the three months leading up to the 1963 election, FALN carries out ninety-one acts of violence. But in the end, Betancourt prevails. He is able to complete his term and preside over new national elections. Amid threats of electoral violence, over 92 percent of the population defies the insurgents and cast their votes. Acción Democrática wins again, appointing Raúl Leoni as their next president.[47]

In 1968, Rafael Caldera of Copei wins the presidency and, for the first time in Venezuela's history, there is a peaceful transfer of power from an incumbent government to the opposition. Caldera honors the Punto Fijo agreement, but simultaneously pursues a policy of Latin American solidarity aiming to ease tension with Cuba, the Soviet Union, and the extreme left. He re-legalizes the Communist Party, as well as the MIR, and offers political amnesty to leftist guerrillas. Many accept and re-enter electoral politics.[48] But power remains concentrated in the hands of incumbent AD and Copei, winning about 90 percent of the votes between them. During the second half of the twentieth century, power essentially alternates between these two main parties whose members are known as "adecos" and "copeyanos." Whoever is not in power at the time is still able to keep influence and perks. At the top, everyone is getting rich, and as long as there is enough money, things are fine.

In 1976, President Carlos Andrés Pérez of the AD nationalizes the oil industry.

By 1980, petroleum accounts for 70 percent of the nation's revenue and 26 percent of the total gross national product. The energy crisis causes the price of oil to soar, enabling Pérez to increase the role of the state in the economy to unprecedented levels. Between 1974 and 1979, the government spends more money than the other Venezuelan governments during the previous 143 years combined. Pérez launches ambitious state-owned industrial projects, including the production of hydroelectric energy and massive infrastructure projects. His investments attract immigrants from across the continent, but the drastic increase in public spending also produces waste and corruption, increasing rather than decreasing the gap between the rich and the poor. When the price of oil begins to fall in the 1980s, the bonanza ends, plunging Venezuela into unemployment and inflation.[49]

The crisis exposes the flaws of the Punto Fijo agreement. While it might have served the purpose of safeguarding a frail democracy, it has also turned into a corrupt club for the privileged few. The AD started out as a left-wing party and Copei as a Christian Democratic party, but over time their politics have grown increasingly similar, with a center-left tendency.[50] Government has become impenetrable for anyone but the incumbents, and immune to new influences and ideas. It is a corrupt, but stable democracy, supposedly built on the legacy of the Liberator who always argued for "the cessation of party strife."

Since his death, countless rulers have relied on Bolívar to justify their policies or positions of power. As Bolívar left behind countless speeches and writings, full of contradictions, most political standpoints can find support somewhere in his canon. He was both liberator and tyrant. Brave and principled, he gave up his fortune and heritage to fight for what he believed. But his beliefs underwent a drastic metamorphosis along the way. The man who started out professing that "a nation in which one man rules is a nation of slaves" later conceded that dictatorship was the only way to accomplish anything when ruling an uneducated and "immature people." "Everywhere I look, I see only misery and distrust ... a dictatorship will solve everything."

Bolívar was the first, the prototype, in a series of democratically elected rulers who went on to become dictatorial. It is a pattern that has created chaos in Latin America, yet it continues to be emulated.

In 1969, the first criticism of the abuse of Bolívar's legacy appeared. In *El culto a Bolívar* (The cult of Bolívar), Venezuelan historian Germán Carrera Damas argued that Bolívar had been transformed, through systematic political manipulation, from a figure of popular admiration, to a mechanism used by the ruling political elite to consolidate their power. Natural admiration, he claimed, had been turned to state policy and converted into a single point of view, allowing control of society.[51]

Over the years, many other historians would criticize how the ideas and actions of the Liberator were manipulated to promote conflicting political agendas. Among politicians, however, criticism of Bolívar is still considered blasphemy.

While Bolívar's legacy continues to affect all of Latin America (both Ecuador and Bolivia currently have presidents who call themselves *bolivarianos*), nowhere has it influenced society more than in Venezuela. During the rule of Chávez, the cult of Bolívar would achieve its apex. Chávez would transform Bolívar from a noun to an adjective, from a historical figure to a characteristic, embraced by all his supporters. But Chávez was not the first, nor would he be the last, to invoke Bolívar. Generations of political leaders, and their opponents, have manipulated the legacy of the Liberator to enhance their own interests. Because of this long tradition, and his ability to accommodate ideologies from the extreme right to the extreme left, the cult of Bolívar will remain, and continue to adapt to an ever-changing present. New generations of leaders aspiring to the throne find themselves compelled to walk that same well-trodden hero's path, searching for ways to mold Bolívar's image to fit their own aspirations. Whether through subtle references or direct invocations of his name, his words, his deeds, or even his cape, they will attempt to convince the public that they are the new, true, Venezuelan hero, and the most worthy vessel for Bolívar's unyielding spirit.

As such, Bolívar's legend continues to give rise to new heroes and new villains, in perpetuity.

III

It is August 20, 1950. The emigrant ship *Portugal* docks in La Guaira at the end of its fifteen-day journey from Italy. Annamaría Frojo descends the gangplank with her five-month-old baby boy Giampiero, taking in her first impressions of a new land. She has crossed the Atlantic to join the rest of her family; her husband Brunello Riccio, a young architect from Naples, and her father Achille Frojo, an Italian engineer.

The family is one of many thousands of immigrants escaping the depression of post-war Europe and the looming threat of the Korean War. Having lost everything, they arrive by the boatload hoping to discover a land of work and opportunity.

And they do.

During this period, Venezuela's economy leads all of Latin America. The discovery and exploitation of vast oil reserves has fueled impressive growth. In 1950, Venezuela is the fourth wealthiest nation per capita, ahead of nations such as Canada and Sweden.[52]

While ruthless with his critics, dictator Marcos Pérez Jiménez is passionate about turning Venezuela into a modern, prosperous nation. He invests heavily in world-class infrastructure like roads, skyscrapers, and telecommunications, creating a massive construction boom.

For foreign educated and skilled labor, the Venezuela of this time is indeed a land of opportunity. With an over-abundance of resources, but not enough educated people to develop them, the country desperately needs engineers like Achille and architects like Brunello. They find more work than they dreamed possible.

In Italy, few of Brunello's designs were ever built. But Venezuela is different. Here, Brunello sees most of his ideas materialize; lines on a paper convert into a tangible legacy and considerable wealth. Brunello feels accomplished, and he looks the part. He begins to dress in fine suits and starts wearing his dark hair slicked back. He relocates his family to their own apartment and grants his wife Annamaría her wish for a second child. In 1954, their son Folco is born.

On January 23, 1958, the military ousts Pérez Jiménez, and soon after Venezuela holds democratic elections. Left-oriented politicians, who fled the persecution of the Pérez government, return to Venezuela. Social democratic Acción Democrática wins the election later that year, but President Betancourt excludes the communists from his government of national unity. Inspired by the Cuban Revolution, the Communist Party radicalizes and launches a guerrilla war against the newly elected AD government in the early 1960s.

While the Riccios are excited about the shift to democracy, the guerilla war and the deteriorating security situation frighten them. On June 24, 1960, there is an assassination attempt on President Betancourt. He survives but is badly burned as a result of a car bomb detonation. That same summer, the Riccios take a trip to Italy for the 1960 Summer Olympics in Rome. They are impressed with what they see. Italy has pulled through the depression and the country is booming. "Come back home!" family and friends tell them.

In Venezuela, 1962 is marked by bloody military uprisings and attempts by the extreme left to disrupt society and discredit the government through terrorism. There are widespread acts of sabotage, arson, and robbery.[53] The Riccios decide to return to Italy. Appalled, they follow the news as the guerilla group Armed Forces of National Liberation (FALN) sabotage oil pipelines and carry out kidnappings, and bombings. In 1963, FALN famously seizes Venezuelan cargo ship *Anzoátegui* and shortly thereafter they kidnap Real Madrid soccer star Alfredo Di Stéfano at gunpoint from the Potomac Hotel in Caracas. They also bomb the US Embassy in Caracas and a Sears Roebuck warehouse.

The Riccios move to Rome where Brunello gets a job in government. But he finds it difficult to readjust to life as an employee. In Venezuela, he was his own boss. Now, after five years in Italy, he is still taking orders from someone else. His wife Annamaría also struggles to readjust. She hates the cold winters and misses her parents who have stayed behind in Caracas.

Meanwhile, in Venezuela, the situation begins to stabilize as the communist guerrillas fail to mobilize enough support from the Venezuelan peasantry to pose a serious challenge to the new regime.

In 1967, the Riccios return to Caracas to start over. Having spent most of their savings in Italy, they move into a run-down apartment in Caracas. This time, progress is slower, but Brunello still does well. After a couple of years, the family moves to a nicer area. Brunello starts working at the Ministry of Public Works. Unlike his previous assignments, which were purely commercial, Brunello now works on projects focused on social impact, such as low-income housing for the poor.

In one such government house, in a different part of the country, thirteen-year-old Hugo Chávez lives with his widowed grandmother, Rosa Inés.

Hugo was born in 1954, the same year as Folco, in the dusty village of Sabaneta, on the Venezuelan plains. His parents were teachers at the local primary school, and the family lived in a simple home with earthen floors and a roof made from palm leaves. With the birth of their sixth son, the overcrowded parents sent the two oldest—Adán and Hugo—to live with their grandmother in her recently awarded government house.[54]

While many slum dwellers receive state housing, the government cannot keep up with the growing need. There seems to be a never-ending supply of poor people. Destitute immigrants from all over Latin America flock to oil-rich Venezuela. Unlike the Europeans that came in the previous decade, most of the new immigrants lack education and struggle to get ahead. Many end up in the ever-expanding slums. While the country grows richer, the oil wealth never reaches these areas. As a result, millions live in abject poverty, and the tensions created by the growing economic disparity begin to affect the political agenda.

IV

It is 1975. The door of an affluent Caracas home flings open to energetic sounds of young María Corina Machado and her three sisters. The house is ideal for children; old, vast, and packed with secrets. In special closets, under certain carpets, and in some parts of the roof, there are hidden passages to secret rooms and secret exits. In the 1920s and '30s, young students who were persecuted under dictator Juan Vicente Gómez's rule used to hide here. Sometimes, Enrique Machado Zuloaga, the girls' father, takes them on enchanting tours through these places, telling stories of their occupants, which over time evolved into rich family legends.

While her sisters rush off to play, María Corina goes straight to her grandmother Ana Teresa Machado. She finds her, as always, in her rocking chair, basking in the light flooding in through the massive window in her room. She leaps up in the old lady's lap and hugs her. Then, as on most days, she begs her to tell the story again, the story of her great uncle Armando Zuloaga, her grandmother's youngest brother. He was killed in a rebellion against the dictatorship of Juan Vicente Gómez in 1929, at the age of twenty-four.

As far back as she can remember, María Corina has been fascinated by Armando Zuloaga. He gave his life fighting for his country. For freedom. What greater destiny could there be?

Ana Teresa Machado is the dearest grandchild of Eduardo Blanco, acclaimed author of *Venezuela Heroica*—the epic tale detailing the battle for Venezuelan independence, published in the late 1800s.

"In *Venezuela Heroica* everything pulses, everything inflames, everything overflows, explodes in sparks, smoke, and sparkles. It is like a storm of glory after which the earth remains covered in gold dust. ... One feels capable of all the glory that is well sung. ... Every adult should write it, every child should read it, every honest heart should love it. Contemplating the stature of such heroes awakens in us the irresistible desire to imitate them," writes José Martí in the books preface.

María Corina treasures that connection. She knows she is her grandmother's favorite grandchild, and since her grandmother was Eduardo's favorite, María Corina senses a special bond between herself and her great Venezuelan ancestors. She too must be destined for great things. Only eight years old, her face already bears the look of determination and intentness of purpose.

In the morning, her grandmother sends her off to school at the Merici Academy, an exclusive Catholic girls' school, taught by Ursuline nuns. María wears a marine blue cardigan over a white blouse, a folded blue skirt, and white, knee-high socks. Her long brown hair is tied back with a white ribbon. Her little hand clutches a red leather briefcase. She is her father's daughter, the daughter of steel magnate Enrique Machado Zuloaga, president of the massive Sivensa company.

In the 1950s and '60s, the Venezuelan steel industry flourished. With the lowest domestic prices in the world for iron ore, natural gas, and electricity, the prospects for developing exports into international markets were great. María Corina's grandfather saw the opportunity and became an early investor in Sivensa.

His son, María Corina's father, did his part to build on the family legacy. An engineer from Universidad Central de Venezuela, Enrique Machado Zuloaga completed his postgraduate studies abroad in France and the United States. When he returned to Venezuela, it was with knowledge and ideas uncommon to the country at the time. He developed new steel applications such as auto parts and value-added byproducts. As he grew these businesses, he gained greater responsibility, until eventually he took over as president of the whole company.

V

Caracas, 1960. Six-year-old Folco sits on the floor of the living room waiting for his next assignment.

"Design an apartment building for me," his father Brunello requests.

Every night, the Riccios gather in front of the TV. They love Italian film and the directors of the neorealist tradition like Roberto Rossellini, Vittorio De Sica, and Federico Fellini. Between the sofa and the chairs is a big square table made of white marble. This is the center of young Folco's universe. Here he can spread his papers and design anything his imagination can conceive.

"Give me a three-story-building where each apartment has four rooms," Brunello continues.

He likes to provide Folco with the framework to make his designs more realistic. Using Lego for building bricks, Folco then puts his designs to the test. He builds skyscrapers of Lego, taller than himself, to determine which structures support the greatest heights.

At seventeen, Folco begins to study architecture at university. He is a young man of his time. As a student in the 1970s, Folco identifies strongly with the hippie movement. He grows his hair long, and for years his daily attire consists of a pair of Swedish clogs and technicolored T-shirts his father bought for him on Carnaby Street in London.

For Folco and his friends, life is about communal living, sharing resources, and artistic experimentation.

VI

"A horse riding school?" Folco and his friends Sony, Enrico, Azier, and Taku look incredulously at each other.

"Superficial," comments Enrico.

"Completely meaningless," echoes Sony.

It is 1976, and as usual, the five friends are scattered around the living room at Sony's place. Having lost both his parents in an accident, Sony lives alone in a big apartment in central Caracas. As aspiring architects, the young friends love the classical beauty of his place. Light floods the entire apartment through floor-to-ceiling windows. In the center, around the rectangular, black glass table at the heart of the living room, they gather to work on their university assignments, often long into the night. Except for Taku, who is Japanese, and Azier who is Basque, the friends are all of Italian descent. This, in combination with their leftist sympathies, has earned them the nickname "the Communist Mafia."

The big student movement at the time is called "Formate y Lucha!," roughly translating to "Educate Yourself and Struggle!" But many young people, including Folco and his friends, have also joined Movement toward Socialism, MAS. MAS was founded in 1971 by former guerilla fighters who decided to re-enter electoral politics to shine a spotlight on the growing inequalities in Venezuelan society.

It is nearing the end of their six-year architecture program at the Simón Bolívar University, and Folco and his friends are frustrated. While their teachers exude a deep love for their profession and for architecture, the students wish they would focus a little less on design and a little more on solving social problems.

The country faces a severe housing shortage. Over one million homes are needed and the deficit is growing by the day. Yet the students receive assignments they consider completely irrelevant. And now this business of a horse riding school. It's the worst yet. Folco lets out a deep sigh of frustration.

"These types of assignments were fine for the first three years when we were still learning how to design, but not anymore. By now we should be working to meet the real needs of Venezuela! Let's focus on a problem that matters!" he exclaims.

The others look up inquisitively from their drawing boards.

"Let's build houses for the poor."

"Okay, but it can't just be about return on investment," says Sony.

"Or about squeezing as many people into the same building as possible," says Azier.

"No, it's got to be about creating communities!" Taku suggests. "With the right infrastructure. Education. Jobs."

Convinced that architecture can act as a tool to bring about social change, the five friends devote the following two years to developing their ideas on how to best design low-income community housing. In a document they call "the manifesto," which they later hand in as their final thesis, they create a model for an entire ecosystem, complete with green areas, public space, schools, and sports facilities.

They suggest communities be laid-out in flower patterns with a plaza in the center. Along the main boulevards there would be buildings with shared housing and retailing opportunities suitable for small family businesses. By a gradual transition from the private to the public sphere, pedestrians would be drawn toward the center of the flower: the plaza. This would be the social and commercial hub of the community. There would be kids riding their bikes, playing soccer in the park, or skipping rope on quiet pedestrian streets. There would be local bakeries, grocery stores, and businesses—communities designed to promote the vibrant street life portrayed in the Italian neorealist film classics of their childhood.

VII

In 1971, Hugo Chávez moves from the Venezuelan plains to attend the military academy in Caracas. He dreams of pitching for the military baseball league, and while he does become one of the army's champion players, he soon realizes his calling is on the field of battle, not on a baseball diamond.

While at the academy, Chávez develops an interest in politics and finds like-minded friends among the other young cadets. Together, they dream of liberating their country from the poverty and inequality they experienced growing up. Inspired by their idol Simón Bolívar, they start a secret revolutionary movement within the military.[55] Filled with warnings of excessive reverence toward Bolívar, Carrera Damas's 1969 book *The Cult of Bolívar* is viewed negatively at the pro-Bolívar Caracas Military Academy. But Chávez and his comrades admire it, regarding the book as a crucial guide. "We thought the same as Carrera: Bolívar had become so mystified, and he was just a man. We considered it necessary to study the contradictions of these men, of Bolívar, of Zamora," Chávez later recounts.[56] The young cadets realize the myth of Bolívar could help "get people and ideas moving." By fusing left-wing nationalism with military might, they conspire to finish the economic and social liberation Bolívar started. In 1977, Chávez addresses Bolívar directly in his diary: "Come. Return. Here. It is possible ... I have to do it. Even if it costs me my life. It doesn't matter. This is what I was born to do."[57]

On December 17, 1982, the anniversary of Bolívar's death, Chávez and his fellow military officers Raúl Isaías Baduel, Felipe Acosta Carlez, and Jesús Urdaneta Hernández create a Bolivarian revolutionary army called Movimiento Bolivariano Revolucionario, MBR. Under a very old tree known as Samán de Güere, beneath which Bolívar once rested, they repeat the same oath that Bolívar had first uttered in 1805 when he pledged to devote his life to liberate Venezuela from Spanish oppression: "I swear before you, and I swear before the God of my fathers, that I will not allow my arm to relax, nor my soul to rest, until I have broken the chains that oppress us."

The following year, in 1983, the suffix "200" is added to the movement's name in celebration of the 200th anniversary of Bolívar's birth.[58]

But the cadets of the Movimiento Bolivariano know that in order to succeed with their plan of liberating the country, they will have to be patient.

VIII

It is 1969. Eight-year-old Antonio Rivero stands on the patio of his home in the south of Caracas, staring up at the sky. His perceptive brown eyes follow two fighter jets until they disappear behind the lush hills of El Avíla. During parades or airshows, military airplanes like Mirages and Canberras fly over his house. They always come in from the south. He watches them as they make their way across the sky and eventually disappear into the mountains in the north. The idea of being able to travel like that, suspended in mid-air, enchants him. That's what he wants to be: a pilot flying one of those fighter planes.

The years pass, but his passion remains unabated. As a teenager, he visits private airfields, begging pilots to take him along.

When he finishes high school, he applies to become a pilot in the air force. He should be a perfect fit. He is intelligent with fast reflexes, physically fit, and not too tall. But the examiners discover some hidden defect with his vision and he is rejected.

So Antonio settles for his second choice—studying oceanology and marine biology on Isla de Margarita. In his forth semester, his studies are put on hold because of a student strike. In the vacuum, Antonio returns home to Caracas. He has always been very religious, and now, with no school to attend, he finds himself devoting more and more time to prayer. He becomes involved in the Charismatic movement of the Catholic Church, and eventually the Jesuits. He finds a mentor in an older priest, Father Rafael Benito Araujo. Araujo preaches in many different locations, including the Military Academy of Caracas. Antonio accompanies him there to attend Mass and catechism. After a while, the priest suggests that he apply to the academy. The Society of Jesus thought of its members—the Jesuits—as soldiers of God, fighting for the defense and propagation of the faith. Araujo is about to become a military priest and regards it as an excellent option. Why should Antonio waste any more time waiting to return to his old studies when he can enroll straight away?

Antonio hadn't contemplated a career as an officer, but, after all, his childhood dream was to join the air force. So in 1980, at the age of nineteen, Antonio Rivero applies and is accepted into the military academy.

Hugo Chávez, by now a captain, teaches communications engineering. He introduces Antonio to the world of frequencies and transmissions and teaches him to operate radios and phones.

Rivero's first impression of Chávez is that of a charismatic leader with great potential. A natural storyteller, Chávez would interrupt classes to deliver a compelling anecdote from Venezuela's struggle for independence, tell a *llanero* legend,[59] recite a poem, quote Bolívar, or suddenly break out in a traditional *llanero* song about beautiful Barinas, a state in northwestern Venezuela dominated by plains. Chávez has a nice voice. As a young boy he was frequently asked to sing at birthday parties and similar events. Now, as a young adult, he still loves to sing. He sings whenever and wherever he feels like it, though never in a way to compromise military discipline. He is very formal, always well prepared, and very ambitious.

After he graduated, Chávez was appointed as the communications officer of an armored division. The communications systems of the tanks were unfamiliar, as were his colleagues. The officers here were tougher. Stronger. He feared he would never gain their respect. Communications officers did not become generals. For that he needed a specialty like artillery, infantry, or armory. So Chávez chose armory.

With his students, Chávez goes out of his way to make it clear that he did not abandon communications for lack of passion; his motivation was ambition. He wants to become a general.

Like Chávez, Rivero thrives in the military. The discipline, order, and camaraderie of the armed forces impress him and suit his personality well. It isn't long before a bond of mutual respect and affinity begins to grow between the young cadet and his superior.

IX

It is 1979. Folco is in his father's office working on the design of a private sports club to be located in southern Caracas. It is to be built around an Olympic pool, complete with volleyball courts, tennis courts, and a soccer stadium. Very modern. Very exclusive.

Since graduation, Folco has worked at his father's architectural firm. It's a great opportunity to learn the trade and a rare chance to work on complex developments at such an early stage of his career. He knows he should be grateful. And he is. But still he can't stop thinking about his thesis. He wants to develop his vision further: to create a manual for sustainable, cost-efficient, and comprehensive low-income housing that will improve quality of life for its residents.

He is also sick of the bureaucracy and corruption in Venezuela. Whenever he goes to apply for a permit, there is the unspoken expectation of a bribe, a habit he refuses to adopt.

So after four years working for his father, he applies to postgraduate school in the United States. Accepted at MIT, UC Berkeley, and Harvard, he decides on Harvard, enrolling in their postgraduate program in urban design. For two years, he studies the scientific theories behind what he already knows instinctively: that the design of space can impact social behavior, decrease crime, and influence health and happiness.

After graduating from Harvard, Folco works a few years in Boston before returning to Venezuela in 1987 hoping to build his holistic community project.

Upon his return, he seeks out the minister of urban development to pitch his idea. But the minister is completely uninterested, and after about ten minutes, he cuts Folco off and wraps up the meeting.

Folco then turns to some private sector developers, but few seem to care about innovation. They want to keep doing things the way they have always done them. Folco struggles to get anyone to understand that something that is socially beneficial can also be a good investment.

Finally, he turns to CONAVI, the national council for housing. There, he is initially met with great enthusiasm, but this soon withers through lack of progress, and lack of resources. After about a year of submitting countless proposals and paperwork, which are all eagerly received but never put into practice, he is no closer to realizing his vision. In the end, his proposals are neither approved nor rejected, but remain in limbo until Folco finally gives up.

X

It is 1982. Fifteen-year-old María Corina is lying in her room staring at a worn black-and-white photograph of Armando Zuloaga Blanco. There is something eagle-like about his face. The nose is sharp and the eyes fearless and penetrating. He is wearing a meticulously done-up suit jacket, a bowtie carefully fixed to his white collared shirt. On his head, a perfectly placed black beret.

Ever since she was about eight, María Corina has been in love with a dead man. She knows it worries her mother, Corina Machado, an accomplished psychologist, but what can she do? How can any boy of her own age possibly compete with this historic figure? He gave his life in the fight for freedom. What drove him? Where did he find the courage?

Over the next few months María Corina tracks down his old friends and acquaintances. In an old-age-home she finds his old girlfriend, Nory Acosta, now in her eighties. Despite the age difference, the two women become great friends. María Corina begins to write Armando's biography.

2

THE CALL TO PURPOSE

"When the trumpet of the homeland sounds, even the weeping of the mother falls silent."

Simón Bolívar

I

It is March 1, 1989, and Caracas is shaking from violent protests. Antonio Rivero watches as a group of officers of the national guard force protestors to the ground. Then they fire plastic bullets at them point-blank. All around him, guardsmen are firing, many at random, into the crowd of protestors.

During the past decade, Venezuela's economy has been hit hard by collapsing oil prices. Poverty is rising fast.

In February 1989, Carlos Andrés Peréz, the newly elected president, implements a series of unpopular reforms recommended by the International Monetary Fund, including the privatization of state-owned companies, reduction of customs duties, and tax reform. He also removes the heavy subsidies on petroleum, which Venezuelans are used to getting virtually for free. On February 27, when public transport operators respond to the drastic increase in gas prices by doubling fares, massive protests erupt throughout Caracas, quickly spreading to other towns across the country.

After three days of uncontrolled rioting, arson, and looting, Peréz declares a state of emergency and imposes martial law. The police are unable to cope, so the government sends in the security forces to conduct a violent crackdown on rioters and looters.

Rivero is on leave studying engineering when the riots erupt. His commanders recall him and send him to reinforce a national guard division in his native Los Teques.

There, he is shocked by the brutality of the guardsmen tasked with upholding public order.

Rivero's assignment is to prevent looting and vandalism. He settles for preventing excess. The looters are poor and hungry, and he can't help but sympathize with them. In supermarkets torn open, he watches desperate parents stuff their pockets with cans of food and old ladies dragging big bags of rice and flour. Many pile on more than they can carry. Rivero tries to be pragmatic. If he sees someone stealing five loaves of bread, he leaves them with one, while making sure the rest is returned. The desperation of the people, coupled with the aggression of his fellow soldiers, leaves him feeling terrible.

When it's all over, as many as 3,000 protestors and looters have been killed in what becomes known as the "Caracazo."

While the Caracazo understandably traumatizes the public, it also deeply affects members of the armed forces, including Rivero and Chávez. Although neither was present at the hotspots where the worst offenses took place (Chávez was hospitalized with chickenpox), both felt stronger support for the people and their expression of frustration than for the orders given. They were on the wrong side of justice.

II

In 1991, Chávez and his co-revolutionaries are promoted into commands across the country. Moved by the increasing public cries for military intervention, the group begins to prepare in earnest for a military coup d'état they codename Operation Zamora.

In the twilight hours of February 4, 1992, five army units under Chávez's command move into downtown Caracas. Their objective is to capture the president, senior generals, and strategic military, political, and communications sites.

A third of the troops head straight for the presidential palace of Miraflores, one unit advances to attack the defense ministry, while another takes on La Carlota military airport. Chávez heads for the Military Museum from where he intends to lead the operation. But he has been betrayed.

Upon their arrival at the Military Museum, Chávez and his men are greeted by machine-gun fire. They return fire, driving back their opposition. Then they make their way into the building, only to find that none of the necessary communications equipment needed to coordinate the operation is there. Chávez is cut off with a small group of rebels, unable to convey orders to the rest of his troops.[1]

At Miraflores and the other locations, the other battalions struggle to break through. Reinforcements are cut off outside the city, the civilian supporters fail to show up, and the air force generals decide it's too risky to send air support.[2]

They battle through the night, but by morning, Chávez realizes they are doomed. He assumes responsibility for the failed coup and agrees to turn himself in on the condition that he is allowed to appear on live national television.

Wearing a bright red beret and a crisp, green, camouflage-patterned uniform, he addresses his fellow coup plotters and the nation:

"First I want to say 'good morning' to all the people of Venezuela, but this Bolivarian message is directed specifically to the courageous soldiers of the parachute regiment of Aragua and the tank regiment of Valencia. Comrades: unfortunately, *por ahora*, the objectives that we set have not been achieved in the capital. That's to say that those of us here in Caracas have not been able to seize power. Where you are, you have performed well, but now, to avoid more bloodshed, it's time to reflect. New possibilities will arise again, and the country will be able to move definitively toward a better future. So listen to what I have to say. Listen to *Comandante* Chávez who is sending you this message. And, please, think deeply. Lay down your arms, for the national objectives that we set are not within our grasp. Comrades, listen to this message of solidarity. I am grateful for your loyalty, for your courage, and for your selfless generosity; before the country and before you, I alone shoulder the responsibility for this Bolivarian military uprising. Thank you."

His charisma and presence penetrate the screen. He has probably not slept in days, yet here he is, handsome, radiant, confident, addressing the nation like a liberator who has just put his life on the line in the fight against corruption and repression. The hidden promise in his defiant "por ahora," or "for now," turns a failed military coup into a successful media coup. He is an instant hero among the Venezuelan people.

The following morning, the first page of daily newspaper *El Nacional* reads: "Chávez is the salvation of Venezuela." "Chávez is the closest thing to God that exists."

Chávez goes to prison a martyr.

III

While Chávez becomes increasingly radical as he ages, Folco does not. Disillusioned by the social indifference and lack of vision among politicians, he abandons his dream of developing holistic communities for the poor and returns to his father's firm to work on housing and hotel developments.

In 1992, Folco wins a commission to design a housing development on the island of Margarita, just off Venezuela's northeastern coast. Arriving off the plane, he is moved by the contrast between the island's supernatural beauty and its terrible poverty and decay, especially that surrounding the old port in the center of the island's main city of Porlamar.

At the beginning of the 1900s, the port had been a bustling hub for trade and commerce. But, in 1975, a cargo port was built on the other side of the island, and the old port became little more than a fish market. Around the same time, the entire island was declared a duty-free zone. Overnight, Margarita became a popular destination for mainlanders seeking cheap cigarettes, blue jeans, and whiskey. Commerce shifted entirely to the busy streets of downtown Porlamar, leaving the old port as little more than a run-down parking lot littered with trash.

Now, the coastline is covered with empty cans and garbage that has drifted to shore. A moldy, abandoned mattress is floating about. Given the location at the heart of the city's waterfront, only five blocks from the city's main square Plaza Bolívar, the state of the port defines the town. In the midst of the decay, Folco sees immense potential. Margarita is a beautiful place; a paradise. And this old, decrepit port could be its gateway to the world.

Folco's dream of social and financial transformation through architecture is refueled.

In the early 1990s, cruise ship terminals were still largely thought of as bus terminals of the sea: mere transit points to more interesting destinations. They frequently shared facilities with cargo ships, far from the heart of the city. Folco finds it strange that, while cruise ships become more and more extravagant, their ports of call remain shabby, off-the-beaten-track locations. Such is the case for Margarita. The few cruise ships that stop on the island do so at the inconveniently located cargo port.

Aruba receives three cruise ships per day during high season. The Cayman Islands welcome 1.6 million passengers per year. Why is it that Margarita's Caribbean neighbors are able to attract more than ten times the number of visitors? Margarita is just as pretty if not more so. Its sea just as turquoise. Its beaches just as inviting.

Folco figures that if he designed the most beautiful cruise ship port in the region, the community would attract nearly every ship that sailed past. As he stands there on the deserted parking lot, overwhelmed by the beauty of the sea, his mind sees past the cans and the litter. Over there would be an arcade. Over there a fountain. There a patio and arched corridors, all contained in stoned walls with fort-like details. Stoned floorings. Ramps. And the plaza! Outdoor restaurants and cafés with shaded terraces, enlivened by music, arts, and folkloric dances. And over there would be an open-air stage designed as an amphitheater. Next to it a spacious port house. And over there, a marina. Some shops would line the main floor, but it wouldn't be a shopping center. The main street has enough of that. This would be a marketplace, like Boston's Faneuil Hall, a cultural destination and meeting place.

The cruise ships would anchor out at sea so as not to overshadow the city center and block the magnificent sea views. Passengers would be transported the last mile in motorboats. After spending time in the port itself, inviting pedestrian boulevards would inspire visitors to explore downtown Porlamar a mere few blocks away. They would inject well-needed energy and capital into the decayed city center, stimulating commerce and development. With time, the development could grow to include a hotel, a casino, a convention center, office buildings, residences, and maybe even a recreation center.

His passion rises with the vision. Standing among the garbage and the ruin, Folco sees the future: Venezuela open to the world, its full potential realized.

IV

Caracas, 1993. Young boys are locked behind bars in rooms with hardly any light. Their gaunt arms reach desperately for María Corina as she walks past. She has agreed to accompany her mother on a visit to an orphanage. Twenty-five years old and pregnant with her second child at the time, the experience catches her completely off guard.

Fifteen boys between the ages of six and eighteen crowd together in each dormitory, locked up all day without access to education or proper healthcare. The place reeks of urine and feces. To María Corina, it seems more like a prison than an orphanage. Mixed in with the abandoned kids are drug addicts and delinquents, some convicted of crimes as serious as murder.

* * *

The oldest of four sisters, María Corina grew up with her father's expectation that she would one day take over the family business. Eager to prove to him that he didn't need to have a son in order to continue his legacy, María Corina studied industrial engineering at the Andrés Bello Catholic University, where she graduated first in her class. She then went on to get her master's degree in finance from the IESA business school in Caracas.

Straight after graduation, she pursued a career at Sivensa. Being part of the family didn't mean automatic employment at the company. On the contrary, for María Corina it meant working extra hard to prove herself. As a young engineer, she moved to Valencia and worked in the auto-parts division where her father had started his career. There, she worked her way up, becoming the total quality manager in charge of redesigning operations to maximize competitiveness.

At this point, her passions are efficiency, quality, and competence. Social injustice and poverty are the furthest things from her mind. She knows they exist, of course. Anyone who grows up in Caracas has witnessed poverty. The dwellings of the poor cling to the hills for everyone in the valley to see. From the western side of the city, the poor look across at the mansions crowning the eastern hills of Caracas. In the east, the affluent stare back from their poolside terraces. For the wealthy, the poor are abstractions; their homes like tinderboxes made for dolls.

María Corina has visited poor, rural areas with her mother before. She has met people of few means, but always found them to be hardworking and clean. Urban poverty is different. Less dignified somehow. And here, in the orphanage, she smells abject urban poverty for the first time. The stench makes her vomit.

When María Corina returns home, she walks straight to the phone. She picks up the receiver and calls her boss to resign. "I don't know if this is going to be for a few days or for the rest of my life, but I won't be able to sleep again if I don't do something," she tells him.

María Corina visits state-run shelters across the country. Similar conditions prevail. She contacts the government. Different representatives repeat the same story in different ways: without the budget to improve the facilities, little can be done.

Unwilling to accept the status quo, María Corina and her mother create a foundation, Atenea, and persuade the government to let them take over the management of the orphanage.

Through a carefully planned awareness program, they raise the necessary resources, donations, and volunteers to turn the orphanage around. Volunteers remove forty-five truckloads of garbage and weeds. They convert the abandoned garden into a beautiful space for the children to use. Within a few years, Atenea builds a health center, a small school, vocational training facilities for the older kids, and restores the abandoned swimming pool. The center becomes a place of hope and second chances.

Building on its success, Atenea moves to expand its influence, lobbying for important legal and policy reforms to protect children and adolescents. Encouraging partnerships between government, NGOs, and the private sector, they hope their example inspires others.

As for María Corina, in a few short months she transitions from building steel to building support for a cause, from leading workers in a plant to inspiring unpaid volunteers, and from improving an industrial process to improving society through politics, sheer willpower, and good, old-fashioned, hard work.

V

February 7, 1992. Three days after Chávez is incarcerated, Father Rafael Benito Araujo, Rivero's spiritual mentor, goes to visit the Comandante in prison. There, he finds a depressed and troubled man who talks of ending his own life. The failure weighs heavy on Chávez. Full of regret, he feels personally responsible for the ruined careers of all the officers and soldiers he persuaded to join him. Father Araujo tries to comfort him. He brings him a Bible and tells him that although violence is not the way, the coup has served to open the eyes of many people to the realities of the country, convincing them of the need for change.

Among the officers, the incarceration of Chávez dramatically increases support for the resistance.

Rivero did not participate in the coup of February 4. Chávez had invited him to a meeting, but not understanding the significance, Rivero chose to attend his engineering course instead. When news of the coup breaks, he realizes what he missed.

Through Father Araujo, Rivero reaches out to Chávez. The two begin to communicate and eventually conspire to stage a second coup.

Chávez believes the success of any plot depends on gaining control of the media. During the February 4 coup, President Pérez managed to flee to the studios of Venevisión and address the people from there. They can't let that happen again. Pérez must be prevented from leaving Miraflores. In order to control the flow of information to the public, the antenna for Venevisión and two other private television stations will need to be taken out. The state channel, Canal 8, will have to be taken over and used to engage the public.

The plan is simple: liberate Chávez and take him to the studio of Canal 8 where he will once again address the Venezuelan people in an attempt to convince them of the need for change. Rafael Caldera and other personalities from the opposition are also scheduled to appear. They will advocate for a democratic transformation.

Initially, Rivero's assignment is to take over the television station, but as the relationship between the two men deepens, Chávez asks him to help plan and execute the most important piece of all: his liberation. They code name the operation "*León de Profecía*." The biblical story of Daniel the Prophet, who survived a night in a lion's den, had always appealed to Rivero. The suggestion suits Chávez's sense of destiny.

In prison, Chávez records a message to be broadcast to the nation in case he doesn't arrive at the television studio in time:

> Comrades in arms, *por ahora* [for now] and forever, the Bolivarian Revolutionary Movement 200, returns to battle with the people's flags held high, onwards towards final victory. Since the glorious day of February 4th, the men and women of Venezuela have exhausted all peaceful means of achieving the changes we need to make to the organization and management of the Venezuelan state. These changes can no longer be postponed.

Dressed in uniform and red beret, Chávez sits against the background of the Venezuelan flag, above which black block letters announce "MBR—200." He is calm and collected. His—by now famous—presence and charisma radiate from the screen:

> The whole world witnessed the days of creativity and hope of a people who awoke to their liberating force. Still, we suffer a leadership that is blind and deaf to the voice of the people; that continues to turn its back on the nation, trying once more to deceive the public, entering into secret pacts that are contrary to national interests. Enough disgrace, enough betrayals. We, the sensible men and women, committed to the future of this country, have gone out to fight in the streets of Venezuela, to reclaim with our own hands, the stained honor of our homeland. To begin to build a system of government that will provide the greatest possible amount of happiness, the greatest amount of social security, the greatest amount of political security, as our highest leader General Simón Bolívar, the Liberator, said. This system of government is and always will be the Bolivarian democracy. The defeated, mistaken members of government should immediately lay down their arms and change their perspectives to join the Bolivarian majority, which has taken control of the country's fate. The new transitional government, made up of the Patriotic Bolivarian Junta, will address the nation in a few minutes. People of Venezuela, we ask your support for the Patriotic Junta. Today is a day of national rejoicing; today is a day of Venezuelan celebration. Decorate your doors and windows with the tricolor of hope! Brothers and sisters! Fill the streets and squares of the homeland to celebrate the people's victory! Invite the civilized world to follow the example of Caracas once more!

3

TESTS, ALLIES, AND ENEMIES

"Damned be the soldier who turns the weapons of the Republic against his own countrymen."

Simón Bolívar

I

In the early morning hours of November 27, about forty men wait impatiently in the lush hills surrounding the Yare Prison. Among them are Antonio Rivero and Chávez's brother Argenis. They have come to liberate their Comandante and the other military prisoners.

The previous evening, Rivero attended a Christmas party at Fuerte Tiuna. He left around 11 p.m. to say goodbye to his mother in Los Teques and to drop off some checks for her.

"You won't see me for a while. Be careful," he tells her.

When Rivero returns to Caracas at around midnight, he notices the security forces are searching all cars arriving and leaving Fuerte Tiuna. It is not standard procedure. His pulse picks up, but now there is no going back.

Meanwhile, just after midnight, Admiral Hernan Grüber Odremán and his men take over the Military Museum in Caracas, where Chávez headquartered himself during the February 4 coup attempt. Once again it will serve as command central. This time, they have the equipment they need.

Under the command of General Francisco Visconti, members of the air force take control of the El Libertador Air Base in Maracay, La Carlota in Caracas, and Rafael Urdaneta Air Base in Maracaibo.

It is just after 4:30 a.m. when Rivero and three of his men arrive at Fuerte Guaicaipuro military base, near Yare Prison. They have come to pick up reinforcements. One hundred soldiers are to join them in their mission to liberate Chávez, while 300 soldiers are to head to Caracas to reinforce parallel operations under the command of Admiral Odremán.

They park some distance from the first roadblock of which they are to take control. Before leaving the car, Rivero takes off the white neckerchief that the rebels have agreed to wear to recognize each other. It looks strange with his uniform and he doesn't want to draw unnecessary attention to himself. But just as he reaches the roadblock, two buses pull up. Armed men start pouring out. With raised weapons, they shout: "Down on the ground!"

Rivero thinks it's the secret service and readies his pistol. The others raise their weapons instinctively to fire, when one of the attackers recognizes him.

"No! No! He is one of ours," the man shouts.

It's Rivero's civilian point of contact for the operation. The people on the buses are the civilian and military participants whom Rivero and his men were meant to meet further down the road at Yare.

The aggression and obvious lack of coordination among the civilian rebels shakes Rivero's confidence in the plan, but it's too late for doubts. After securing the roadblock, he sends the buses on their way to Yare while he and his men go in search of the reinforcements as planned.

When they arrive, the fort is on high alert. Rivero approaches one of the guards. The searching of vehicles earlier in the night was no coincidence. A mole has informed the Ministry of Defense that a military uprising is underway. At Fuerte Guaicaipuro, orders are to detain anyone attempting to enter. While Rivero and the others are not detained, the soldiers from the base have backed out. They pledge not to engage the rebels, but they want to wait and see how things develop before committing troops. Either they will join in the morning, or remain passive, they say. Rivero and his men continue alone in the hopes that the air force will make up the difference.

It is 6 o'clock, almost an hour behind schedule, when they finally arrive at Yare Prison. They meet up with about thirty-five other rebels, military as well as civilians, involved in Chávez's liberation. The plan is to use the nearby waste water plant as their forward operating base. But as the men approach the plant, they notice the presence of armed men with vests. They assume they have been exposed and that the leak has compromised more units than originally thought. They continue another 500 meters past the waste water plant and gather around their vehicles on an abandoned road. A lieutenant and two of his soldiers change into civilian clothes. They approach the armed men to find out what's going on. It turns out they are police officers from the forensic unit looking for a man who has been kidnapped. The soldiers seize the opportunity, take them prisoner, and return to the others.

By now, the sun is up. Rivero and his team head up one of the surrounding hills from where they plan to launch mortars. The idea is to intimidate and distract from the sides, while the others attack from the front, attempting to force their way in through the gates. When Rivero reaches the top of the hill, the prison is completely covered in mist. It is impossible to target properly. He waits a while, hoping the mist will clear, but time is running out. He and his team quickly review the intelligence they have gathered, and making the best estimates possible, he orders his men to fire into the mist. The sound of detonating mortars is the signal for the others to launch their attack on the entrance.

The counterattack from the national guardsmen at the prison is almost immediate. They were ready. Rivero and his men draw back quickly to avoid being hit. The attackers by the entrance are also swiftly turned away. Regrouping with Rivero in the hills, they hear for the first time the updates from the missions across the rest of the country.

The early morning operation to take out the antennas of the private television stations and occupy Canal 8 has succeeded, although not entirely according to plan.

At about 4:30 a.m., thirty rebels approach the station. At the major intersection of avenues Monte Cristo and Romulo Gallegos, they begin to pull citizens over, seizing their cars to build a makeshift barricade. Those who do not immediately surrender their vehicles are shot and left dead in the streets.[1]

Once outside the Canal 8 building, the rebels execute the elderly watchman by the entrance. Neighbors report that the old man has his hands raised, trying to surrender when the bullet hits him. He is left lying dead in his booth. Inside, the rebels come across a second watchman who is also executed with a bullet through the mouth.[2]

Having seized control of Canal 8, the rebels proceed to transmit the recording of Hugo Chávez. But the second tape prepared by other prominent leaders backing the coup has been lost in the confusion. Furthermore, the company of soldiers meant to arrive from Fuerte Tiuna to provide reinforcements never arrives. Without their backup, the television station is an easy target for the tanks of national guardsmen loyalists that show up shortly thereafter. It is now impossible for Admiral Odremán, and the other leaders meant to make live statements, to reach the studio. Panicked, the rebels lock themselves in the studio. Odremán orders them to speak in his place. But the adrenaline-charged soldiers were neither recruited nor trained to handle communications.

"People of Venezuela, in the name of the 5th of July Movement, I call on you to take to the streets and overthrow this government which has left you nothing but misery," Captain José Valera Rumbos shouts.

It is he who has taken Rivero's place as head of the Canal 8 operation, along with Lieutenant Jesse Chacón (who would later go on to assume a wide portfolio of ministries in the government of Chávez, including the position of minister of the interior and justice).

Valera Rumbos stares into the camera wild-eyed, his face contracted in anger. The words sound more like an order than a plea.

"I ask my brothers in arms to join this struggle to finish off the defeat of Carlos Andrés Pérez!" he shouts. "I repeat ..." Then he begins to stutter.

One of the civilian participants tries a softer approach: "We call on the people of Venezuela to support decisively our movement in the streets. Without hesitation! It is time that this people take a stand for a different road, a truly democratic road, for a true democracy!"

But the incoherency of preaching democracy in the midst of a coup is further underscored when Lieutenant Arné Chacón takes the microphone in a fit of aggression: "Comrades! We do not want us to kill one another! Please put down your weapons, because if you don't ... our airplanes will bomb you!"

His crude, unpolished demeanor is not doing the rebels any favors. Then mustachioed Jesús María López, the team's electrician, enters the television studio wearing a pink shirt and dark sunglasses. With his rifle pointing straight up in the air and his finger on the trigger, he and another civilian rebel displaying a pistol, position themselves with their chins slightly raised in defiance behind Arné Chacón as he shouts: "Long live our liberator

Simón Bolívar! ¡Viva Ezequiel Samora! ¡Viva Simón Rodríguez! ¡Viva el Comandante Hugo Chávez! ¡Viva el Comandante Arias Cárdenas! Long live all the heroes of February 4th! And long live the rest of our comrades! And finally, long live the fine people of Venezuela!"

Jesús María López then takes the microphone and encourages the nation to "finish off this usurping, treacherous government."

Rivero listens to them with growing horror. What is this? The speakers were meant to be polished commanders and politicians who could lend credibility to the coup, who could reassure the population that the goal was a democratic transition; who could gain their support. Admiral Odremán and politicians like Rafael Caldera were supposed to deliver a call for reconciliation, unity, and a safe and democratic way forward. In the recording, Chávez told the nation that the leadership of the Patriotic Bolivarian junta would address them next. They were to inspire the population to join and encourage the soldiers who still hesitated to participate. Instead, here are these intimidating thugs preaching violence and revenge, talking about a new movement—5th of July—of which Rivero, let alone the population, has never even heard. It is a disaster. No one will join them now.

The national guardsmen outside the studio increase the pressure, launching grenades. The rebels grow increasingly desperate. Trapped and scared, one of the civilian rebels addresses the nation again: "People of Caracas, especially those in the main streets of Los Ruices, we call on those of you who have been banging pots, on the mothers whose sons they have killed, on the students ..."

He stops, shifting his glance to something taking place off screen. He becomes anxious, then, as if remembering where he is, he turns to the camera again and continues: "Students, where is your valor? ... We call on you to support the group of civilians and soldiers who have taken this channel. The national guard is trying to put us down but we're keeping them at bay."

But no one comes, and the rebels are outmatched. At 8 a.m., they agree to surrender. With their hands on their heads, they exit the building. Antonio's brother, Wolten Rivero, is among the first group to exit. As they walk out, the officer in front of him is immediately shot dead. Wolten is shot in the leg. As bullets fly, the men behind him turn around and run back into the building. They are not about to walk out into a firing squad. After some further negotiations, the national guardsmen agree not to shoot. All of the remaining rebels hand themselves over, except for a cameraman who is discovered three days later hiding in a ventilation duct inside the building. A journalist helps Antonio's brother to a clinic where his leg is operated on. He manages to evade detection by the police or national guard, but never regains full mobility.

Despite the failure at Canal 8, the coup continues. At around 5:30 a.m., airplanes piloted by rebels take off from Maracay, Maracaibo, and Barquisimeto, unleashing their 40-millimeter cannons on the Miraflores presidential palace, the presidential residence La Casona, the military airport La Carlota, El Helicoide—the headquarters of the national intelligence service—Fuerte Tiuna, and the Sucre municipal police. Seeing the rebels dominate the skies lends new strength to the troops on the ground. And although no soldiers from Fuerte Guaicaipuro join the coup, they keep their word and do not attempt to interfere with the rebels in the hills around the prison.

The success of the air force emboldens Rivero and the team, and they decide to make another approach. The mist has cleared and it's turning into a hot, blue-sky day. The men are discussing how best to proceed when a tractor approaches not far from where they stand. Improvising, they stop the tractor, forcing the driver to charge the main roadblock of the prison. Using the tractor as their shield, a handful of men follow behind, while an additional twenty or so prepare to charge once the entrance has been breached. The remaining men, including Rivero, spread out in the hills surrounding the prison. The vegetation is dense and bushy, but Rivero finds a spot about 300 meters away where he can observe the only road leading up to the prison as well as the roadblock which the tractor is approaching. But in plain daylight and with no element of surprise, the national guardsmen take the tractor out effortlessly with a single rocket, injuring the driver and the soldiers using it for cover.

They have failed again and now they have injured comrades who need medical care. Over the radio, Rivero and his men reach out to the director of the prison, hoping to negotiate the release of Chávez and the other prisoners. But to no avail.

As they regroup for one last approach, Rivero learns the other teams around the country have been defeated.

Channel 10 has managed to keep its signal alive and uses its news show *Televen* to broadcast the government's side of the story. They display gruesome footage of dead civilians, killed by the rebels during the takeover of Canal 8.

From Miraflores, President Carlos Andrés Pérez addresses the nation: "Venezuelans, what is at stake here, as on February 4, is not a government or even a party; what is at stake is Venezuelan democracy. The Armed Forces have responded with dignity and with the loyalty we saw on February 4. There is nothing to fear."

The people don't take to the streets to join the rebels. And once again, the ability to use the media strongly influences the outcome of the coup.

In the lush hills surrounding the Yare Prison, Rivero and the others realize it is time to cut their losses. They gather their arms and get ready to disperse. The civilians scatter. Some of the soldiers head back to their units to turn themselves in, and some go into hiding. Rivero heads to a friend's house in Los Teques to hide and plot his next move.

El Libertador Air Base is the last to fall. At around midday, government tanks seize the base. Shortly thereafter, a Hercules carrying close to 100 insurgents manages to take off for Peru. Three fighter jets under rebel control escort the fugitives to the border, before returning home to surrender.

Through the media, Rivero learns that the air force officials who escaped to Peru are blaming the failure of the coup on the events that transpired in Canal 8. He is enraged, but also feels partly responsible. Rivero sends a letter to the Venezuelan media, assuming responsibility for the planning of the Canal 8 operation. He laments the violence and loss of life, but also criticizes the national guard for their excessive use of force in repelling the violence. Instead of remaining hidden in Venezuela as he had originally intended, Rivero decides to head to Peru. He wants to explain to the officers what really happened. The last thing the rebels need is division within their own ranks.

II

It is 1993. Folco stands before a spellbound crowd at the Hilton Hotel on Isla de Margarita, gathering support for his dream.

"The cruise ship industry is booming." He pauses for effect. "The last report we have is that average spending is 104 dollars per person per port or destination. There are places like the Bahamas where there is an inflow of 1,800,000 passengers a year. One of the islands we are competing with, Aruba, will be receiving 475,000 cruise ship passengers this year. It is almost inconceivable that Venezuela, having 3,000 kilometers of coastline and so many islands, has not even one cruise ship port of call. Now we have the opportunity to not only develop a new port, but to build one that will stand above all others as world class," Folco exclaims.

On the surface, little remains of the young hippie he once was. His hair is cut short. A receding hairline and a few extra kilos testify to the twenty years that have passed. He is wearing a conservative dark blue suit with the exaggerated shoulder pads typical of the early '90s. On an island where no one wears a suit, he is the odd bird, intriguing and intimidating at the same time. The Italian in him is still very apparent. He speaks as much with his hands and arms as with his mouth. His passion makes him perspire. Every now and then he takes out his handkerchief to wipe the sweat from his brow. There is so much potential. He has to make them see that. Convince the skeptics. In a few years, the island could be receiving 600,000 passengers annually. According to his calculations, there would be 7,000 new direct and indirect jobs created, transforming the economy of the entire island.

It is a big dream. Brave. But not unrealistic. Folco has done his research, but he needs investors. After two years, he finally finds them. The municipality of Mariño, as well as the two most important companies on the island—food retailer Rattan and the ferry company Conferry—agree to take on 25 percent of the ownership each. Together with Folco, they form the development company Desarrollos Puerto de La Mar.

The plan is to attract four cruise ships per week. This inflow of tourists directly to the heart of the city is expected to generate 64 million dollars in economic development every year. Benefiting from Margarita's duty-free status and this massive injection of customers, downtown retailers are expected to flourish. This, in turn, will reverse the trend of decay and neglect that has plagued the city.

To get the permits from the Venezuelan government, Folco needs the approval of various ministries. That means commissioning studies of the potential impacts on the environment, local fishery, pollution, and so on. The ministries of environmental affairs, infrastructure, tourism, agriculture, urban planning, transport and communication, health, and defense, each have to sign a letter of "no objection." Approval from other institutions, such as INEA (the National Institute for Water Management), the coast guard, the navy, and the local government, is also needed. All in all, Folco submits dozens of studies to each of the different ministries, institutions, and government organizations involved.

Folco also assures himself of the support of the local fishing community and traders. There will still be a pier in Puerto de La Mar where the *tapaditos*[3] and traders of fresh vegetables can sell their goods. But more importantly, in cooperation with the fishermen associations from Pampatar to La Isleta, Folco creates Fundepet (Foundation for the Development of Fishery and Tourism), an organization that will build a brand new marina called Puerto de Los Cocos, dedicated to traditional fishery. It will offer moorage for fishing boats and a home to the headquarters of the various fishing institutions so that fishermen can get the permits they need in one place instead of having to visit multiple offices across the island. The location will also host the main fish market and a university for oceanology, fishery, and tourism. 20,000m^2 of land are purchased and set aside for the project in an even more deteriorated part of downtown Porlamar.

Most local fishermen are excited about the opportunity. Folco collects 6,700 signatures from supportive fishermen and neighbors, many of whom publicly declare their support for the project. From posters around the city, their faces beam: "Give the tourist your best smile—Tourism and fishery is our future!"

III

It is January 21, 1993. Antonio Rivero stares at his own reflection in the mirror. The man looking back is a savage. His beard is long and bushy, his face worn. Even the eyes seem different somehow, more animal-like, as though the wilderness has crept into them.

For one month and twenty-one days, he walked the Great Venezuelan Savanna, crossing the border into Brazil. Hitchhiking when he could, but traveling mainly on foot to minimize his contact with people, he averaged eight to ten hours of walking a day. Sleeping in his hammock in the wild, and living off whatever food he could find in nature, he made his way across the Amazon and on toward Bolivia. By the time he arrived in Beni, the Bolivian part of the Amazon, he was broke. Surviving on fruit and the odd river fish caught on a simple hook and line, most nights he fell asleep hungry. At one point he met a Swiss couple—backpackers separated on either side of a river by a flash flood. He helped them reunite and accompanied them for a few days through the jungle.

When they parted ways, the couple gave him some Peruvian sols in thanks. While it wasn't much, it was enough to cover his stay in a six-bed dorm here at the Hostel España, a clean backpackers' hub in the center of Lima.

As he looks himself in the mirror for the first time in a long time, he is surprised he was allowed to check in. He takes a long shower, shaves, then lies down on his bed and closes his eyes. The clean, stiff sheets feel strange against the skin of his back.

* * *

Rivero finds the bulk of the Venezuelan exiles in Chosica, a community about two hours northeast of Lima in the valley by the Rímac River. Most of them are from the air force. They are suspicious of him. The incredible story of how he got here doesn't help. Some believe it. Others don't. Rivero's hopes of reconciliation are only partly realized.

Through Chávez's family and friends, Rivero stays in touch with his Comandante. Chávez is more isolated than ever. After the second failed coup of November 27, all his allies are either in exile or jail.

IV

It is April 1994 outside San Carlos military prison in Caracas. Antonio Rivero stands motionless. His face is turned upward toward the hot noon sun. His eyes are closed. Three weeks of legal proceedings are finally over. He savors the moment. He is a free man.

In May 1993, President Pérez was impeached on charges of corruption. The unpopular reforms and the two coup attempts had caused confidence in the government to plummet, until, finally, even his own party turned on him. In his place, Congress elected Ramón José Velásquez as interim president until the end of the year when new elections could be held.

The favorite candidate, Rafael Caldera, founder of incumbent Christian-democratic party Copei in 1946, had left his party and founded a new, more left-leaning party—National Convergence. In a speech to Congress after the attempted coup on February 4, Caldera had expressed sympathy with Hugo Chávez and the 1992 coup plotters:

"We cannot ask people to immolate themselves for freedom and democracy, when freedom and democracy are not able to feed them or to prevent the exorbitantly rising costs of subsistence; when they are not able to put a stop to the dreadful disease of corruption, which eats away at our institutions every day, before everyone's eyes. This situation cannot be hidden. The military coup is reprehensible and condemnable in every form, but it would be naive to think that this is only an adventure of a few ambitious men who rushed ahead without realizing what they were getting themselves into. There is a context, there is a tide, there is a serious situation in the country and if this situation is not confronted, the fates will have many and very serious concerns in store for us. ... I would like the heads of state of the rich countries, who called President Carlos Andrés Pérez to express their solidarity in defense of democracy, to understand that democracy cannot exist if the people are hungry."[4]

The speech gained him the support of former political opponents such as the Movement for Socialism and the Communist

Party of Venezuela. In his presidential campaign, Caldera promised to pardon the coup plotters should he be elected.

But factions within the military conspired against him. There were rumors of another coup. From prison, Chávez asked Rivero, still in exile in Peru, to gather intelligence. Rivero returned to Venezuela clandestinely through Colombia. Again, he modified his appearance, staying underground. In a fifty-day operation, Rivero uncovered a military plot to create chaos through a series of explosions that would justify military intervention and the ousting of interim President Velásquez. Then the election schedule was to be accelerated and rigged against Caldera.

Working with others loyal to the cause, Rivero thwarted the plot against Caldera by identifying his enemies among the military ranks.

Today, the verdict is the reward for his efforts. Caldera kept his word. In April 1994, he pardons Chávez, Rivero, and most of their compatriots.

On his first day of freedom, Chávez visits Bolívar's tomb at the National Pantheon. He places a wreath beside Bolívar's grave, a symbol to mark the start of the "Bolivarian hurricane."[5]

V

"Come here Hugo, there is someone who wants to see you."

Señora Carmen Reyes de Díaz ushers Chávez into the small bedroom of her apartment in Los Teques. Then she leaves.

It is June 1994. Chávez is dressed in a grey *liqui-liqui*, a traditional *llanero* outfit consisting of full-length trousers and a jacket with a rounded Nehru-style collar, fastened by a chain link. As part of his "Bolivarian hurricane," Chávez is touring the country to rally support and reorganize his Bolivarian movement. In passing through Los Teques, his first stop is the home of Señora Reyes de Díaz. She is the mother of Carlos, a major who was also imprisoned on February 4, and she supplied her son and Chávez with food and other necessities during their time in prison.

Chávez squints as his eyes adjust to the dim light. Then his face opens up in a wide grin.

Waiting in the shadows is Antonio Rivero.

"*¡León de Profecía!*" Chávez exclaims as he enters the bedroom.

Although the two men have exchanged countless letters over the past two years, this is the first time they are able to meet in person since before the coup of February 4.

Visibly moved, Chávez approaches Rivero and grabs him by both shoulders.

"I don't kiss men," he says. "But I will give you a kiss for everything you've done for me and for the struggle." He leans over and plants a kiss on Rivero's cheek.

Then they embrace, remaining silent for a long time.

"We are organizing the movement again," Chávez says once they are seated on the old lady's bed. "I'm taking care of the civilian side, but I need help from officers inside the forces to reorganize the military side."

As a condition of his release from prison, Chávez was forced to leave the armed forces. Rivero, on the other hand, was allowed to remain in active service. To avoid rumors of new conspiracies, it is best that they are not seen together.

Like many of the coup-plotting officers who were allowed to stay in the armed forces, Rivero was stationed in the remote jungle regions of Zulia, near the Colombian border. Chávez insists they keep in touch and meet whenever Rivero is home on leave, which is every two months or so.

"For now and forever we'll keep up this struggle! Homeland or death! We will prevail. Be strong, my friend! Fuerza!"

Shortly thereafter, Chávez travels to Latin America in search of foreign support for his Bolivarian movement. Most significantly, he visits Cuba where Fidel Castro attends to him personally, gripping him by both shoulders as soon as he steps off the plane. Cuba is in crisis. With the fall of the Soviet Union, Fidel lost his chief ally and financier whose subsidies had kept his fragile economy afloat. He needs new friends and has long hoped to find them in oil-rich Venezuela. In the 1960s, Castro supplied weapons and training to Venezuela's leftist guerrillas. While their efforts failed, he has reached out to every Venezuelan president ever since. Chávez, while not a president, is an important potential ally. Shadowed by an official photographer, Chávez and Castro quickly bond. They have a great deal in common. Both come from rural backgrounds and both grew up with ambitions of becoming professional baseball players, until politics and revolution superseded all other dreams. Like a boy who had won a meeting with his idol, Chávez is sent home star-struck with a photo book filled with the moments he and Fidel had shared.[6]

Chávez's visit to Cuba concerns Rivero. He does not believe that communism is the right solution for Venezuela. But Chávez assures him he has no such intentions. He is merely being polite, accepting an invitation extended to him by a foreign chief of state.

Between 1994 and 1996, Chávez and Rivero meet regularly in Caracas to discuss the best ways for the movement MBR—200 to develop and reach power.

Though figures vary, several hundred people are estimated to have died in the two coup attempts of 1992. The dead haunt Rivero, convincing him that violence is not the way to bring about change in politics. So, in 1995, when Chávez raises the option of taking power by force again, Rivero is disappointed. At first he stays quiet, hoping Chávez will change his mind. There are still many other non-violent options and plans being developed simultaneously. But in the beginning of 1996, Chávez announces that it is time to finalize a plan. The best plan, he has decided, is to seize the strategic state of Bolívar. The state has large garrisons across all four military branches—air force, army, navy, and national guard. It also has plenty of veterans from the former coup attempts, since many officers were stationed in this border jungle as a form of punishment. Bolívar state is relatively easy to defend, as the jungle and the Orinoco River make it difficult for tanks to maneuver. And of course there is Guri, the massive energy plant generating between 70 and 80 percent of the energy consumed in Venezuela. From Bolívar, Chávez plans to apply military and economic pressure on the government until he can seize all of Venezuela.

Chávez asks Rivero if he would secure access to the National Parks and the weapons stashes of the units located there.

"I will be honest, I don't agree with this. I think you should opt for the electoral route. You have a lot of followers. You can form a successful political movement. We will provide the military backing for your victory, but after all that has happened, I cannot be part of pushing it through by force," Rivero says.

"I'm sorry you feel that way, but I appreciate your honesty. We'll talk later," says Chávez.

Though Rivero detects no change in Chávez's expression or tone of voice, Chávez never calls Rivero directly again.

But Rivero is not the only one to oppose the plan. The governor of Bolívar state and leader of leftist party Radical Cause, Andrés Velásquez, also rejects the plan. As do several of Chávez's military colleagues and allies. In the end, he is unable to rally the support he needs.

Chávez's mentor, Luis Miquilena, former communist leader and well-known politician, urges Chávez to rely on the ballot box. A frequent visitor of his in prison, Miquilena provided Chávez with a political education while trying to convince him that change could be achieved democratically. Chávez remains skeptical, believing that most elections are rigged in order to legitimize an established order. He is convinced the oligarchy would do whatever possible to prevent a Bolivarian like him from becoming president. But Miquilena insists that Chávez has enough support to win such an overwhelming victory that the establishment can't deny it. Putting this theory to the test, Chávez organizes a poll. The results show he has a clear majority.

With the support and guidance of Miquilena, Chávez and his supporters in the Bolivarian movement found a new political party. In July 1997, they register the Fifth Republic Movement (MVR—Movimiento Quinta República) in order to support Chávez's candidacy in the 1998 presidential elections.

Rivero is enthusiastic. It is precisely what he has hoped for: an approach focused on defending the rights of the people.

VI

"I hope that you will live in a Venezuela of democracy and prosperity!"

Juan Carlos Requesens still remembers the exact words of his grandfather. It was not so much what he said, but how he said it, in that tone of voice he reserved for important announcements.

It is 1998. Juan Carlos is nine years old and the whole family is anxiously anticipating the election results.

Born in 1989, the year of the Caracazo, Juan Carlos's rise to influential student leader twenty-five years later was preceded by a childhood of political and economic turmoil.

In the 1980s, collapsing oil prices hit Venezuela's economy hard. As oil was the country's main source of income, the consequences were far-reaching. The number of people living below the poverty line nearly doubled from 36 percent in 1984 to 66 percent in 1995.[7] In 1996, inflation peaked just shy of 100 per cent. Industrial wages and the minimum wage, once the highest in Latin America, dropped to a level below that of the 1950s.[8] By 1998, the purchasing power of the average salary was only a third of what it had been in 1978.[9]

It is against this backdrop that the charismatic Hugo Chávez takes the stage as an anti-establishment candidate in a country that has come to distrust politicians. He promises to eradicate poverty, put an end to cronyism and corruption, purge the elites, and open up political power to all.

Everyone in Juan Carlos's family votes for Chávez: his mother—an English teacher—his father—a knee surgeon with the Venezuelan armed forces—as well as other family members, and friends.

On December 6, 1998, Hugo Chávez is elected president of Venezuela, with 56 percent of the vote.

In his inaugural address, Chávez echoes Bolívar's speech before the Congress of Angostura: "Happy is the citizen who, displaying the armorial shield of his command, has the privilege of convoking the representatives of national sovereignty so that they might exercise their will, which is absolute."[10]

"Why Bolívar?" Chávez asks. "Our Bolivarianism is not merely rhetorical ... It stems from an urgent need for all Venezuelans, for all Latin Americans, to look to the roots of our own existence for the formula to get out of this horrible labyrinth in which we all find ourselves, in one way or another."

VII

It is 1999 in Caracas. Folco is at the Ministry of Transport and Communications. In an office that looks more like a living room, four friendly officials smile at him from across a big, round table. Bookshelves and paintings line the walls. On the table before him rests the document he has been waiting for. The government of Venezuela has finally granted Folco's company the concession to build, operate, administrate, and maintain the cruise ship port for fifty years. The concession is approved by the new president himself—Hugo Rafael Chávez Frías.

Folco has come alone, wearing his best suit. He has waited so many years for this moment that he almost can't believe it is happening. They all gather around, and with the expectant faces of family members watching a birthday boy blow out his candles, they watch as Folco carefully writes his name on the contract.

With the permit in place, the state-owned bank, Banco Industrial de Venezuela, approves loans of 12 million dollars in bolívares. In the years of construction, Folco and his investors will put in an additional 10 million dollars of their own funds. Ground is broken. Construction is underway.

* * *

A few months later, Margarita's newly elected Chavista governor, Alexis Navarro, shows up at Puerto de La Mar unannounced. Folco walks over to receive him.

"Hello Alexis! How are you doing?"

Navarro continues past Folco without returning his greeting. Except for the age difference, accentuated by Navarro's white hair and beard, he is the spitting image of Comandante Chávez. The same nose, the same rounded lips.

"Come with me!" he shouts as he heads toward the water. He walks up the stairs to the top of one of the buildings under construction. From there, he points to a small fishing boat with three fishermen out in the bay.

"Look!" he exclaims. "People fish here!"

Folco can't believe it. This is the first time he has seen any fishermen in this polluted bay. He senses a plot, as if Navarro asked them to be there.

"Listen, Alexis," Folco says, turning to face the governor. "You know very well nobody has ever fished in those waters ... I have been working on Puerto de La Mar for nine years. You have been governor for a few months. When your time as governor is up, I will still be here."

The two men stare at each other a moment. Without saying a word, Navarro walks away.

A few years earlier, when another entrepreneur had attempted to get a permit to build a cruise ship port on the island, the fishermen of El Morro had objected. In an open letter, they suggested the location of Puerto de La Mar as a better option. There, they said, a cruise ship port would not interfere with their fishing. When Folco first picked the location recommended by the fishermen, Wilmer González, leader of El Morro, called and congratulated him.

But now, it turns out, González has changed his mind. Having recently returned from a six-month "ideological training" program in Cuba, sponsored by Navarro, González joins the governor and a few other local Chavista deputies in an effort to undermine support for the port development.

After their meeting at the site, Navarro refuses to recognize Folco's concession to build, operate, and maintain Puerto de La Mar. Even though the permit has been approved by the Comandante himself, he requests Folco to redo all the studies.

Inspectors show up with greater and greater frequency. The pace of progress slows.

"Folco, have you heard, they found a big rock by the entrance of Puerto de La Mar so the cruise ships won't be able to enter without great risk of getting damaged," Folco is told by an acquaintance one day on his way to the port. "Folco, have you heard, your dredging will create problems with the quality of the water," someone else comments. Folco tries to explain that they haven't, nor will they need to, do any dredging. But it doesn't matter; the person simply raises the next topic from a long list of rumors: "The location of your port will disrupt traffic circulation in the downtown area ..."

Every week, there is a new story about Puerto de La Mar and why it won't work.

Until finally, they strike upon sardines.

Based on studies by local marine ecologist Alfredo Gómez, the opponents of Puerto de La Mar declare that a cruise ship port would threaten the traditional sardine fishery for which Margarita is famous. Folco cannot believe it. No other study had indicated that the sardines in Margarita would be hurt by a cruise ship port. With the level of contamination in the bay right in front of Puerto de La Mar, outlined in his environmental studies, sardines could not possibly live there. But just to be absolutely sure, Folco asks a number of experts, including the navy and the School of Applied Marine Sciences, to redo their studies. Their previous findings are confirmed: there are no sardines in front of Puerto de La Mar. It is agreed that the bay has not been a habitat for sardines for thirty years. The sardines of Margarita are concentrated in other areas of the island. Following the study, the Ministry for Environmental Affairs grants Puerto de La Mar its permit, for the third time.

By this point, fifty-eight cruise ships have expressed interest in making Puerto de La Mar their port of call. Ironically, this interest becomes fodder for the cargo port of El Guamache, on the other side of the island. Since the change to a Chavista government, the cargo business has slumped, so management broaden their scope to include cruise ships interested in Puerto de La Mar. They offer cruise liners to be their temporary port-of-call while construction of Folco's port is being completed.

VIII

It is 2001. María Corina is heading home from her Caracas office where she now runs an Internet-based start-up for home services. After six rewarding years, she left Atenea having contributed everything she could. She was ready to take on new challenges. But her return to business is not proving as fulfilling as she had hoped.

As she crosses the street, she hears someone call her name.

"María Corina! María Corina!"

She turns around. A young man who appears to be in his early twenties is beaming at her. She doesn't recognize his face.

"Don't you remember me?"

"I'm sorry," she says.

"You don't remember?" the young man asks again, playfully.

María Corina studies his face more carefully, but is unable to place him.

"My name is José Manuel. We met at Atenea," he says.

"My God! José Manuel!" María Corina exclaims surprised.

José was one of the troubled young teens she worked with at the shelter.

"I work for a security company now. I'm married. I have two kids! It is all thanks to you, all of you! You changed my life!" he says, glowing.

The moment stays with her. Back in her office the next day, she struggles to concentrate. How she misses working with things that matter! That sense of purpose. Her eyes scan the barren office: the desk, the computers, the neatly piled papers of purchase orders. Her ancestors left their mark on history. What will her legacy be? What will be her impact?

IX

It is 2002. María Corina Machado and engineer Alejandro Plaz are chatting in the lobby of a hotel in downtown Caracas. As usual, the conversation turns to the increasing social challenges of Venezuela.

"I've been thinking," Plaz says. His brown eyes are full of life, in youthful contrast to his prematurely grayed hair. "What if we were to start an NGO that could channel the growing differences peacefully, in a democratic and electoral way? Think about it María Corina ... It's time to go from words to action."

Machado never pictured herself becoming involved with politics, but with the rise of Chávez, she feels compelled to act. Like her great uncle Armando Zuloaga, she is passionate about freedom and about her country. Now it's her turn to take a stand for the Venezuela she wants.

She leaves the lobby overcome by the feeling of destiny. "It's a choice of ballots over bullets," she reflects.

Shortly thereafter, Machado and Plaz form the NGO Súmate (Join up).

X

It is in the midst of the Iraq war. Hugo Chávez takes to the air on *Aló Presidente*, his daylong variety show broadcast every Sunday on all the major channels. Surrounded by cows and rural supporters, with a panoramic savanna unfolding in the background, Chávez addresses President Bush directly:

"Eres un burro, Mr. Danger!" he exclaims, repeating his message several times in Spanish. Then, presumably to make sure the message is understood by the American president, he adds in broken English: "You are a donkey, Mr Bush!"

After criticizing the invasion of Iraq and President Bush's cowardly tactics, Chávez dares his fellow president to invade Venezuela.

"If one day you were to come up with the crazy idea of invading Venezuela, I'll be waiting for you in this savanna, Mr Danger." His eyes burning, he stares into the camera and shouts in broken English: "Come on here, Mr Danger! Come on here!"

The cameraman turns to film the officers in the audience. Some applaud. Others shift uneasily in their seats. But Chávez is not done. He is worked up.

"Come on here Mr. Danger!" Then, shifting back to Spanish, he shouts "Coward!"

But he seems dissatisfied. It's not strong enough. He tries again: "Assassin!" he barks.

Still not good enough.

"Genocist!"

Chávez seems pleased and repeats it, eyes burning: "Genocist! You are a genocist! You're an alcoholic, a drunk ... a drunk Mr Danger. You're an immoral Mr Danger. You're the worst ever, Mr Danger!"

He turns to his audience.

"How do you say 'the worst' in English?"

He picks up a faint, inaccurate, response from someone in the audience.

"The last! You are the last!" Chávez roars in English and smashes his hand through the air.

"The worst of the worst that has existed on this planet is called George W. Bush. God free the world from this menace! Because he is an assassin. A sick man. A psychologically ill man!"

Stupefied, the world watches as Chávez continues to heap abuse on Bush for three and a half minutes.

* * *

Chávez has often been called the world's first virtual president. From the very start, he understood the power of mass media and used it to give himself a permanent presence in people's life.

"The media has for us a fundamental priority because it is a weapon in the armed struggle and a weapon to tell the people of our intentions," he announced in one of his first TV broadcasts.

Once elected, Chávez created seven new state channels. He also made frequent use of *cadenas*, which literally translated means "chains." A *cadena* is a broadcast that has to be shown by all channels, public or private. *Cadenas* were meant to be used for emergency announcements that needed to reach the public without delay. As such, they had precedence over regular programming, and on the president's order they would interrupt movies, soap operas, or sports events without warning. Chávez employed this "emergency" measure several times a week, often for hours at a time, and rarely for any valid cause.

And every Sunday there was *Aló Presidente*. It started on the president's orders, usually around 11, and lasted for as long as he wished, almost always the whole day.

It was advertised as a variety show, and it lived up to its billing. Chávez would tour the country, recording each show in a different place. One show he could be talking about a law proposal at his desk in Caracas, the next he'd be operating an oil drill, or singing a song, or reciting a poem, or riding a horse. He invited his viewers in, sharing everything—childhood memories, anecdotes, history lectures, policy decisions, hopes, and fears.

In one episode, Chávez decided, seemingly at a whim, to create a unique half-hour time zone for the country, moving the clocks back half an hour so that there would be daylight when children went to school.

"I don't care if they call me crazy, the new time will go ahead," he said.

The change was implemented within a week.

"These children have to get up at five in the morning ... they arrive at school dead tired," said Chávez. "And why? Because of our time."[11]

Other television highlights include his argument that capitalism could have killed life on Mars: "I have always said, heard, that it would not be strange that there had been civilization on Mars, but maybe capitalism arrived there, imperialism arrived and finished off the planet."

Someone in the audience burst out laughing, but quickly stopped when noticing that nobody else was laughing. It was apparently not a joke.

The drama, unpredictability, and real-life implications of *Aló Presidente* made it famous all over the world. The *New York Times* called it "The Realest Reality Show in the World" with a degree of absurdity comparable to that of the American 1980s show *Mrs. Mouth* featuring an upside-down chin and mouth dressed as a woman.

"A TV show in America, no matter how engaging or successful or artfully put together, is always, in essence, a distraction from life. 'Aló Presidente' inverts this formula, at least for Venezuelans," wrote Rachel Nolan for the *New York Times*:

"Chávez's show not only reflects reality, it also affects reality. Whatever he says on air, whatever he orders his inferiors to do, however he decides to spend public money, becomes law and policy right away. It's not Monopoly money that he's throwing around. In that sense, it's the only really real reality show out there."[12]

Chávez's constant media presence allowed millions of citizens to forge a personal bond with him. After being ignored by the elite for so long, many welcomed this illusion of direct presidential contact. Chávez talked to the people. In the early days of the show, it was even possible to call in and tell the president about one's problems or challenges. Faithful followers would spend their entire Sunday with him. Maybe not glued to the television set for all eight hours of the show, but listening to him in the background, while cleaning, cooking, drinking beer, or doing chores.

In most homes, even in the barrios, the TV was always on, and Chávez was on every channel.

4

THE ORDEAL

"Damn it, how will I ever get out of this labyrinth?"

Simón Bolívar

I

January 2001. The system begins to consume Folco.

The state-owned bank, Banco Industrial de Venezuela (BIV), has yet to release his funds. Folco writes, calls, and visits bank officials repeatedly. After many mixed messages, the bank finally sends a technical evaluation commission to review the documentation related to Desarollos Puerto de La Mar, the same process used to approve the loan in the first place. The commission scrutinizes the permits, legal paperwork, the environmental studies, the impact on the local fishing industry, port operations, administration, finance, accounting, budget, costs, commercialization plans, and sources of revenue. Folco's staff struggle to cope with all the requests for documentation and meetings. Construction comes to a complete standstill. Potential tenants begin to question the future of the project.

May 2001. After four months of additional diligence, the commission finds that Puerto de La Mar complies with all the requirements. They present their conclusions to the credit department of the bank, recommending once again that the bank proceed to lend the funds previously granted.

Two days later, the president of BIV, its management, and the entire board of directors are suddenly replaced. The new president, Jorge Castillo, and his board disregard the work of the previous leadership, and construction of Puerto de La Mar remains on hold pending funding.

Folco writes. He calls. He lobbies through friends and contacts. After a few months, Castillo agrees to carry out a new commission to inspect the viability of Puerto de La Mar. After six months reviewing the very same documentation, the new leadership reaches the very same conclusion as the previous commission. Credit is granted.

February 2002. The bank makes its first payment. At this point, construction has been on hold for fourteen months, save for some small progress made using the partners' own capital.

April 2002. The president of BIV is discharged, and with his discharge loan payments stop.

July 2002. Folco appeals and the new president of BIV and his various vice presidents begin yet another inspection of Puerto de La Mar, reviewing the very same documentation. Again, they reach the same conclusion. Everything is in order. Credit is extended. Loan payments resume.

November 2002. There is another change of management. President Luis Orozco and his management team have just put up their names on their desks when they are replaced by Leonardo Gonzalez and another management team. Payments stop. Due diligence starts all over.

April 2003. Management agrees that all is in order. Payments recommence, but the recurring standstills and uncertainty have scared off many retailers planning to open shop in the port.

By October 2003, the port is finally ready to start receiving ships just in time for the upcoming cruise ship season. It is just as beautiful as Folco had imagined. Terracotta-roofed structures in off-white contrast beautifully with the turquoise sea.

Representatives from the Florida Caribbean Cruise Association, representing the thirteen biggest cruise lines in the world, arrive in Porlamar to conduct an inspection of Puerto de La Mar. The facilities exceed their expectations: "After 15 years in the cruise industry, I have traveled the world inspecting many ports, in order to approve them for use by the Royal Caribbean International Cruises, and I must congratulate you for the professional work you have done in Puerto de La Mar," nautical superintendent, Captain Tellef Lie-Nielsen, writes in a letter to Folco.

Now the only remaining obstacle between Folco and his dream is a written certificate of compliance from INEA, the National Institute for Water Management. But although they have already conducted several successful inspections of the port, INEA refuses to issue the necessary document. Folco loses another cruise ship season.

II

"Eddie Ramírez, General Director, until today, of the Palmaven division. You're out!" shouts Chávez.

It is April 7, 2002. Episode 101 of Chávez's weekly TV show, *Aló Presidente*, is being broadcast live to 15 million viewers.

"You had been given the responsibility of leading a very important business, Palmaven, a subsidiary of PDVSA. This Palmaven belongs to all Venezuelans. Anyway, Señor Ramírez, thank you very much. You, sir, are dismissed."

Chávez goes on to fire and humiliate a list of officials from the state-owned petroleum company Petróleos de Venezuela SA (PDVSA). The audience cheers after each name. No saboteurs trying to prevent the advance of the revolution will be tolerated, Chávez explains. Then he picks up a whistle, as if he were a soccer referee, blows it and shouts: "Offside!"

Venezuela's oil wealth was crucial to Chávez plans of reducing poverty. As such, one of his first moves as president was to revitalize the Organization of the Petroleum Exporting Countries (OPEC) and use it to drive up the price of oil by restricting supply.

In March 1999, at an OPEC meeting in Vienna, Venezuela stressed the importance of respecting the agreed upon cuts in production and even suggested further cutbacks. OPEC, conceived by Venezuela and created in 1960, had set production quotas for its members, but these were not followed. Before Chávez, not even Venezuela adhered to them. When Chávez came to office in late 1998, the price of oil was less than 10 dollars a barrel, but his sleek maneuvering caused oil prices to rise sharply. Early on in his presidency, Chávez toured all ten of Venezuela's fellow OPEC members, including Iran and Iraq. Oblivious to criticism, he was the first foreign head of state to visit Saddam Hussein since the end of the Gulf War.[1]

Venezuela had exploited its oil since the early 1900s. At first, big Western companies drilled the country's oil, but after President Carlos Andrés Pérez nationalized the industry in 1976, state-owned PDVSA would take on this task. It did so very well, employing 30,000 people, pumping three million barrels a day and competing successfully with multinational giants like BP, ExxonMobil, and Chevron.

Most of the state's revenue came from oil, but Chávez still felt that PDVSA kept too much of the profit. He resented the elitist mindset of the management with their air of superiority and their condescending attitudes toward the workers. He wanted control. So Chávez decided to replace the existing board of industry insiders with his own people.

On February 26, 2002, all the presidents and directors of the various subsidiaries of PDVSA responded to what they perceived as an attack on meritocracy by launching a campaign to protect PDVSA. They warned Chávez not to make the mistake of politicizing the company. Then, on April 4, 2002, they went on strike. But Chávez would have none of it. Referee whistle in hand, he seized control of the match.

III

"We are no longer Chavistas," Juan Carlos's father informs him one day.

It is April 2002 in Caracas. Juan Carlos shrugs. He is thirteen years old. Politics is the last thing on his mind. But for his father it matters.

Within the first year of his election, the Requesens were already starting to regret having voted for Chávez. On his first trip abroad as president, Chávez went to visit Fidel Castro in Cuba. Increasingly, the Requesens felt there was a hidden agenda to launch a socialist revolution. They felt deceived.

* * *

Once in power, Chávez prioritized the drafting and implementation of a new constitution. The old elite still held a majority of seats in Congress and needed to be neutralized while momentum was with him. Before a hostile Congress, Chávez echoed Bolívar's denunciation of those who had rejected independence in 1811. He called for Congress to join his Bolivarian revolution. "Today gentlemen, to join those who want to conserve things as they are now, to seek consensus with those who oppose those changes that are necessary, I say today like Bolívar: it is a betrayal!"[2]

Chávez swiftly announced and won a referendum to approve a constituent assembly. In July, its members were elected. Before the end of the year, they had drafted a new constitution, which was approved by over 70 percent of voters in a referendum held on December 15, 1999.

With the adoption of the new constitution, the country's name officially changed from the "Republic of Venezuela" to the

"Bolivarian Republic of Venezuela." The constitution itself was referred to as the "Bolivarian Constitution" because its ideology supposedly stemmed from the thinking and political philosophy of Simón Bolívar.

While the document enshrined additional human rights guarantees, free healthcare and education, protection for the environment, and the right of indigenous minorities to uphold their own traditional cultures, religions, and languages, it also enhanced the powers of the president. The presidential term was extended from five to six years with the right to immediate reelection. The two houses of Congress were merged into one National Assembly, eliminating the Senate. The president also attained control over promotions within the armed forces.

Soon, Venezuela became Cuba's main trading partner, far ahead of China, Canada, or Spain. Through a combination of direct investments, subsidies, soft loans, and profitable trade contracts, where Cuba acted as the intermediary on Venezuelan imports of food, goods, and equipment, Venezuela essentially kept the Cuban economy afloat.[3]

* * *

In his third year of office, tensions between Chávez and the opposition intensified.

In November 2001, Chávez pushed through forty-nine laws by decree, several of which the opposition deemed unconstitutional. The most controversial new laws were the oil law, which doubled the royalties paid to the government, and the land reform law, which allowed expropriations.

The infected conflict with PDVSA further outraged the opposition. The public dismissal and humiliation of Ramírez and his colleagues became the final straw. Two days later, the Confederación de Trabajadores de Venezuela (CTV)—a federation of labor unions representing over 1.2 million workers—as well as Fedecámaras, the national federation of private businesses, joined the oil executives in their strike.

IV

"Vamos a Miraflores! Let's go to Miraflores!"

Malvina Pesate first hears the rally cry from a young boy in the crowd.

"Why to Miraflores?" she asks him.

"Why not? Let's tell Chávez we don't like what he's doing."

It is April 11, 2002. Hundreds of thousands of protestors, some claim over a million, gather for a march to PDVSA's headquarters in Chuao where they will demand the reinstatement of the dismissed executives. But as the march kicks off, it becomes obvious that the crowd wants more.

Marching on the presidential palace is forbidden. Afterwards, no one could say who suggested it first. All Malvina knows, as the march changes course and heads for Miraflores, is that it feels right.

Television cameras follow the march, broadcasting it live to the nation. As it closes in on Miraflores, the marchers stop. National guard troops and pro-Chávez groups flood into the streets. Rocks hail down on the marchers.

At home, Malvina's mother anxiously watches the events unfold on television. Suddenly, the screen starts to shake as though the cameraman is running. Malvina's mother rushes to the phone to warn her daughter.

"Get out of there, Malvina! The Chavistas are throwing rocks!"

"Don't worry, Mama!" High on adrenaline, Malvina hangs up the phone and ignores her mother.

The gray vapor of teargas creeps in, shrouding the picture. Then, Malvina's mother and the millions of Venezuelans watching the unfolding drama are cut off. The distressing images of the live broadcast are replaced by the government symbol and a blowing trumpet. "This is a special announcement from the Ministry of Communication and Information."

Seconds later, Chávez appears at his desk. Dressed in a suit, he sits by the ever-present portrait of Simón Bolívar.

"Good afternoon, my dear fellow countrymen and countrywomen of Venezuela. Here we are, as ever, facing our responsibilities."

The speech is broadcast as a *cadena*, which means all channels are obligated to air it, and thus prevented from showing the events unfolding outside.

Chávez speaks for ninety minutes, urging the marchers to reflect and repent. He ends by assuring the population that the situation is "under control."

Meanwhile, Malvina and her friends close in on the palace. They carry placards stating: "We want justice! We want democracy!"

"Watch out for the teargas," someone shouts.

A lady in the crowd offers Malvina a jug of vinegar.

"Dip your shirt in it," she says. "Then put it over your mouth!"

She is wrapped in a Venezuelan flag reeking of vinegar.

Malvina looks at the lady blankly. Why would she want to do that? What is she talking about?

"It will help you breathe through the teargas," the lady explains.

They continue straight ahead until they can proceed no further. The metropolitan police have blocked the road to separate the marchers from the Chavista crowd ahead of them. By now, big rocks are falling all around them. Malvina and the other women in her group of friends seek shelter behind a newspaper stand while the men continue ahead with the placards. Malvina is peeking out from behind the stand when she sees a man about 3 meters in front of her hit the ground. She rushes out to warn her boyfriend. Searching for his head in the crowd, she feels an impact to her face. *Concha*, she thinks, they got me in the face with a rock.

Malvina can't feel her face. She hits the ground. Someone pulls her to the side and loads her on to a motorbike. She tries to object. She is terrified of motorbikes. Then, the world goes black.

"Are you in a lot of pain?" A woman with bright red lipstick leans over Malvina. She is in an ambulance.

"No," she replies. She can't believe she passed out. How embarrassing.

When they arrive at the clinic, she walks in on her own. At this point, everybody but Malvina knows she has been shot.

The bullet entered her face just next to her mouth, leaving a 5-millimeter entry hole, crushing the jaw and exiting through her neck, leaving a hole of 2 centimeters. A video recording of the event shows Malvina tilting her head back slightly as she is calling out for her boyfriend just before the bullet finds her face. That slight movement probably saved her life.

Outside Miraflores, bullets keep flying. Bodies fall to the ground. Unidentified snipers are spotted, but whom do they represent? Panic spreads as people in the crowd appear to be executed at random, with both Chavistas and non-Chavistas targeted.

Defying Chávez's attempt to monopolize the airwaves, four private television stations choose to split their screens, showing the president's speech on one side, and live images from the turmoil outside Miraflores on the other. The contrast between the president's words and the murdered marchers makes Chávez look like a liar.

When it is all over, nineteen people have been killed and hundreds wounded.

Throughout the evening, private television channels show reruns of footage recorded earlier in the afternoon of armed pro-Chávez supporters firing their pistols. Then they show footage of the wounded and the dead. With nothing to substantiate their claims, the media convey, in no uncertain terms, that Chávez is the one responsible for it all. Weaved in with the distressing footage, oppositional leaders start appearing on live television denouncing the president and urging the military high command to intervene.

V

It is 11:30 p.m. on April 11, 2002. A commission of generals arrives at Miraflores. They have come to ask the president to resign.

On duty inside the presidential palace is Antonio Rivero, now the head of communication security. As part of the group in charge of the president's security, Rivero is responsible for all telephone, radio, fax, satellite, and electronic communication. He ensures phones aren't tapped and microphones aren't planted inside Miraflores. Thirty people, including phone operators, radio installers, technicians, and informatics personnel, work for him.

Upon the arrival of the generals, Chávez summons about thirty of his closest men to his office, including Rivero. He orders phone calls to be made to all the command units and most important military garrisons—Caracas, Valencia, Maracay, and Zulia. Nobody picks up, not even Raúl Baduel, commander of the 42nd Paratrooper Brigade, and supposedly Chávez's most loyal general.

"I don't have the high command, I don't have the armed forces, I don't have anything," Chávez tells Rivero and the others present in his office. Realizing he is on his own, Chávez agrees to resign, but his resignation will not be unconditional. The constitution must be followed, Chávez insists. The vice president must take over and new elections must be called within the stipulated time. Chávez also asks that he and his family be allowed to leave the country and go to Cuba or Spain.

Then Chávez is left alone with Lucas Rincón, who has been appointed Minister of Defense less than two weeks previous. After their private meeting, Rincón heads back to his office at the ministry where he calls a press conference to announce to the nation that the president has resigned.

Only he hasn't. Back at the military headquarters, the generals have decided to reject Chávez's conditions. He will not be allowed to leave the country. They want an unconditional resignation or Miraflores will be attacked. The generals return to Miraflores to bring in Chávez. They place a resignation letter on his desk for him to sign. Chávez makes some manual edits in the document and sends it to be adjusted. He is presented with another version, which he edits and rejects. Finally, a third version is placed on Chávez's desk.

Watching all this from the corner of Chávez's office is Rivero. He can't see if Chávez actually signs the third version, but he sees him hand it to Major Jesús Suárez Chourio, head of Chávez's personal security, who rolls up the paper and puts it in his inside pocket. "I'll take this," Suarez announces.

"Tell me, Comandante, what must we do?" Rivero asks as Chávez stands up to leave.

"You already know, León de Profecía," Chávez replies. He picks up a book from his desk, a biography of himself, *In the Shadow of the Liberator* by Richard Gott, scribbles something on the first page, and hands the book to Rivero. It reads: "Antonio León Profecía Rivero; In this moment of life, of memories, of dreams, of hopes. Para siempre!!"

He finishes with his famous signature and the date, by now the early hours of April 12, 2002.

Then the generals and Suarez escort Chávez to the presidential car to take him away. Rivero and another major accompany them in a different vehicle to the gates of Miraflores.

Chávez leaves in uniform, but when the delegation arrives at the high command he is ordered to take it off and remain in his undershirt and undergarments. The military police then place him in a holding cell for the rest of the night.

Among the opposition, celebrations erupt. Generals, tycoons, bishops, and media-owners cheer, but Rivero is left with a foul taste in his mouth. So this is over, *menos mal*, but it shouldn't have happened like this. Why wouldn't they accept Chávez's conditions?

In the morning, a helicopter takes Chávez to Turiamo, a Caribbean naval base. Meanwhile, the military high command asks Pedro Carmona, head of the national federation of private businesses, to form a provisional government at Miraflores. Carmona is a well known business figure in Venezuela who has managed several petrochemical companies in the 1980s and 1990s, before becoming president of the federation.

At 5:30 p.m., Carmona hosts a televised ceremony in the Salón Ayacucho at Miraflores. Short and slight, he stands in a dark blue suit before a room full of supporters.

Right hand raised, he swears himself in. "I, Pedro Carmona, as President of the Republic of Venezuela, swear before God almighty, before the nation and all Venezuelans, to re-establish justice, equality, solidarity, and social responsibility."

"We love you Pedro!" shouts someone in the crowd.

Carmona smiles restrainedly, with lips tightly sealed as though holding back a wide grin. He raises a clenched fist in gratitude.

"We hereby decree that a democratic transitional government shall be established in the following manner," announces the newly appointed attorney general.

"We hereby dissolve the National Assembly," he continues.

The crowd cheers, pumping their fists in the air.

"We also dissolve the Supreme Court."

More cheers.

"We dismiss the Attorney General, the Head of the Central Bank, the Ombudsman, and the National Electoral Board."

By now the cheers are deafening.

Then, Carmona revokes the constitution.

Meanwhile, Rivero and most of the remaining officers at Miraflores gather in a nearby office.

"This is illegal!" Rivero exclaims to his colleagues. "An encroachment and a coup!"

The cheers from Carmona's supporters next door are so loud he has to raise his voice for the others to hear him.

"If the president resigns there are procedures to be followed, procedures outlined in the constitution. This is illegal!"

Rivero, a major at the time, has no access to troops of his own. The command of autonomous troops is reserved for officers with a rank of lieutenant colonel and above. And among the few remaining high-ranking officers, many are still undecided as to the appropriate course of action.

"It's our duty to defend, if not Chávez, then at least the constitution," Rivero insists.

Inside Salón Ayacucho, Carmona is still talking: "Thanks to this brave mandate, which we received from the Venezuelan people, a mandate more valuable than any referendum, with the support of all sectors of society, we accept this responsibility. ... I call upon the international community to support this profoundly democratic process."

* * *

The following morning, Chávez's supporters pour down from the barrios. Rumor has spread that Chávez didn't resign. Outraged, they take to the streets to demand their president's return.

That afternoon, Chávez is to be transferred to the island of La Orchila, but before leaving Turiamo, he manages to persuade a national guardsman to transmit a letter back to the mainland. It reads: "Turiamo, 13 April, 2002, at 14:45. To the people of Venezuela (and to whomever it may interest). I, Hugo Chávez

Frías, Venezuelan, President of the Bolivarian Republic of Venezuela, declare: I have not resigned from the legitimate power that the people gave me. Forever! Hugo Chávez Frías."

This sparks new discussions between Rivero and his military colleagues at Miraflores.

"If Chávez really didn't sign the resignation and those who have taken him prisoner won't follow the constitution and let the vice president govern until new elections can be called, then how can this be called anything but a coup?" Rivero asks.

As the highest-ranking officers left it is their responsibility to defend the palace from illegitimate pretenders.

"It's no longer about Chávez. He has made mistakes and if he chose to resign because of them, we have no right to interfere. But he didn't resign. This is an usurpation and we cannot allow it. If they had called for elections it would have been different. We must restore the constitution and if need be we must do so by force. That's what the armed forces are for! It's our duty!" Rivero insists.

As supporters march to the palace, the private media stations do the opposite of what they did during the unfolding coup. They mention nothing of the unrest, but broadcast cartoons and Hollywood movies as though everything is fine. But the river of people will not be ignored, and for the undecided officers, the rise of the barrios becomes the final push to action.

General Raúl Baduel, who has been incommunicado ever since the coup, reappears as the cry from the masses grows louder. He rallies the entire 4th Division against Carmona. Other divisions follow. Carmona manages to escape from Miraflores, but is soon arrested. Rivero and the other officers at Miraflores detain the remainder of Carmona's entourage and the newly appointed ministers.

A helicopter from the air force is sent to rescue Chávez from La Orchila. The idea is to fly Chávez to Maracay where Baduel and the other generals will have a serious chat with him. He might still be their president, but there is widespread discontent with the way he is governing the country.

Rivero has also started to lose faith in his Comandante. He feels that Chávez isn't being open about his relationship with the far left, the Colombian guerrillas, the Cuban regime, and more specifically Fidel Castro. It bothers Rivero that Chávez wears a military uniform. The presidency is a civilian appointment. There is no reason for Chávez to dress in military attire.

Things have to change. But once in the helicopter, Chávez is not interested in going to Maracay. He orders the pilot to take him straight to the presidential palace in Caracas. When the pilot tries to object, Chávez simply reminds him that he is, after all, the president.

VI

It is April 14, 2002. Rivero and two-dozen officers wait beneath the deafening whirr of helicopter blades. The air force Super Puma comes in for landing, doors open, and out jumps Chávez, wearing a long-sleeved, navy-blue jacket and a radiant smile.

"Welcome Mister President!" Rivero shouts.

Chávez takes his hand, grinning at him and the others.

"We came straight from La Orchila," he shouts happily. He ushers the group away from the noise, toward the presidential palace, then continues: "But tell me, what happened here? How did you manage to free Miraflores?"

As they approach the palace, ministers and staff rush out to embrace the Comandante. Outside the perimeters, the crowd is ecstatic, chanting: "He's back, he's back, he's back ..."

* * *

Though he was eager to put things right, Rivero did not want to see Chávez return with the same air of majesty and the same flaws as before. Yet, here he is, walking around like a resurrected Messiah. Rivero is disappointed to learn that the talk Baduel planned to have with Chávez never took place. Anxiously, he waits to hear what the Comandante will say to the nation.

In the Salón Ayacucho, where Carmona betrayed him mere hours before, Chávez delivers one of his more memorable speeches, broadcast on every channel. Dressed in a dark military uniform, against the backdrop of Simón Bolívar's portrait, he solemnly announces: "The people came to this palace to never leave again. The Venezuelan people and their armed forces have written a new page, and what a great page, in the history of Venezuela."

He picks up a small crucifix and holds it up in front of the cameras.

"From this moment on we will reflect and put God first. We invoke Jesus Christ our Lord, bringer of peace, to reunite the country. These events that brought blood and suffering are, and should be, an immense lesson to all of us. ... Let's put things right for the good of all, for the good of Venezuela. We all have to rectify many things in order bring back tranquility and continue building the homeland for our children and grandchildren."

This day, he says, is "memorable, historic, unforgettable, for ever and ever."

"If I loved you yesterday—today I love you so much more!"

The words of Chávez ease Rivero's concerns. He seems reconciliatory. After the television broadcast, the two of them ride the elevator together as Chávez is on his way to give his second speech of the day, this time addressing the masses from the People's Balcony of the presidential palace.

"Here, put this on!" says Rivero and takes off his bulletproof vest.

"Thank you!" Chávez puts it on underneath his jacket.

"You know me," Rivero tells him. "I believe in what you just said down there, but rest assured that if we don't correct our flaws, I will not remain here."

"Don't be so dramatic," Chávez replies. "You have to understand the situation. I am not the enemy. The enemy is another. The enemy is worse."

In a meeting ten days after the coup, Rivero hands over three newspaper articles to Chávez. They are pieces Rivero has authored anonymously, criticizing Venezuela's relationship with Cuba. Chávez puts them aside to read later. That is the last time the two men speak.

Although the full truth is never uncovered, the most widely accepted explanation is that the coup was planned by a few elite members of the opposition, in collaboration with some high-ranking officers. Despite lack of evidence, Chávez remains convinced that the CIA was the puppeteer orchestrating it all.

The coup removes any last hesitations Chávez might have had toward fully embracing Cuba and its revolution. It proves Fidel Castro right. Fidel had long feared, and prepared for, real and imagined CIA plots. No doubt, he had warned his protégé of the relentless efforts of "the empire," as Chávez henceforth calls the United States, to overthrow people like him. On *Aló Presidente*, Chávez tells the nation: "Venezuela is at the very top of the Empire's list of its laboratories for psychological warfare, economic warfare, sabotage." And: "The CIA is everywhere. Recently, Fidel told me, 'Chávez, watch out, because this is the most perfect killing machine that has ever been invented.'"

As head of communication security, Rivero is an important player in the "situation room," the intelligence management center of Miraflores. After the coup, this responsibility is given to Cuban intelligence officers. Having fended off countless coups against Castro, they are considered better suited for the job. Rivero and the other Venezuelan officers failed, it is assumed, either because they were in on the plot or because of incompetence.

Rivero is put under surveillance and even accused of being a coup plotter. It isn't long before he is pushed out of Miraflores and given a non-military posting as head of civil protection at the Ministry of Justice.

VII

It is February 2004. Folco is sitting in his office when the phone rings. It is the captain of a big cruise liner on its way to Guamache cargo port.

"Folco! We are right here in front of Puerto de La Mar. I see that the port is ready. Can we come in?"

Folco jumps to his feet, runs out of his office, and out onto the pier. He stares at the massive cruise ship, stopped in the bay, just beyond the 1-mile barrier.

He takes a few deep breaths, shakes his head, and replies. "I'm sorry but we are not yet authorized to accept any ships ..."

"But all we need is the pier," the captain insists. "It doesn't matter if the surrounding facilities aren't ready. I assure you it will still be better than the cargo port."

However tempting, Folco knows this is exactly what his opponents are waiting for. Summoning all his willpower, he forces his mouth to form the words: "I'm sorry, I can't. ... Next time we'll be ready."

"I understand. It's a pity. Thank you!"

Folco hangs up, deflated.

"Do things by the book and sooner or later common sense will prevail," he reminds himself. "Nothing rash."

Every night, from the balcony of his home in Pampatar, Folco watches the cruise ships sail past Puerto de La Mar, using the very same navigation routes that his opponents claim will destroy the sardine fishery. Meanwhile, he loses one season after another to yet another study, yet another minister, yet another bureaucratic process.

While waiting for his final authorization, Folco focuses on perfecting the surrounding facilities: the marketplace and the

Gourmet Plaza. But then, in April 2004, the latest in a long row of presidents of Banco Industrial de Venezuela, resigns.

Folco's financing is once again frozen.

In July, a new president and management team are appointed. Folco asks them to come and carry out their inspections urgently. But there is not even time to schedule an appointment before they are replaced—the fifth change of president in six years.

In September 2004 yet another inspection is requested and conducted.

In December, there is finally word from the bank. But instead of a check, it is a request to start making repayments. Folco now owes more in accumulated interest than in capital received. With loan repayments pending, and still no ability to make income, Folco travels to Caracas to seek out José David Cabello, minister of infrastructure.

When Folco arrives, Cabello is busy. His secretary takes Folco to see if the vice minister is available. They wander the hallways of four floors in the massive building, but except for the rooms immediately surrounding that of the minister's, practically every office is empty, void of furniture as well as people. There is no sign of the vice minister, nor of anyone else. Folco is stunned. Where is everyone?

After a few minutes, Cabello lets the secretary know that he is ready to receive Folco.

Dressed in a red sport's jacket, Cabello remains sitting behind his desk when Folco enters. His round face is clean-shaved as he looks up to greet his visitor. Folco is struck by the sterility of the office. It is spacious, but totally void of character. There is a desk and a disorganized bookshelf, but no pictures of important buildings or sites, no traces of anything to do with infrastructure. The walls are as bare as Cabello's face is expressionless.

Cabello extends his left hand to greet Folco. His right hand is deformed and hangs limply by his side.

"Please, take a seat." Cabello motions with his left hand for Folco to sit down.

Then he leans across the desk and, in the voice of a robot, delivers what strikes Folco as an overly rehearsed, twenty-minute long speech on the benefits of socialism.

Folco lets it wash over him without hearing. Now and then he picks up a familiar platitude: the people, the Comandante, the empire. This could be coming from Chávez himself or any of the faceless officials acting as his knights.

When Cabello grows silent, Folco takes out the documentation he has prepared and starts to explain the case of Puerto de La Mar. He only gets a few sentences in before he is interrupted.

"I don't need to see this. We already know about it and we like it very much. You don't need to sell it to me," Cabello says.

Then he leans forward and continues in a lowered voice:

"It's an important development and we want it to work, but there is a little group of fishermen who are a pain in the ass. Chávez doesn't want to go inaugurate the port and have them cause a problem. We need your help. You have to speak to them and convince them to not be against the project anymore."

Folco nods in agreement, though he can't quite understand what he can tell Wilmer González that he hasn't already said.

Back in Margarita, at the next fishermen's meeting of Fundepet, Folco tells the men that he intends to reach out to Wilmer one more time. All fishermen's associations except Wilmer's El Morro are already members of Fundepet. Excited about the prospect of being reunited, the fishermen give him their blessing. So Folco sets out for the pier where Wilmer usually fishes. Wilmer is out at sea, but his father is there mending nets.

"Wilmer is under a lot of pressure," the father tells Folco, "but I will talk to him."

"Great," Folco replies eagerly. "Please let him know I stopped by and ask him to call me."

Folco reports back to the Ministry of Infrastructure that the mission is accomplished. Cabello is not in, but his deputy seems pleased and informs Folco that Chávez wants to inaugurate the port by the end of 2005.

But Wilmer doesn't get back to Folco, and Chávez doesn't come.

VIII

It is April 2006. The last few months have been marked by silence, the days quietly receding into a wasteland of lost opportunity. Folco's port is ready, the interest on his loans accumulating, but he still has yet to receive any word regarding the status of his one missing permit.

Once again, Folco travels to Caracas. As the representative of Margarita's business community, he has the personal cellphone number of Venezuela's vice president, José Vicente Rangel, who wants to maintain good relations with the private sector. Now, at the end of his rope, Folco decides to turn to him. He calls and is granted an appointment with Leopoldo García, director of land development.

Folco brings two full suitcases of permits and approved environmental studies with him. García and two of his colleagues attend to Folco. This time, Folco is not interrupted. For four hours he explains all the twists and turns in the case of Puerto de La Mar, showing his approvals and studies. Visibly impressed, García asks Folco to prepare a summary and get ready to present his case at the Vice Presidency.

In May 2006, the first meeting takes place. Folco arrives with his lawyer and two co-workers. They are invited into a very large room. About thirty people sit around tables laid out in the shape of a horseshoe. At the head, sits García and the representatives from the Vice Presidency. Spread across the rest of the room are representatives from the navy, the coast guard, the municipality of Mariño, the INEA, the National Institute of Fisheries

(INAPESCA), the governor's office of Margarita, the leaders of the different fishermen associations, the ministries of tourism, infrastructure, and environmental affairs. Folco is stunned by the caliber of people present, as well as by the sheer numbers. Between May and November 2006, they participate in a series of nine meetings convened by the Vice Presidency.

For the last meeting, the vice president flies the leaders of the nine fishermen's associations to Caracas. Wilmer González arrives together with Alfredo Goméz, the only marine ecologist arguing that the sardine fishery would be threatened by a port, and the admiral from INEA who has consistently denied Folco his permit. Together, they gather in the usual conference room. The first person to speak is the admiral of the navy, Carlos Castellanos Materan. Distinguished-looking in his uniform and graying temples, he informs the group that the navy has conducted a three-month study. They've concluded that there are no sardines in front of Puerto de La Mar and that, furthermore, there haven't been for the past thirty years.

"In our office there is no project development file as complete and exhaustive as the one of Puerto de La Mar," says the official from the Ministry of Environmental Affairs, who is next in line to speak.

The official recounts how the ministry has been asked to review the case over and over, year after year, always reaching the same conclusion: the bay of Porlamar, where Puerto de La Mar is located, is not a sardine habitat. Cruise ships or tender operations will not interfere with the activities of the local fishermen nor impact the environment.

"If there is one of development in all of Venezuela that has all the permits and approvals required by the law, it's Puerto the La Mar," the official from the Ministry of Environmental Affairs concludes.

When it's Wilmer González's turn, he gives a PowerPoint presentation based on Goméz's research arguing that the sardine fishery will be damaged. The leaders of the other eight fishermen's associations disagree with his conclusions and a heated argument ensues.

In the end, the representatives of all ministries and associations except González, Goméz and INEA, give their approval of Puerto de La Mar. INEA gives neither approval nor disapproval but refers to the opinion of the Ministry of Environmental Affairs.

"It doesn't interfere with the sardines nor does it affect the eco system," minister of the environment and natural resources, Jacqueline Faría, tells local newspaper *El Sol de Margarita*.[4]

On December 15, a few weeks after the final meeting, Folco contacts the office of the vice president hoping to get a hint about the verdict.

Leopoldo García takes his call.

"Stay calm. Don't say anything. You are swimming with sharks. But I believe you will have a very nice Christmas present," he tells Folco.

But Christmas comes and goes without a word.

IX

On January 12, 2007, after two more weeks of silence, Folco travels to the office of the Vice Presidency in Caracas.

He is shown to a small barren room, with a table and a couple of chairs. The bare gray walls of the room add to his feeling of uneasiness. When he is finally attended to, it is by a middle-aged woman he has never seen before. Folco finds her unattractive. She has dark, greasy hair and lips painted exaggeratedly red. He senses the feeling of aversion is mutual.

"Leopoldo García doesn't work here anymore," she tells him.

He asks for the other officials of the Vice Presidency who attended the meetings. She shakes her head. It is not only Leopoldo García who has been replaced; so have the rest of his staff.

"But what about the meetings? The nine months of meetings we had here last year!" Folco exclaims, fighting to hide his rising sense of panic.

"I don't know anything about that," the woman replies coldly.

"But how is that possible, we spent almost a year in meetings?"

"I don't know anything about this. I don't have anything for you."

"But ..."

She cuts him short: "You are wasting your time."

X

It is April 2007. The vice governor of Margarita calls Folco to tell him he has just returned from a meeting at the Ministry of Infrastructure in Caracas.

"We're close now, Folco!" he exclaims excitedly. "All that's needed is a meeting with the leaders of the different fishermen's associations."

"What are you talking about?" asks Folco. "We've just been through a nine-month trial involving all of them."

The phone call leaves Folco with a feeling that something terrible is about to happen.

A few days later, Chavista deputy Rosario Pacheco calls a meeting with the newly appointed representatives of different ministries and the fishermen to decide the future of Puerto de La Mar.

Folco is not invited, but he cannot stay away. On the morning of the meeting, Folco drives to the venue. He parks his car across the street and waits. In horror, he watches as Pacheco arrives and unloads a bus of supporters outside the local hotel where the meeting is to be held. One by one they pour out of the bus, wearing new, bright red T-shirts and baseball caps. They carry massive banners that read: "Abajo Puerto de La Mar": "Down with Puerto de La Mar."

Folco waits in his car for the meeting to be over and for people to leave. He counts at least fifty people dressed in red. How many actually attended the meeting and how many are just hired supporters he doesn't know. Among them is the recently appointed president of the fishermen's association and about a dozen of Wilmer's men. Finally, he sees three fishermen he knows. He rushes up to them.

"They didn't let us talk," says one.

"I found out by chance," says another. "Why would they hold the meeting at 9 a.m. when everybody is out fishing? Practically nobody showed up."

Rosario Pacheco calls for quiet, then faces the rolling cameras of the media outlets to announce her verdict: Puerto de La Mar will not be permitted. It would wipe out the sardines.

XI

Folco rushes to Caracas. He still hasn't heard anything regarding the outcome of the nine meetings held at the Vice Presidency the previous year. He heads straight to the Ministry of Infrastructure, but this time José David Cabello is not available. Instead, one of his vice ministers attends to Folco.

The vice minister's office is small and stuffy with piles of documents occupying every available surface. Folco takes a deep breath in an attempt to gather the patience he needs to recount the latest developments once more. The vice minister stops him before he gets started.

"I know the case well. I've been working on it. Take a seat, please," he tells Folco. Then, from a drawer in his desk, he pulls out a folder.

"You didn't get this from me," he says, as he pushes it across the desktop toward Folco.

Folco nods without really understanding. Then he opens the folder. Inside are the letters with the recommended course of action from all the institutes that attended the meetings. They all give a vote of no objection; all except INEA who defers to the Ministry of Environmental Affairs. But the document that stands out above all others is one signed by the vice president of Venezuela, José Vicente Rangel himself. It is an order of approval for Puerto de La Mar.

"As you can see, Chávez wants to see Puerto de La Mar open," says the vice minister. The decree is dated December 2006—six months earlier. The decision is based on the outcome of both the studies and the meetings with the different ministries. The document declares that the pre-existing permit was perfectly legal and that it has been demonstrated that cruise ship operations will have no impact on the marine ecosystem nor will they damage the fish population or interfere with traditional fishing practices. And to be absolutely sure, the vice president finishes by recommending extra environmental monitoring for the first two years of operations (as suggested by Folco), after which there will be another environmental impact study to detect any unforeseen consequences.

The letters on the document blur together as Folco reads it over and over, unable to comprehend. This is exactly what he has hoped for. Why has he not been informed?

Rather than wasting time dwelling on who has kept the letter hidden, Folco proceeds to make copies of the document to send to all the people on the island who are in any way involved with the Puerto de La Mar conflict, including the eleven mayors of Margarita and the main newspapers.

He puts up posters with a copy of the letter: "This is the Order of Aperture for Puerto de La Mar." "Those who continue manipulating the truth delegitimize the Vice-Presidency of the Republic."

Then, he sits back and waits. But it is as though nothing has happened. The president of INEA will still not give the final authorization. For the eighth cruise ship season in a row, Folco is forced to watch the ships sail past Puerto de La Mar to dock in the cargo port across the island.

5

THE PUNISHMENT

"Our hatred knows no bounds, and the war shall be to the death."

Simón Bolívar

I

Upon his triumphant return to Miraflores in April 2002, Chávez reinstates the dismissed PDVSA executives in an effort at reconciliation. Eddie Ramírez is once again head of Palmaven. He and his colleagues return to work. Ramírez is at the end of his career, and six months later he retires. Two months into his retirement, Ramírez is in Canada visiting family when he hears that his former colleagues have re-ignited the conflict.

On December 2, 2002, the managers of PDVSA shut down operations; 90 percent of the employees—workers and executives—walk off the job, supported by the country's businesses and unions. Still fearing that Chávez will seize control of the oil company, the management launches a pre-emptive strike.

The strike goes on for weeks. Weeks turn into months. All ships stand still. Oil can't go out, gasoline can't come in. The economy suffers. Factories have to shut down. Livelihoods are destroyed and billions lost. There are shortages and queues. The country is paralyzed. But there is no uprising. Instead of channeling their pain at Chávez as the strikers had hoped, many victims are disgusted with the elite they refer to as the oligarchy. Finally, Wilmer Ruperti, president of Maroil Trading, decides to help Chávez. He has worked at PDVSA for fourteen years and is convinced that the management is committing a terrible mistake.

"You cannot be over the country, you cannot be over the government, you cannot be over the people who are elected democratically in order to satisfy the needs of the population that was very poor," he says.[1]

Ruperti uses his contacts and influence with the shipping companies to rent tankers and transport gasoline and oil in and out of Venezuela. Soon, the other tankers join in. Whether his motives stem from true altruism or not, Ruperti is handsomely rewarded. He is decorated by Chávez and goes from having one tanker to having nineteen.[2]

The strike is broken, and for Chávez it is payback time. As far as he is concerned, there will be no more attempts at reconciliation.

"I sheathed my sword and I was wrong," Chávez tells a cheering crowd of supporters. "I have been forced to draw it again, and I will never ever sheathe it."[3]

On state television, Chávez and other officials make it clear how they feel about the strikers. They are described as "saboteurs," "traitors of the homeland," "vagabonds," and "delinquents." Then they are dismissed en masse through the publication of long lists of names and identification numbers in newspapers. Around 20,000 workers lose their jobs.

The children of dismissed workers are no longer allowed to attend PDVSA's school. The law states that any school financed by a state company is to be considered public and hence open to anyone. Still, children of dismissed workers are not let back in, and mid-semester their parents scramble to find new options.

The former employees are also immediately ousted from their corporate housing. As many of the petroleum plants are based in remote locations, special housing, so-called *campos petroleros*, or oil camps, were built back when the oil industry first started to develop. Many of these houses are now part of the communities that have developed near the oil plantations, but a few thousand still remain, forming part of the benefit package offered to employees. Once dismissed, the workers have to vacate those houses. Having challenged the legality of the dismissals in court, many refuse to leave until the labor court returns with a verdict. In response, Chávez sends in the national guard to evict families by force. Some try to resist by forming human shields or throwing rocks. The conflict escalates, and finally some families—adults and children alike—are dragged out of their homes in the middle of the night, amid clouds of teargas.

The dismissed workers become pariahs, barred not only from working at PDVSA but from working at any state company or even any private company that provides state companies with services. This includes other oil companies active in the country, such as Shell and Total.

Between 5,000 and 7,000 former PDVSA employees are essentially left with no option but to emigrate, relocating across twenty-six different countries, including Canada, Norway, Mexico, and Angola. Others change industries or start their own businesses.

As for Eddie Ramírez, he loses his pension. Having retired, he was no longer personally affected by the way PDVSA was run, but when the strike was first announced, he decided to give some public declarations announcing his support for his former colleagues. The result: at the age of seventy-two he is forced to try to find work. He takes on odd jobs, but dedicates most of his time to Gente del Petróleo (Petrol people), an NGO documenting the violations of the former PDVSA employees' rights.

II

It is August 15, 2004. The offices of Súmate are buzzing with activity when a group of police officers barge in to conduct a raid. Chaos erupts as frightened volunteers run for the doors. María Corina Machado's reaction is immediate. She stands up from behind her desk and exclaims: "No one leaves!"

Her staff stop in their tracks. After a moment of stunned silence, they return to work, quietly emboldened, ignoring the police officers milling about.

In the 1999 constitution, Chávez included the right for the people to recall officials who had served half their term. If 20 per cent of the electorate signed a petition requesting a recall, that would trigger a referendum.

Using this new clause, in 2003, Súmate launched a campaign to recall the president himself.

Chávez's ratings had dropped, even among his strongholds in the barrios. The economy was stagnant, and many felt he had failed to deliver on his promises.

By August 2003, Súmate had collected 3.2 million signatures for delivery to the National Electoral Council (CNE), more than enough to trigger a referendum. But the CNE, a state body with close ties to Chávez, claimed the petition was flawed and refused to accept it.

Unfazed, the Súmate volunteers hit the streets again, with a more diligent process. Meanwhile, Chávez turned to Fidel Castro to plot his defense and recover his popularity.

Castro suggested the creation of social programs called *misiones*, or missions. In return for 95,000 barrels of oil a day, he offered to send thousands of Cuban doctors and nurses into the barrios to run medical clinics, providing free healthcare to those who previously lacked access. They called it "Misión Barrio Adentro." Other missions were launched: "Misión Mercal," a chain of grocery stores offering subsidized food; "Misión Vuelvan Caras," a skills and training mission for agricultural and industrial cooperatives; "Misión Robinson," "Misión Ribas," and "Misión Sucre," educational initiatives addressing illiteracy, high-school graduation rates, and university access.[4]

While it would take years to measure the impact of these efforts on people's quality of life, the impact on the polls was nearly immediate.[5]

In November 2003, Sumáte once again submitted more than 3 million signatures to the CNE. Again, they were rejected. This time, the CNE claimed that fewer than 2 million of the signatures were valid; that the list contained names of deceased people and those pressured to sign. The CNE launched a *reparo* (rectification) process where owners of disputed signatures were given three days to show up to confirm or withdraw their signature. Rather than a verification process, it was promoted as an opportunity to repent and withdraw one's name from the petition.

"Whoever signs against Chávez will be registered for history because they are going to have to give their name, surname, identity number, and fingerprint," Chávez warned on national television.[6]

Still, from May 28 to May 30, over 600,000 of the disputed signatories showed up to verify their signatures, keeping the total number above the required 20 percent.

* * *

In August 2004, the referendum takes place. But the yearlong delay proved enough for Chávez to rebuild his popularity. He wins with 58 percent of the vote.[7]

After the election, Chávez keeps his promise to never again sheathe his sword. He tasks Luis Tascón, a young National Assembly member and specialist in information technology, to collect copies of the petition signatures. Tascón then posts the identities of the signatories on the Internet, effectively creating a blacklist. Elected officials use it to cleanse non-believers from government and state positions. New jobs are denied, contracts lost, careers ruined, and social benefits taken away. The "Tascón List," as it is henceforth called, formalizes the political division of the Venezuelan people.

Chávez calls the leaders of Súmate "conspirators, coup plotters, and lackeys of the US government." The state prosecutor charges Machado, Plaz, and two other members with treason and conspiracy for accepting 53,400 dollars from the National Endowment for Democracy (NED), a nonprofit organization founded and funded by the US Congress. Prominent leaders from around the world protest. The trial is postponed several times, and in the end nothing comes of it, but Machado and Plaz have earned a permanent place on Chávez's list of enemies, along with two and a half million other Venezuelans.

III

It is February 2005. Chávez decides to shut down Fundación Atenea and take back management of the orphanage. María Corina sits in her Súmate office when a friend calls to deliver the news. She finishes the call unable to stand.

Before the takeover, the shelter received 80 percent of its funding from private donations. After the takeover, they get nothing but subsistence from the government.

María Corina and her former colleagues from Atenea make several attempts to visit, but are barred entry. Visitors are no longer allowed, they are told.

To Machado, the message is clear. The government doesn't want anything associated with her name to receive any credit, especially not if it has to do with social justice. As she walks away from the gates of the orphanage for the last time, she realizes she must cut all ties with everything that matters to her.

IV

It is May 31, 2005. María Corina Machado sits in a blue striped chair before a white marble fireplace. She is wearing a short, black skirt, a black jacket over a white top, and black high-heeled shoes. To her left, in an elegant black suit, sits the Devil—as Chávez likes to call President George W. Bush.

Bush has her hand locked in a firm handshake. He and Machado hold their pose, basking in the light of the countless flashes delivered by the crowd of journalists who have come to cover the meeting. This is the Oval Office, the inner sanctum of the White House and a place to which Bush has never invited Chávez.

In Venezuela, the visit is a provocation and a statement to Machado's detractors. To most Chavistas, the image seals her fate as a traitor.

V

It is just before midnight, May 27, 2007. Employees of Radio Caracas Television (RCTV) chant "freedom" and sing the national anthem. Then, precisely at midnight, the signal of Venezuela's oldest and most popular private television channel goes dead. As the screen goes blank, thousands of employees and supporters break down in tears. Sobbing violently, they try to comfort each other, but Venezuela can no longer hear them. The new, state-sponsored TVES has already replaced RCTV. According to President Chávez, TVES will better reflect the socialist revolution.[8]

Chávez has recently won his third presidential election with 63 percent of the vote, the widest margin and highest voter turnout since Venezuelan democracy began in 1958. He is more popular than ever, largely thanks to his new social programs (the missions) and soaring oil prices.

On this wave of support, Chávez announces his intent to change the constitution. His list of priorities includes nationalizing "strategic" industries, abolishing presidential term limits,[9] putting the president in control of the central bank and gubernatorial appointments, extending social security benefits, and reducing the workday to six hours.[10]

He also takes the opportunity to take RCTV, one of his strongest critics, off the air.

"There will be no renewal of the license for that coup-plotting TV channel called Radio Caracas Television. The license has ended!" Chávez declared.

RCTV had supported the coup against Chávez in 2002. They had deliberately manipulated footage and withheld information in order to encourage the uprising. They provided ample coverage as the coup unfolded, helping to ensure sympathizers knew where to go, but later neglected to inform the public that the coup had failed, preferring to broadcast reruns of Looney Tunes and the film *Pretty Woman* while the barrios were rising to restore Chávez to power. And while most channels toned down their attacks on the president after the coup, RCTV continued its aggressive anti-Chávez stance.[11]

Chávez waited five years for the license to expire before acting. So when he does, with clear motives and his popularity at a high, he is caught off guard as Venezuela explodes in response. Chavistas and non-Chavistas alike take to the streets in protest. While there are also demonstrations in favor, the vast majority of the population is against the decision. RCTV was Venezuela's most popular channel, broadcasting the people's favorite shows and soap operas since 1953. And while it is still available on cable, losing its public broadcast frequency has made it inaccessible to most of its audience.

At the forefront of the protests are the students. For decades, the students have stayed out of Venezuelan politics, but now they take to the streets in defense of freedom of expression. If the government could close down a television station just like that, against the will of the people, what else could they do? Although it has nothing to do with other suggested reforms, the closure of RCTV becomes a wake-up call, prompting the students to scrutinize government policy. Socialist or not, they are not prepared to hand the president absolute power. So when Chávez announces his intention to modify the constitution, the students declare war.

Across the country, they mobilize for a "no" vote in the referendum. But as protestors take over the streets, Chávez remains unaffected. He devotes countless television hours to explaining the benefits of the new constitution, which he claims will facilitate Venezuela's transition to "twenty-first-century socialism." Sixty-nine articles are to be modified, increasing the state's involvement in the economy and centralizing power. In his weekly *Aló Presidente* show, Chávez sings that he is in love with the constitutional reform: "Estar enamorado es leer la reforma en la mañana ..."

He says that approval of the constitution is essential for the revolution: "I am sure that the great majority will approve it."

The possibility of defeat does not even appear to cross his mind.

Then, on December 2, 2007, against all odds, Chávez loses the referendum. It is his first electoral defeat, and initially, he accepts it. On live television, he comforts his shocked supporters: "Don't be sad or downcast. I believe that the Venezuelan democracy will become more mature. Every process like this that we live through, every election day, every political event permits our democracy, our country, to continue maturing."

But as the opposition celebrates, Chávez runs out of goodwill. Two days later, again on live television, he calls it a "shitty victory" and declares that there is nothing to celebrate: "We have not lost anything. And get ready because a new offensive is coming for the proposed reform."

It is not over, he announces: "For me, this is not a defeat. For me, this is another *por ahora* ... for now."

VI

"Good evening comrades, we are here today to destroy Puerto de La Mar," a crackling voice announces over the radio. The dial has shifted slightly, and instinctively Folco adjusts his tuner to 97.7 FM until the voice of Jakeline Vergara rings clear. Vergara is a municipal councilor from Mariño. Lately, she has adopted the habit of starting her daily 8 p.m. radio show in this fashion.

Folco turns off the radio. There's no reason to torture himself. Ever since he published the order from the vice president, local political resistance against Puerto de La Mar has intensified. Deputy Rosario Pacheco and her ally Vergara now devote more time than ever to badmouthing the port.

Folco is at the point where he dreads going out. Every time he leaves his house, he seems to run into someone eager to echo the latest excuse for why Puerto de La Mar is destined to fail.

VII

"Good morning! Good morning to all of Venezuela. It is Sunday March 2 [2008] and the month of March has arrived with marvelous sunshine. This is the *Aló Presidente* show number 306. It is five minutes past 11 in the morning. Here we are at the heart of Caracas. I was remembering that old song ..."

Chávez turns his back to the camera and starts to sing: "Caminando por Caracas, Caracas. La gente me saludaba y andaba ..."

He stops, then shouts, his back still turned to the camera: "Good morning to everyone!"

"Security. Security in the streets," he continues, presumably announcing the theme of the show. He still has his back turned toward the camera, as though unaware that the cameraman is behind him.

"How beautiful Caracas is! And we keep restoring it. This is the old Plaza Diego Ibarra." He lashes out with one arm and points to somewhere in the distance, beyond the reach of the camera. "Isn't that right, Ramón Rodríguez Chacín?" He spins around to face the camera and a nervous man steps into the screen. "Hello Ramón? How are you?" Chávez pats Rodríguez Chacín, minister of interior and justice, on the shoulder and shakes his hand. "Have you been able to get some rest?"

"Si, Señor," the minister replies. He is wearing circular glasses and a bright red shirt, matching that of Chávez.

"This is the old Plaza Diego Ibarra," Chávez repeats and gestures once more out in the distance.

"Diego Ibarra," Rodríguez Chacín echoes.

"That was occupied for many years," Chávez continues. "By the so-called informal economy. They destroyed it."

He lets out a little laugh and continues: "I want to congratulate Bernal. Where is Mayor Bernal?" Chávez spins around to face the camera and his invisible entourage again: a skinny, gray-haired man dressed in a red shirt and a red jacket comes stumbling into the picture, as though pushed in front of the cameras.

"Epa Freddy ¿cómo estás?" Chávez exclaims. "Do you remember this song: Caminando por Caracas, Caracas ..." he sings. "Who sang it? Don't you remember?" Bernal and Ramón shake their heads. Chávez continues to sing: "La gente me saludaba y andaba ..."

"Bueno. Greetings to all the people of Caracas, the people of Venezuela. Now what?" He turns to Mayor Bernal and slaps his shoulder. The stunned mayor mumbles something about walking, and together they proceed to wander the streets of Caracas. Chávez chats to police officers and random citizens, talking about the problems of security in Caracas and about his plans to restore the city center. He stops every now and then to sing a little, or to tell an anecdote from his youth.

About an hour and a half into the show, he finally arrives at his desk, which is transported to a different location for each broadcast. This time it has been placed in the center of Plaza Caracas. His daughter María Gabriela appears out of nowhere and escorts Chávez the last few meters to his desk. He kisses her cheek before taking a seat and proceeds to give a few quotes by Simón Bolívar, as is his custom. Then he welcomes all the specially invited guests. Today, the show will be unusually short, he announces, as the party congress of Partido Socialista Unido de Venezuela, PSUV, is taking place. He has to be there, he says, to ensure that the party remains a true revolutionary party of the people. A party that guarantees the continued existence and advancement of the Bolivarian revolution, the construction of twenty-first-century socialism and the strengthening of Latin American unity. This unity, Chávez says, has been badly bruised of late because of the "cowardly assassination" of Raúl Reyes.

Reyes was a Colombian FARC guerrilla fighter who had been killed the previous day when the Colombian government launched an attack on a guerilla camp in Ecuador.

Chávez picks up a copy of newspaper *Diario Vea* and points to its headline "Raúl Reyes Assassinated by Missile on Ecuadorian Territory."

"There's the truth," he exclaims, "but the press of the oligarchy tells a different story. The press of the Colombian oligarchy says there was combat. There was no combat. It was a cowardly assassination! ... Yesterday we heard CNN heaping disgrace on to the assassinated leader. That is what imperialism is like. Accusing him of being a drug dealer, leader of a powerful network of drug dealers. Accusing him of crimes, including the rape of children. CNN—the voice of the empire."

No trace remains of the look of gaiety and ease with which Chávez started the show.

"We pay tribute to the good revolutionary that was Raúl Reyes!" he says solemnly and pauses for effect. "I knew him personally," he continues.

There is a feeble trickle of applause from the sea of red supporters so Chávez repeats it again: "I knew him personally!" This time, his cue is impossible to miss. The applause grows louder and is accompanied by cheers.

Chávez goes on to tell of his various encounters with Reyes before launching a full attack on the Colombian government and on Colombia's President Álvaro Uribe who had ordered the bombing.

"Álvaro Uribe can lead a mafia, but can never be president of a country. A Mafioso cannot be president, especially not of a South American country, of a country like Colombia, a brother nation. President Uribe is a criminal. Not only is he a liar, a Mafioso, a paramilitary; he heads a narco-government. He's a lackey of the US empire. He's a subordinate of Bush. Uribe does whatever Bush tells him to."

Over the course of the show, Chávez becomes more and more agitated, layering criticism after criticism on the Colombian government and President Uribe.

"The Colombian government has become the Israel of Latin America and for sure there are Israeli mercenaries in Colombia. They have come to instruct the mercenaries, paramilitaries, and unfortunately also the militaries of Colombia how to kill. And of course there is the hand of the United States; North American and Israeli mercenaries, training for death, for the war of death. ... And now they want to bring this to the neighboring countries. We will not accept it! Señor Mafioso Uribe, we will not accept it! ... This is a very serious matter. It could be the beginning of war in South America."

Then he shouts: "Señor Minister of Defense, get me ten battalions to the Colombian border immediately!"

A surprised minister wearing a well-decorated uniform and black beret stands up in the audience and bows his head obediently.

"Battalions of tanks! Deploy the air force!" Chávez continues. "We do not want war, but we will not allow the North American Empire, who is the master, and their puppy President Uribe, and the Colombian oligarchy, to divide us, to weaken us. We will not allow it! I order the immediate retreat of all our staff at the embassy in Bogotá. Close down our embassy in Bogotá! Señor Foreign Minister Nicolás Maduro, ... I put Venezuela on high alert ... Colombia is a terrorist state, subject to the great terrorist of the world, which is the government of the United States and all of its imperialist apparatus. ... We will free Colombia from the hands of the North American empire!"

* * *

Attending *Aló Presidente* every Sunday was mandatory for ministers, and they had to come prepared for anything. The show was where Chávez drafted and announced many of his policies, with the entire nation watching. Failure to answer a question or provide the requested input meant humiliation on national television, as well as the possibility of losing one's job.

Being filmed meant every comment and facial expression was preserved for posterity. Not only did Chávez review footage after each broadcast but there were millions of viewers and one could be sure that any unintentional smirk would be recorded and spread online by the opposition or even rivals within the same party. In Venezuela, freedom of expression did not seem to apply to Chavistas. Loyalty constituted the number one priority determining whether or not someone would be successful. Ministers were not to take initiative or come up with ideas of their own, but they had to be quick to obey and carry out orders given by the Comandante.

This was how Nicolás Maduro rose through the ranks. In his youth, Maduro belonged to the Marxist–Leninist Socialist League Party. In 1986–7, he underwent political training in

Cuba. An ally of Chávez since the 1992 coup, he was both loyal and obedient. As such, he soon became Chávez's favorite. Before his political career, Maduro was a bus driver and union activist in Caracas. In 1999, he was a member of the National Constituent Assembly that rewrote the constitution and was later elected to the newly formed National Assembly, of which he eventually became chairman. In 2006, Chávez promoted Maduro to minister of foreign affairs, even though he lacked both education and foreign-language skills. Maduro kept this post for six years—a remarkable feat given that, in just over a decade, Chávez went through more than 180 ministers.[12] Some ministers lasted only a few weeks. And frequently their fates were discussed, and their replacements introduced, live on *Aló Presidente.*

* * *

Three hours into an episode filmed on February 10, 2008, in his hometown Barinas, Chávez brings up the subject of unused land. In certain areas, he says, it is understandable that there is unused land, but not here, not a mere 5 kilometers from the state capital city of Barinas.

"Señor Mayor, how can that be?" he shouts. "Señor State Secretary, Señor General Commander of the garrison. How can you permit this? I don't know how we can permit it. Where is the president of the Institute of Land? How can you permit this? Explain it to me! Let's hear!"

The camera scans the audience, sweeping the faces of the accused, seeking its target from the crowd. Most sit eyes lowered, like schoolchildren being scolded by a headmaster. The camera stops and zooms in on the face of a young man wearing a brown baseball cap, black glasses with thick frames, and a khaki-colored shirt. It is the president of the Institute of Land, Juan Carlos Loyo.

"Certainly Comandante. The agenda ..."

Chávez interrupts him.

"What is happening? Do I have to come myself and take this land?"

"No, Comandante, the ..."

Chávez interrupts him again: "What do we do? Are there no representatives of the armed forces here?"

His attention shifts from Loyo as he starts scanning the audience for men in uniform.

"Where are the armed forces in all of this?" he repeats. "Where is the government?"

By now the audience is clapping and whistling. All except the ones who have been named and scolded. The cameraman zooms in on them, offering no respite until finally they too succumb to the pressure and start clapping, however reluctantly. "Where is the Regional Institute of Land?" Chávez continues. "Where are you all? Is there no one here? Do I have to come here to take the land?"

Chávez returns his gaze to Juan Carlos Loyo, and with a slightly softer voice addresses him again: "Loyo, what do we do? Tell me!"

"Comandante, the only possible reflection is that there is no excuse. I assume total responsibility."

The audience applauds approvingly, and after promising to do better Loyo is let off the hook. For now. And in this way Chávez remains the defender of the people, standing up against a government that is never doing enough. *Boligarchas* were enriching themselves on the back of the revolution and at the expense of the people. But somehow none of this touched Chávez. If his grandiose plans failed, it was not his fault, but the fault of the ministers or officials assigned to implement them. On *Aló Presidente* he held them responsible, playing the part of both prosecutor and judge, separating himself from poor decision-making by transferring the responsibility onto someone else. Soon, a new slogan had taken root among the people: "Viva Chávez, abajo el gobierno": "Long live Chávez, down with the government."[13]

VIII

It is almost midnight when the phone rings, waking Folco.

"You have to open Puerto de La Mar ... Chávez is coming to town tomorrow!"

It is October 1, 2008. Local elections are coming up and polls suggest several of the Chavista candidates on Isla de Margarita will lose. In order to prop up the candidates, Chávez decides to hold a rally—at Puerto de La Mar. This will not be the first time Puerto de La Mar is used for official ceremonies. Government representatives have hosted a few events here since 2004, when Folco began leasing the space to avoid bankruptcy.

Although they never offer to pay anything, Folco accepts in the hopes of both placating them and increasing awareness of the facility. There is no doubt that denying them would only add to his challenges.

* * *

The following morning, a sea of red washes in as thousands of supporters with red T-shirts and baseball caps fill Puerto de La Mar. Giant posters and banners of Hugo Chávez and the PSUV candidates are plastered hastily at the entrance and hung from the archways; 2,000 chairs are placed in the main auditorium. On stage, a podium is prepared for the commander himself.

Around midday, Chávez appears and gives a speech to support his candidates. Folco does not attend. He stays in his office to finish a letter to the Comandante. Chávez's unexpected visit is the perfect opportunity to make his case and defend against the campaign of sabotage.

Suddenly, there is a knock on the door. It is one of the presidential guards.

"I'm sorry to disturb, but we'd like to use your office for the day."

"Of course," Folco says. He pauses a moment, before continuing.

"But perhaps in return, you can help me," he adds tentatively. "For years now, someone has been trying to sabotage Puerto de La Mar. I'm at the end of my rope. As a matter of fact, I've just finished writing a letter to the president himself on this matter."

The man nods sympathetically. "I'm not sure I'm the right person to help you, but what I do know is that Chávez is keen to see Puerto de La Mar operational. Give me your letter. I'll be traveling back with the Comandante and I will see to it personally that he receives it."

As Folco hands him the letter, a big roar erupts outside. Folco steps out to see what is going on. Amid the celebrating crowd, he finds one of his employees. She is crying.

"What's going on?" he asks.

"Didn't you listen?"

"No, what happened?"

"They are taking Puerto de La Mar!"

The woman, who has attended the speech, recounts the words of Chávez:

"This is a very beautiful place. It was conceived to be a cruise ship port of call. This is a private place, right? Well, from now on it will not be private anymore. I will return it to the people. We are going to have a Bolivarian University here!"

"Return what?" exclaims Folco. "It didn't exist before! There was nothing here!"

Folco rushes back to the presidential guard.

"What is going on?"

The guard seems equally surprised.

"I had no idea," he tells Folco. "He must have decided now that it was a good idea."

Desperate, Folco tries to find Chávez to talk to him, but the president has already left.

The following day, the official press reports:

> Chávez: I Want Nueva Esparta Bright Red
>
> 2 October 2008
>
> The spaces of Puerto de La Mar proved too small to accommodate the large red tide that flocked to its doors for the visit of the undisputed leader of the Bolivarian Revolution and President of the Republic, Hugo Chávez, who among the eleven mayoral candidates of the United Socialist Party of Venezuela in Nueva Esparta state, gave his backing to Milka Olivero, in the upcoming elections on November 23.
>
> Under the song "uh ah Chávez is not going away," the National President felt the warmth and support of his revolutionary people from all corners of Nueva Esparta, who with flag in hand and chest swollen with red, listened attentively to the Presidential address, urging the recovery of the Nueva Esparta state for the revolution.

Folco, wearing a final look of resignation, gathers his twelve employees together for an early morning meeting.

"They finally found a way to break us," he says.

"Go and find yourselves new jobs. I don't think we will have a future here."

The employees watch Folco incredulously. They still can't accept it.

"But Folco, do you really think this is it?" his assistant finally asks.

Folco sees their disappointment. As their leader, he has always kept a brave face and maintained hope in their presence. But now there is nothing left to hope for. Now he must focus on transitioning them into new jobs; moving on.

The meeting is disturbed by noise from the outside. The first invaders are already at the front gate, demanding entrance.

IX

After a few days of trying to fend off local Chavistas, Folco calls the regional admiral of the navy. Ever since they conducted their three-month study of the fishing waters around the island, the navy and the coastguard have been staunch supporters. Outraged to hear of the unwanted guests, the admiral immediately sends thirty soldiers with machine-guns to help Folco keep watch over the premises. They stay for a few days and the admiral then agrees to leave four men on a long-term basis. All Folco has to do is provide them with food and a place to sleep.

Defying advice to stay away from Puerto de La Mar, every day at 7.30 Folco walks over to give the soldiers their breakfast. At noon, he returns with lunch. And in the evenings, he brings dinner. They don't talk much, just exchange a few sentences about the food and whether or not any invaders have shown up that day.

For six months, the soldiers keep watch. Then the admiral is replaced. The new admiral does not approve of the arrangement, so Folco hires private security guards to take their place, until he runs out of funds a couple of months later.

With no guards to deter them, people push through the gates like weeds, occupying every available surface. Staff members from the university take over Folco's office. A few of the fishermen who fought against the port begin hanging about, but the representatives of the university soon chase them away. Alfredo Gómez, the ecologist who claimed the cruise ships would harm the sardines, applies for permission to turn the facility into a marine museum under his control.

In November 2008, Chávez is the host of a graduation ceremony at Puerto de La Mar for students of Misión Sucre. He beams at the crowd and exclaims: "How beautiful it turned out. We have to thank the private sector for building it. ... They had a project here to destroy the fishing grounds. A private project to make lots of money, that's capitalism. But socialism arrived, expropriated it, and now this is the headquarters of our Bolivarian University of Venezuela in Nueva Esparta."

6

DEATH, RESURRECTION, AND DELUSION

"When tyranny becomes law, rebellion is a right."
Simón Bolívar

I

"Be aware, what I'm about to tell you is a state secret and must be treated as such," the Cuban instructor cautions his Venezuelan audience.

It is November 2008, and Antonio Rivero is at the Military Academy in Caracas attending the inauguration of a new course for officers who will be supervising the construction of military tunnels.

Rivero has recently returned to the armed forces from the Ministry of Justice, where he did well for himself. He stayed out of politics, and after a few years as head of Civil Protection he was promoted to general. But the homecoming is proving cold.

Seated in the front row of the auditorium, he stares at the instructor in disbelief. Rivero's superior, a two-star general, has introduced the Cuban officer as a colonel, yet he is dressed in civilian attire: blue jeans and a checkered short-sleeved shirt, exposing his tanned arms. His hair has started to turn white. Rivero estimates him to be in his early sixties. Though it has only been about fifteen minutes since he arrived at the event, Rivero has already forgotten the Cuban's name. He's convinced it's just made up anyway. He can feel himself growing increasingly agitated.

He stands to address the instructor: "How can you, a representative of a foreign armed force, tell us a state secret?"

"Excuse me one second, general," the colonel raises his hands to suggest that he will attend to Rivero shortly, but Rivero's superior, the two-star general, intervenes.

"Rivero, please take a seat. We'll talk later," he says, anxious not to disturb the event.

"But my general, if these are state secrets, he cannot know them! This can't be."

And with that, Rivero barges out.

* * *

The Cuban influence arose quickly. In January 2005, Chávez officially declared himself a socialist for the first time. He coined the term "twenty-first-century socialism" and announced that this was to be the objective of the Bolivarian revolution. Chávez gathered his political allies in a single socialist party, the PSUV, but also wanted the armed forces, traditionally politically neutral, to embrace socialism. Like Cuba or China, he wanted an army that would defend not just national sovereignty but repel any threat against the revolution as well.

Chávez commissioned a wide range of studies to determine potential areas of collaboration between the Cuban and Venezuelan armed forces, but the analyses conducted by the Ministry of Defense concluded that it would not be advisable for Venezuela to emulate the Cuban defense model. His minister of defense, General Raúl Isaías Baduel, co-founder of MBR—200 and long-term friend and ally, was firmly against any Cuban involvement. But when Baduel's time as minister was up, in July 2007, Chávez replaced him with a much less independently minded general, Gustavo Rangel Briceño. With Baduel gone, significant changes were made to the military doctrine, and the relationship with the Cuban armed forces was solidified through a series of agreements. The in-depth collaboration outlined in these secret arrangements was not approved by, or even raised at, the Defense Commission of the National Assembly.

As part of politicizing the armed forces, in 2007, Chávez adopted Cuba's slogan: "¡Patria o Muerte, Venceremos!" inserting the extra word "socialism" to make it: "Homeland, socialism or death! We will prevail!" It was a way of forcing his officers to show their true colors.

Among those who fail the test is Antonio Rivero, who refuses to repeat the new mandatory motto. Rivero still takes pride in his job, but he has ceased to endorse the regime. He never speaks of socialism, doesn't dress in red, and avoids the mandatory PSUV party rallies. In February 2009, shortly after the incident at the Military Academy, Rivero is appointed second commander of the 4th Jungle Infantry Division, a post in the middle of nowhere, where he will be isolated and without command of any troops.

While he is ostracized both physically and politically for his increasingly open attacks on the Cuban influence, Rivero's exile only furthers his resolve. But he shifts from overt to covert investigation, documenting as much of the Cuban influence in Venezuela as possible.

* * *

Thousands of Cubans enter Venezuela's public administration every year as bureaucrats at the presidency, advisers at the ministries, or analysts at the state-owned companies. Cubans manage the system of identification for Venezuelans, their identity cards and passports; their registers and notaries public. Cubans co-manage the country's ports and airports and have a presence in immigration control points.[1] Cubans even arrive in Venezuela through a separate part of the airport in Caracas, known as Rampa 4. As Cuban officials handle the Cuban immigration process, reliable figures regarding the number of Cuban immigrants are hard to come by.[2]

Rivero's research leads him to estimate that 5,600 Cubans work with intelligence, security, or defense. Around 500 Cubans hold key positions within the Venezuelan armed forces, working with arms, organization, planning, logistics, intelligence, operation, military engineering, and construction of military fortifications.

But the vast majority of Cubans in Venezuela work in the field of healthcare. For Cuba, these exports are an excellent source of income. In 2010, each doctor is valued at 8,225 euro per month, twenty-seven times the average monthly salary of a Venezuelan doctor. In 2011, that number would grow to 9,745 euro per month. But the Cuban government only pays the doctors they send to Venezuela a food stipend of about 50 dollars a month. An additional 225 dollars are deposited each month into the doctors' Cuban accounts. And there is a catch: the money is only paid out to those who return to Cuba.[3]

According to NGO Solidaridad Sin Fronteras, thousands of Cuban workers, most of them doctors, desert the Venezuelan missions every year. Many end up in the United States.[4]

To minimize the number of deserters, the Cubans have to abide by strict rules while in Venezuela. They work long hours and reside in separate, often crowded housing units where they are subjected to curfews and prohibited from making friends with locals. Each mission also has a "legal function," a person assigned to surveillance and investigation of suspect behavior.[5]

II

It is April 2010. Antonio Rivero takes off his medal-covered, dark green uniform and hangs it on the wall. He places his peaked hat on a hook above. Overcome by a combination of pride and nostalgia, he takes a step back to admire it. He wonders when he will wear it again.

Rivero has just resigned from the armed forces.

"The inclusion of Cubans in the military ranks has gone further than what can be, or should be, allowed by the state, and I believe that it has now entered a phase where it poses a threat to the national security and could comprise a future danger," he tells local media.

In May 2010, Rivero also turns to the Ministry of Public Affairs, the State Prosecutor's Office, and the National Assembly to present his evidence regarding the national security threat posed by Cuban infiltration. Allowing the Cubans to manage confidential information is an act of treason, he claims.

"The Cubans have access to and influence over material that is very, very sensitive for the state and that violates the sovereignty and independence of the republic and the national security. I hope that the defense commission will take the political measures necessary to investigate, take corrective action, and revert the damage done in this field," he tells media ahead of stating his case before the National Assembly.

III

On February 11, 2010, María Corina Machado resigns as president of Súmate. The following week, she announces her candidacy for the Venezuelan National Assembly. Seven months later, she is elected as a deputy by the most votes in the country.[6]

As Machado rises to political prominence, the family begins to receive threats that their businesses will be expropriated.

Worried about the potential fallout, María Corina approaches her father.

"You just keep on doing what your conscience tells you is your duty," he says.

So she does.

And sure enough, on October 31, 2010, Chávez reveals that the government intends to expropriate her father's company, Sidetur.

The expropriation, Chávez announces, is a consequence of the inflated prices Sidetur charges for its products. The management insists it has complied with all state-issued price controls. In fact, while prices have been frozen since December 6 of 2006, high inflation rates are decimating the bottom line. The company's board urges the government to consider the impact of an expropriation on Sidetur's nearly 2,000 employees.[7]

On November 1, a number of workers from Sidetur take to the streets.

"We Want to Work!" "Expropriation = More Unemployment" read the massive banners under which the workers have gathered to protest in the streets of Caracas. Some of the men are still wearing their hardhats. Others appear to have come straight from the office, dressed in jeans and shirts.

At the Antímano plant, the minister of basic industries and mining, José Khan, makes a televised speech surrounded by workers supportive of the takeover. Members of the national guard keep all media outlets but the government-friendly VTV from entering the premises. Non-supportive workers are given no airtime.[8]

In 2010 alone, the Venezuelan government nationalizes 220 companies—both foreign and domestic. But not all nationalities are treated equally. In a meeting with Luiz Inácio Lula da Silva, then president of Brazil, Chávez pledges to spare Brazilian companies from the wave of nationalizations. The meeting is supposed to be private, but the microphones have been left on, and local journalists report overhearing the comment.

Official or not, Chávez keeps his promise to Lula. While the rest of the steel industry is expropriated under the pretext that it is a basic and strategic industry, the Brazilian steelmaker Gerdau keeps operating the Sizuca steel mill, producing several hundred thousand tons of raw steel annually.[9]

IV

It is 2011. Juan Carlos Requesens sits talking with a friend on the campus of Universidad Central de Venezuela when chaos erupts. Radical Chavistas have detonated homemade explosives in the restrooms of the university while his sister's friend is inside. The girl, a marathon runner and an athlete, survives, but loses a leg.

A few months later, twenty-two-year-old Juan Carlos is elected president of the student federation. The explosion defines his term. He joined student politics expecting to manage traditional student concerns like academic resources and facilities. The blast reset that expectation. It is not that violence is anything new. Juan Carlos had just started university when he was shot for the first time in a confrontation between radical Chavistas and students who support the opposition. A long scar lines his shoulder, and the place of impact is still clearly visible. Since then, he has been beaten, arrested, and interrogated many times. But somehow the case of the girl is different. She was not involved in politics and she did not attend demonstrations. She was passionate about sports and the blast killed all her prospects. For Juan Carlos, it acts as a wake-up call. Venezuela has serious problems.

V

On June 1, 2010, Puerto de La Mar is officially expropriated. The government publishes a notice in the *Gaceta Oficial* announcing that Puerto de La Mar is to be taken over by the Ministry of Education who will turn it into a Bolivarian university. The owners are told they have fifteen days to provide the documentation needed to calculate fair compensation.

Folco and his lawyers work around the clock to meet the deadline, but although all the paperwork is handed in on time, no compensation is received.

Around the same time, ferry operator Conferry is also expropriated, as is the Hilton Hotel where Folco first tried to raise support for Puerto de La Mar many years ago.

In the period between 2003 and 2011, the Property Rights Observatory records 1,911 land seizures, 915 expropriations, and 529 invasions. Early in the process, the government pays what it deems just compensation for expropriated property. But as the pace of expropriations increases, payments become increasingly rare. By the end of 2012, the Venezuelan government's unpaid debt to the owners of expropriated companies amounts to $13.4 billion.[10]

"There is nothing more we can do," Folco's lawyers tell him. "Since 2007 practically nobody has been paid."

VI

It is 2013. Juan Carlos Requesens loads placards into a taxi in a Caracas suburb. He is tall and corpulent, making the massive placards appear weightless as he lifts them effortlessly and arranges them in the backseat.

"No te quiero Caracas" (I don't love you Caracas), the signs read. Below is the name of the PSUV candidate for mayor in Libertador: Jorge Rodríguez. Blood drips from the letters. The colors and fonts of these student-made versions are the same as those used in Rodríguez's original campaign: "I love you Caracas."

Now twenty-four years old, Juan Carlos is nearing the end of his term as president of the national students' federation. As the representative of nearly a million students, Juan Carlos holds a great deal of power and influence among Venezuelan youth and the opposition overall.

A political science major at the Universidad Central de Venezuela, Juan Carlos is also a member of the political party Acción Democrática. In the upcoming local elections, he is running for councilor in the Caracas municipality of Baruta. The opposition is strong in affluent Baruta, and Juan Carlos is so sure of being elected he doesn't even bother to campaign. Instead, he donates his campaign budget to colleagues running in areas with stiffer competition.

But whether he becomes councilor or not, he intends to remain active in the student struggle. It's a dynamic and powerful movement that can be leveraged in a future political career.

Two young students wait on the driveway while Juan Carlos prepays the taxi. They have volunteered to put up the placards, but as they squeeze into the backseat beside the massive stack, their expressions of determination are replaced by nervousness. "Black campaigning," or badmouthing opposing candidates, is illegal. Not that either side cares. In fact, it often seems to be what the elections are most about. Still, getting caught means trouble.

A few days ago, six students were detained and brought in for questioning by the Bolivarian national intelligence service SEBIN. Immediately, 300 students gathered and marched together to the police station where their friends were kept. Under the lead of Juan Carlos, they threatened to start a riot and burn down the station if the police didn't release them. The stunt had the desired effect and the students were promptly released.

VII

"Let's show the world once more what the people of Bolívar are capable of! Let's write a new page that will remain in the political history of Venezuela and the world. Let's win the YES by knockout on Sunday, February 15. Let's say yes to the future!"

It is February 12, 2009 on Avenida Bolívar in Caracas, and Chávez is once again campaigning to amend the constitution. It is almost exactly ten years since he first came to power, and now, here he is, pleading with the people to let him keep it, indefinitely.

"You know that I, Hugo Chávez, am a soldier, a humble soldier, and I live for you. I will never fail you! Don't fail me on Sunday! Let's not fail the future on Sunday. Let's all go vote YES to open the gates of the new history. Homeland or death! We will prevail! ¡Hasta la victoria siempre!" (Until victory, always!).

In the past year, the opposition had gained some ground. When Chávez lost the constitutional referendum in 2007, it demonstrated that he could be defeated at the ballot box. Invigorated by their victory, on January 23, 2008 a number of opposition parties agreed to select common candidates for the local and regional elections due later that year.

Chávez responded by barring hundreds of them from running.

The most promising was Leopoldo López, mayor of Chacao, the richest district of Caracas. He was to be the opposition's candidate for mayor of greater Caracas and according to polls he was sure to win a landslide. The capital city loved him. He had everything they wanted—charisma, ambition, and such dazzlingly good looks that his female supporters sounded like teenage girls at a boy band concert when they screamed his name: "Leeeoooopoldo!" It didn't hurt that he was also the great-great-grandnephew of Simón Bolívar.[11]

López was the first real threat to Chávez since his rise to power, and the Comandante acted swiftly to thwart it. He accused López of misusing state funds. López denied the allegations and was never formally charged, but it was enough to declare him "inhabilitado"—disqualified from holding public office for six years.

In November 2008, Chávez's PSUV won the vast majority of governorships, but the opposition managed to conquer the most populous states, and Antonio Ledezma, who replaced López, even won the mayoralty of Caracas.[12]

But celebrations didn't last long. *Colectivos*[13], Chávez's brawny street militia, occupied city hall, relegating Ledezma to an obscure office, blocks away. The "coup" was quickly legitimized by Chávez who rather deftly created a new "capital district" of which Caracas would be a part. He then transferred resources and authority over schools, hospitals, and health centers, as well as a TV station, from the city to this new, unelected "head of the capital district," ensuring power over Caracas would be reserved for loyalists.[14]

"It doesn't matter. Even if they only leave me the squirrels in Bolívar square, I am going to show that it is possible to govern Caracas in a different manner," said Ledezma.[15]

Other mayors and state governors suffered similar fates. Some were even threatened with jail. Manuel Rosales, Chávez's former rival from the 2006 election, was charged with corruption after being elected mayor of Maracaibo and soon left the country.[16]

Then, in December 2008, Chávez announced that there would be a new referendum. In the summer of 2008, he had used a special "enabling act" to push through twenty-six new laws, twelve of which closely resembled those of the rejected constitutional reform. But the most controversial amendment—the abolition of term limits—needed voter approval. The first time around, Chávez had only suggested abolishing term limits for himself, but now he also included governors and mayors to make sure they were motivated to campaign hard for a yes vote. And so it was that 2009 kicked off with a massive red campaign. Chavista deputies, governors, and mayors toured the country, distributing free domestic goods. Every day, hours of live coverage of political events were broadcast on every state channel. In Caracas, activists distributed pamphlets outlining the reasons to vote "yes." Topping the list was: "Chávez loves us and love is repaid with love," followed by "Chávez is incapable of doing us harm."[17]

"If the opposition wins power there will be war: that's why it's necessary to guarantee the continuity of the Bolivarian, democratic, revolutionary process and that is what the constitutional amendment seeks to achieve," Chávez said during the course of the campaign. "As long as I govern, the Venezuelan people have peace guaranteed."[18]

At the closing of the campaign, hundreds of thousands of red-clad supporters crowd together on Avenida Bolívar to listen to Chávez's final speech. Dressed in red, standing behind a red podium against a wall of repeating red block letters forming the word "SI," Chávez delivers one of his most compelling speeches yet.

"On Sunday you will decide my political destiny. On Sunday we will know if Hugo Chávez is going away or not. The word is yours. The sovereign decision is yours. I, as a soldier, will stand firm," he pauses to salute the crowd, "and do whatever you decide, because you are my boss. I will always obey the sovereign will of the Venezuelan people. ... On Sunday from 3 a.m. I will be at every electoral table waiting for you to do with me as you see fit, because I am not Chávez, I am a people. I don't belong to me; I belong to the people of Venezuela. My life is not mine. My life is yours!"

VIII

"Victory! Victory! Victory of the people!" roars a seemingly infinite sea of supporters outside Miraflores.

It is February 15, 2009, and an invincible Chávez addresses the multitude from the People's Balcony.

"I told you I would wait for you here, and here we are ... Long live Caracas! Bright-red Caracas! Bolivarian Caracas! ... I knew you wouldn't fail me. Now it is my turn to keep my promise. I will not fail the people of Venezuela, the hopes of the people, the clamors of the people, the love of the people. ... Today, February 15, you have written my destiny—my political destiny, which is the same as the destiny of my life. I want to tell you that I accept with heart and soul ... I swear to the Venezuelan people that from this moment on I devote myself fully to the service of the Venezuelan people ... I swear before the people, before my children and my grandchildren to dedicate all that is left of my life to this path. Long live the people! Long live socialism! ... In 2012 there will be presidential elections, and, God willing and the people willing, this soldier is already an aspiring candidate for the Presidency of the Republic from 2013 to 2019."

"Oh, ah, Chávez no se va!" "Oh, ah, Chávez is not going away!" chants the multitude.

The opposition is rattled. When first elected, Chávez said that he would serve only one term. With each victory, he has extended his expiry date. First 2012, now 2019.[19] Unless they can put their differences aside, Chávez might well rule Venezuela for life. Six of the most important opposition parties meet to discuss the creation of a coalition, and Mesa de la Unidad Democrática (MUD) is born.

Membership in MUD grows quickly, representing the whole spectrum of political ideology, from Marxist Bandera Roja to more conservative parties like the Christian Democratic Party, Copei. Communist to center-right standpoints somehow have to merge and agree on a political framework.

After nine months of workshops, 100 points of consensus have been identified. These are developed and the result presented in a document called "100 solutions for the people." The document, heavy on generic, high-level principles, and light on detail, covers all sectors of government.

The coalition agrees that a number of Chávez's key social and environmental policies should remain, but be structured differently. Most importantly, they believe government must be decentralized, and the economy gradually freed from the inconsistent controls. But there is no doubt the main objective of the coalition is to defeat Chávez. Should the opposition win, they would be left with the challenge of overcoming their fundamental ideological differences.

IX

Juan Carlos Requesens is having lunch at a panadería in Caracas when the phone rings.

"Please don't hurt them!" the caller pleads.

It takes Juan Carlos a few phone calls to get the full story: A group of students have kidnapped some Chavista bikers who arrived at Universidad Central de Venezuela to intimidate students by firing shots in the air. The students shot at the bikers' tires. When the bikers crashed, the students overpowered them, disarmed them, and locked them up.

Conflicts with extreme Chavistas from different *colectivos* are a weekly nuisance and nothing to get agitated about. Juan Carlos makes a few phone calls to make sure the captives are released, while picking away at his lunch.

The phone rings constantly. Things to take care of, favors to grant or request. Juan Carlos leans back in his chair, confident and silent. He listens to the caller on the other end, then makes a quick judgment call to determine the appropriate course of action before attending to the next person. The other day he forgot his phone at home and came back to 530 missed calls, over 1,000 text messages, and several hundred pings.

According to Juan Carlos, between twenty and thirty students have died in direct conflicts at the universities in the past fourteen years. And if one considers the total amount of students who have been killed, the number is much higher. Venezuela has appalling murder statistics and most victims are between eighteen and twenty-four years old. Political motives behind attacks are often suspected, but hard to prove.

Juan Carlos avoids the university after 6 p.m. at night. That's when the bikers come out and attacks are likely. If he has to go he makes sure to go as part of a big group. Most students are left alone, but politically active ones like himself are popular targets. He does not believe that violence should be fought with more violence. But he does not believe in being an easy victim either. Everybody has the right to defend themselves and their loved ones. So when the revolutionary movement Tupamaro came to pay him a visit after he was elected president of the student federation, Juan Carlos was armed and ready to show that he would not take any bullshit.

C, the *colectivo* veteran whom he stood up against that day, is now his friend, or at least no longer an enemy. Juan Carlos gained his respect by showing that he was not afraid.

Intimidation is what most confrontations are about: shots in the air and beatings. Weapons that the students have seized from overpowered Chavistas are used for intimidation and self-defense when the next attack comes.

"In the current situation we have no choice but to get our own hands dirty," says Juan Carlos. "We don't go to university to get killed."

X

"Long live the Libyan revolution!" Chávez shouts. "¡Viva!" the crowd replies obediently.

It is September 28, 2009, and Chávez is back on stage at Puerto de La Mar. This time, he is accompanied by the Libyan leader, Muammar Gadhafi.

"We are here to change history, to put an end to imperialism, to build socialism, the new socialism, socialism in the Arab countries, in Africa, in the Caribbean, in Latin America. Socialism is the road to the salvation of the people, to the greatness of the people, and to the salvation of the world," Chávez continues.

The sea of supporters dressed in red rejoices. A big conference gathering leaders from sixty countries in Margarita has just ended and Chávez is seizing the opportunity to honor the Libyan leader. He has brought Gadhafi to Puerto de La Mar to award him the Collar of the Order of the Liberator, the highest Venezuelan distinction appointed for services to the country, outstanding merit, and benefits made to the community. He also gives Gadhafi a golden replica of Bolívar's sword.

"Fellow President, this is a replica of the sword that freed America 200 years ago. It is a gem, given to Bolívar by the people ... More than 3,000 precious stones. The original is made of pure gold. This sword is alive, and travels over Latin America. On behalf of our people, of the Bolivarian revolution, I give it to you, revolutionary soldier, leader of the Libyan people, of the Libyan revolution, of the people of Africa and leader, as well, for the people of Latin America and the Caribbean. ¡Viva Bolívar! ¡Viva Gadhafi!"

Dressed in a simple black shirt underneath which the top of a red T-shirt can be seen, Chávez goes on to shower Gadhafi with praise:

"One of the greatest leaders of the twentieth century and of the twenty-first. One of the motors, one of the great promoters of the anti-imperial battle, the battle for liberation of people and for unity of people ... I'm by no means exaggerating; what Simón Bolívar is for us Venezuelans, Muammar Gadhafi is for the Libyan people. He is the Liberator of Libya, the creator of the popular socialist Arab republic."

Gadhafi has taken a seat on stage, his eyes so narrow they almost appear closed, his hands clinched together in a firm clasp. He raises and shakes them at the crowd in a gesture implying victory and gratitude.

Chávez continues: "You carry on your chest the supreme decoration, the Order of the Liberator, the medal of Bolívar, because you are Muammar Gadhafi, a great soldier, a great Bolivarian leader."

When its Gadhafi's turn, he declares with equal zeal that Venezuela and Libya "have the same trench, the same fate, the same battle against the same enemy and we will prevail."

From Folco's stage at Puerto de La Mar, Chávez ends his speech by rallying the crowd once more: "¡Viva Gadhafi! ¡Viva Libia! ¡Viva Venezuela! ¡Viva el socialismo!"

XI

Dressed in a green military jacket, Hugo Chávez walks onto the screen, hand-in-hand with his daughter María Gabriela, twenty-five years old at the time. It is February 2010, and the president's weekly talk show *Aló Presidente* number 351 is being filmed and simultaneously broadcast to millions of Venezuelans.

María Gabriela and Hugo wander around Plaza Bolívar in central Caracas.

"Here we are in Plaza Bolívar," Chávez announces. "Bolivarian Bolívar. Walking with María, like in the song. Do you remember?" He pulls his daughter in for an embrace and while clutching her to his chest he starts to sing: "Caminando por Caracas, Caracas. La gente me saludaba y andaba. Yo levantaba mi mano de hermano y Caracas me abrazaba a mi."

They resume their walk.

"Do you remember when you were little?" he asks her. "We would run through here. You would chase doves and cry because you couldn't catch any ... There is one. Catch it!"

She laughs, a little embarrassed. Then, they turn their backs to the camera, facing the impressive statue of Simón Bolívar on horse in the center of the square.

"Look at Bolívar! Bolívar! Plaza Bolívar," Chávez says. Then, suddenly, he turns and points while excitedly exclaiming: "Look a squirrel. Look! Look! Look! There goes a squirrel." Then: "What sort of tree might that be?" The angle changes abruptly as the cameraman is trying to keep up with the switching topics and angles. It feels like watching someone's improvised amateur home video. After shifting topics again and launching a brief assault on capitalism, Chávez motions for a group of people dressed in red to step forward. They've been staying in the background, but now Chávez invites them in and starts to lecture:

"The year they brought Bolívar's remains here, they began to call this place Plaza Bolívar, in 1842. The oligarchy brought his remains here after expelling him in life. Of course, there was a lot of pressure from the family, a lot of popular pressure to bring him back. And there he stayed, resting for several years in the cathedral. Then General Guzmán Blanco came and ordered them to put up the statue. There's the year, look, 1874, after the federal war. Another betrayal! They killed Zamora, and the oligarchy continued owning power. Then they started to use Bolívar, the people who betrayed and expelled him, started to use his myth. They almost turned him into a saint, but for their own interests, to exploit the people ... They made him into something he wasn't, the way some Catholics have made Jesus into something he wasn't. Christ was a great rebel, and for that he died crucified. He was an anti-imperialist. He was born and died among the poor and for the poor and with the poor. But there are some conservative sectors of the Catholic Church that transformed Christ into another, not the real one who existed of flesh and bone. And that's what happened with Bolívar, the bourgeoisie transformed him."

Members of the group dressed in red nod interestedly. They are *voceros*, or spokesmen visiting from municipal councils in Aragua state to share their experiences of *poder popular*, one of Chávez's catch phrases meaning popular power. The theme of the program is a new law affecting the municipal councils. They are all walking along, chatting, when suddenly Chávez interrupts a lady from Aragua in mid-sentence and says:

"Look, this has to be fixed." His foot has detected a loose cobblestone in the square. "All the details have to be fixed. April 19 and July 5 are coming. *El bicentenario* is coming!"

He is referring to the 200-year anniversary of the 1810 revolution. A series of commemorations are planned to honor important historical events, culminating on July 5 when the Venezuelan Declaration of Independence was signed.

"Is the mayor taking notes?" Chávez asks.

He turns to the crowd of people following behind and calls out to Jorge Rodríguez, mayor of the Libertador municipality in Caracas: "Jorge, this plaza has improved, changed, but there are still details missing."

Chávez points to a building behind some trees.

"That building over there, what is it? It was an old theatre, right? But now in government hands?"

"Yes, at this moment it's in government hands," Rodríguez replies.

"And that building?"

Chávez points to another building known as La Francia, a beautiful historic building hosting Venezuela's most exclusive jewelry shops.

"That is a building of private jewelry shops," replies the mayor.

"Expropriate it! Expropriate it!" orders Chávez unexpectedly, his arms still pointing at the building.

"Okay," says Rodríguez in a voice that betrays no emotion.

The face of the lady from Aragua lights up, and she and the group of people dressed in red begin to clap.

"And that building over there, on the corner?" Chávez points to the other side of the square.

"That also has shops," says Rodríguez.

"In that house lived Bolívar when he was newly married, that little house that you see with two balconies."

Chávez keeps his arm pointing so that there can be no doubt as to which house he is referring.

"And now it has shops!" he roars. "Expropriate it!"

The entourage begins to cheer. Chávez is on a roll. He turns to yet another building.

"This building here, what is it?"

"That's also a commercial building. Private property."

"Expropriate it! Señor Mayor, expropriate it!" Chávez rubs his hands together. "We have to make this into a great historic center. Well, it already is, but we have to make more of it, make ... architectural projects, historic projects. We are in the heart of Caracas. Caracas, Caracas, the rebel city!"

Chávez pats the mayor on the shoulder. "How are you, Jorge?" he asks and resumes his walk, a cue that the topic is closed and it's time for the show to move on.

"We were listening to our *compañera* from Aragua," he says and turns to the lady in red who has been waiting patiently during his expropriation spree.

She begins to talk, but doesn't even get halfway through her first sentence before Chávez interrupts again. This time with a song: "Simón Bolívar, Simón Bolívar ..."

XII

It is June 2010. Antonio Rivero braces himself as the wheels of the plane hit the runway at Porlamar's Santiago Mariño International Airport. He has come to Isla de Margarita to meet three Cubans offering classified information.

It all started when Rivero received a message from a man who called himself Carlos. He claimed to be a senior analyst who used to work in "the situation room," the eyes and ears of Miraflores, during Rivero's time at the presidential palace.

"General, you are on the right track. What you are claiming is true. I'd like to speak with you. I can give you more information," he tweeted.

At first Rivero was skeptical, worried it might be a trap. However, after writing back and forth for a few weeks, the analyst managed to convince Rivero that his intentions were sincere.

Rivero has great expectations for his visit. The Cubans have already electronically transmitted a few things, but nothing really game-changing. Rivero is hungry for more. But at the same time, he is scared. He knows he is taking a chance. It could well be a set-up by the government, or by some Cuban agents luring him to the island.

It is thus with a mixture of anxiety and anticipation that he disembarks from the plane, hails a taxi to downtown Porlamar, and makes his way to the 4 de Mayo bakery, the rendezvous point. Here, he will meet the lady housing the Cubans.

Rivero arrives about half an hour early. He buys a pizza slice and a juice and takes a seat outside on the large open patio. At the agreed hour, a lone lady arrives. She is in her fifties and looks like your typical Margariteña: dark hair dyed a warm chestnut color, gray-brown eyes, tanned skin, and apparently very familiar with her surroundings. This must be her. Rivero takes off his baseball cap and sunglasses to enable her to recognize him. He has guessed right, after a quick scan of the place, the lady approaches. They greet each other and she leads the way to her home.

When he enters the house, Rivero immediately recognizes the oldest man as the former intelligence officer he knew as Carlos at Miraflores. A political expert and analyst, Carlos is now in his mid-fifties. He is bespectacled, short, gaunt and a few skin tones lighter than the average Cuban, suggesting that he doesn't get out much. The other two are taller and at least ten years younger. They are IT-experts, specializing in programming.

They tell Rivero they arrived in Venezuela in 1997 as part of a group consisting of twenty-nine Cubans. Initially, they worked in Margarita under a commercial front, but the whole idea was to assist Chávez with matters relating to security, informatics, and intelligence ahead of the 1998 elections.

A report published by newspaper *El Universal* in 2003 corroborates their version. It gives an account of three front firms run by the Cuban intelligence service; two of them registered in Margarita as importers of pharmaceutical products; the third registered in Caracas as a software importer.[20]

"The observations you've made about the Cuban presence are all true," the man tells Rivero and hands over the promised documents explaining how SAI (System of Integrated Authentication) can be used to gain electoral advantage. SAI is a fairly new system of voter verification connecting each ID number to a thumbprint. The Cubans claim that, between 2007 and 2009, they were part of the team developing the system, making it possible to influence the outcome of future elections.

Now convinced that it is not a trap, Rivero relaxes a little bit while the Cubans remain visibly nervous. They have already spent six months in hiding and are not interested in being caught now. Once they've handed over the promised information, they ask Rivero for assistance.

"We need your support to be able to leave the country. We need money and a way out. Will you help us?" the analyst says.

"I'll see what I can do," Rivero replies.

The following day, he returns to Caracas where he begins to put together a plan.

Two months later, they meet in Carabobo. From there, Rivero's network takes them west and eventually across the border into Colombia.

A few weeks later, Rivero is scheduled to participate in an interview with CNN to talk about Cuba's involvement in Venezuelan defense matters. Hours before his interview is due to start, Rivero is summoned to appear for a hearing at the prosecutor's office. He is charged with revealing classified information. But no trial date is set. Instead, he is ordered to appear every week before a military tribunal. Most importantly, Rivero is also banned from speaking to the media on any defense-related matter and from leaving Venezuela. But he is not banned from holding public office, and Rivero soon begins to regard politics as his only remaining method of attempting to forge change.

In November 2010, Rivero runs as an independent candidate in the parliamentary elections. Despite no party allegiance or political connections to speak of, he comes third out of ten candidates in his district. Afterwards, he receives a phone call from oppositional veteran Leopoldo López who is about to register his movement Voluntad Popular as a political party. He wants Rivero to be part of his team. In July 2011, Rivero is elected as the local leader of Voluntad Popular in Bolívar state.

XIII

It is July 16, 2010 in the National Pantheon of Caracas—burial ground of Venezuelan heroes. As the national anthem begins to play, figures dressed in white lab coats, hairnets, gas masks, blue surgical gloves, and blue plastic socks enter marching with knees high in the air. One by one, they gather around Simón Bolívar's sarcophagus. Chávez has ordered the exhumation of the remains of the Liberator to conduct tests on the bones. He suspects that Bolívar didn't really die from tuberculosis, but was in fact poisoned by the Colombian oligarchy.

From every conceivable angle, cameras capture the event.

"We don't regard him as dead," says Chávez, addressing the nation. "No! To paraphrase Pablo Neruda, Bolívar returned when our people awoke. We see the concavities of the cranium as though his eyes were looking at us. ... Bolívar is alive. We don't see him as a skeleton. No! He is like a flash of lightning, a sacred fire."

Any moment now, Chávez informs the viewers, the scientists will uncover the sacred remains of the Liberator.

"Let us kneel to show respect for his supreme memory, his struggle—our struggle, his fatherland—our fatherland. It is 11 p.m. Let us present Bolívar who has returned." The camera shifts from Chávez's face to the white-clad figures inside the tomb who proceed to cut open the lead sarcophagus as if it were a tin of sardines. They peel away the blackened flag covering the body, laying bare before the camera a remarkably intact skeleton. Even parts of Bolívar's boots and the borrowed shirt in which he was buried remain.

"What impressive moments we've lived tonight!" Chávez tweets from the pantheon, making sure to keep followers who aren't watching the televised broadcast up to date throughout the exhumation. "I confess that we have cried—we have sworn allegiance," he continues: "That glorious skeleton has to be Bolívar, because you can feel his flame. My God. Bolívar lives ... We are his flame!"

Addressing the viewers again, Chávez reminds them of how Bolívar was betrayed by the bourgeoisie: "He was defamed and crucified, just like Christ. Maybe that is why Neruda calls him: 'Our Father.'"

To the accompaniment of video footage from the exhumation, Chávez then recites Neruda's poem *Chant to Bolívar*:

> Our Father thou art in Heaven,
> in water, in air
> in all our silent and broad latitude
> everything bears your name, Father in our dwelling:
> your name raises sweetness in sugar cane
> Bolivar tin has a Bolivar gleam
> the Bolívar bird flies over the Bolivar volcano
> the potato, the saltpeter, the special shadows,
> the brooks, the phosphorous stone veins
> everything comes from your extinguished life
> your legacy was rivers, plains, bell towers
> your legacy is our daily bread, oh Father ...

The results of the inquiry into the Liberator's death are inconclusive, but Chávez has grander plans for Bolívar's bones anyway.

On July 24, 2012, during a celebration of the Liberator's 229th birthday, Chávez unveils a portrait of Bolívar reconstructed from digital analysis of his remains. "Happy birthday, Simón Bolívar! ¡Viva Bolívar!" Chávez exclaims at the festivities. "¡Viva!" echoes the audience.

"As Neruda says, everything has your name, Father; the Bolívar hurricane, the Bolívar bird, the Bolívar lightning. ... From now on, your true face, rescued by the loving hands of your scientist sons and daughters, will shine even brighter, because now we know it with precision. We receive the infinite intensity, the luminous presence of this gaze, of this face," Chávez says, pointing to the 3D image, enlarged to cover an entire wall.

"He is alive and will continue to live forever in the struggle for this fatherland."

XIV

"Today, with humility and absolute conviction, I assume the challenge of becoming the first female president of Venezuela."

It is July 17, 2011, and María Corina Machado is announcing her candidacy for the first primary elections in the history of Venezuela. Dressed entirely in white, she faces the television cameras, exuding confidence and composure. She knows she is writing history.

Machado is running on a platform of what she calls "capitalism of the people," with decentralization, social inclusion, education, and security as her main pillars.

"Let's leave poverty behind. With your work and my support you will have property, security, and a future for your children," she promises in one of her televised campaign ads. "You have the right to progress and to live with dignity. That is capitalism of the people. We will all be better off!"

In a short period of time, the MUD coalition has succeeded in propelling a new generation of young leaders. But only one of them will get to challenge Chávez in the upcoming presidential elections. Among the contenders eager to take on the Comandante, Machado is up against Pablo Pérez Álvarez, governor of oil-rich Zulia state; veteran politician and diplomat Diego Arria; and former labor-leader Pablo Medina. But it is Henrique Capriles Radonski, governor of Miranda state, who will be her main competition. His idea of a moderate leftist government inspired by Brazilian President Luiz Inácio Lula da Silva appeals to many voters.

Leopoldo López would have made another dangerous contender. By now the Inter-American Court of Human Rights has overturned the court ruling against López, allowing him to participate in the election. But Venezuela's Supreme Court still bars him from holding office should he win. So López decides to withdraw his candidacy in favor of Capriles. With all of López's supporters joining his own, Capriles is the undisputed favorite.

XV

Juan Carlos sips his rum slowly, allowing his palate plenty of time to absorb the full bouquet of flavor. It makes up for the uncomfortable plastic seats at the Estadio Universitario in Caracas. A giant shark mascot wanders the stadium performing half-hearted cheers for Tiburones de la Guaira, the Caracas-based baseball team playing today. Juan Carlos's favorite team is the Leones, but it doesn't really matter. Baseball is more about hanging out than it is about watching the game. He comes as often as he can.

Juan Carlos controls an entire section of the stadium. About 150 yellow seats are devoted to the student body and he distributes the tickets. He also employs three female students who serve guests beer and rum. As president of the students' federation, he doesn't have any formal salary, but his political benefactors sponsor his lifestyle.

Someone shouts his name. He turns and acknowledges the greeting with a warm smile and a lift of his hand in the general direction of the audience.

The section bordering that of the students is smaller, but also marked by the same yellow chairs. These seats belong to the government. Today, only a few of them are taken. At the beginning of his presidency, Chávez would frequently come to watch his favorite team Magallanes, but eventually the loud heckling from members of the opposition became so disruptive he stopped attending.

Juan Carlos scans the stadium. He recognizes two police officers who detained and beat him during a past clash between students and police. But today their presence no longer worries him. If anything were to happen to him now, the publicity would be enormous.

He makes his way toward the concessions, but only advances a few steps at a time, constantly interrupted by people approaching to greet him.

"Goiko ¿cómo estás compadre?

"¡Epa, pana!"

He shakes hands, slams the shoulders of friends and kisses the cheeks of female acquaintances. Old and young, everybody wants a word. By the time he reaches the concession stands, he has missed an entire inning. He orders a few Venezuelan fast food delicacies: *cachapa*, a type of sweet corn pancake stuffed with cheese, and *arepas*, cornbread sandwiches with delicious fillings. He's on a diet so he really shouldn't be indulging in this kind of food, but a few bites can't hurt. When he goes to pay, the guy working the till won't take his money.

"¡No, Coño!" he exclaims, seemingly pleased about the opportunity to treat the big guy to something.

Juan Carlos leaves before the game is over, shaking hands and waving goodbye to his friends, admirers, and associates. As he is leaving, he greets the parking lot attendants with the Cuban revolutionary motto: "¡Hasta la victoria siempre!"

After all, politics is about staying popular, he reflects.

7

GOLIATH WINS

"Flee the country where a lone man holds all power: It is a nation of slaves."

Simón Bolívar

I

It is January 13, 2012. For the past eight hours, Chávez has spoken without interruption at the legislative palace in Caracas. He is wearing an elegant dark blue suit with the presidential sash in yellow, blue, and red across his chest.

"I still hear people speak of communism. It is not part of our project. We respect communism, but it's not here."

Chávez laughs and continues: "No, communism is something else. Communism even involves the elimination of the state. Our project is socialism, socialism with Venezuelan peculiarities. Bolivarian socialism. Humanist. Democratic! De-mo-cra-tic!" He emphasizes each syllable. Then he falls silent for a few moments, taking in his audience. His gaze finds the face of María Corina Machado among the other deputies, and he says: "So democratic is this socialism that deputy Machado, with all due respect, has told me to get ready to hand in the sash. Well, I wish her luck. This is democracy. If she wins I will hand in the sash and if she permits me I will even give her a kiss of congratulation."

The assembly erupts in laughter and cheers.

"Then accept debate!" replies María Corina. Her voice is barely audible in the big auditorium.

"Debate?" The president frowns and turns his head as though struggling to hear her. Then he laughs and says: "Not yet."

A microphone is extended to María Corina who has risen to her feet.

"President, we have spent eight hours listening to you describing a country far removed from what all the women and mothers of Venezuela experience every day. We have even reached the extreme of hearing that the production of milk has increased when you know that today there are women, mothers, who turn violent at the store over a liter of milk because there is nothing for them to bring home. This is the moment to give answers to the country, to the more than 180,000 mothers and women who in these thirteen years have lost their sons, husbands, and fathers without seeing justice done. This is what we wanted to hear, the decent Venezuela, who definitely don't want to see an advance towards communism. We want respect for property. We want a Venezuela of solidarity, a Venezuela of justice, a Venezuela of achievement. How can you say that you respect the private sector when you have dedicated yourself to expropriation, which is the same as robbing ..."

"Robbing?" Chávez interrupts her.

"Yes, you have dedicated yourself to taking the properties of entrepreneurs, traders, even the owners of small inns. Tell Venezuela the truth! Here we have a decent Venezuela who wants a profound transformation. It is time to face, with seriousness and respect, this historic challenge that we have ahead of us.

Your time is up. It is time for a new Venezuela. Accept debate, president."

Chávez studies her calmly, his face betraying no emotion.

"Well, first of all I would suggest that you win the primaries. That's the first thing you have to do because you are out of ranking to be debating with me," he says.

Then again, more agitatedly:

"You are out of ranking! I'm very sorry, but it's the truth. Now that you have gone so far as to call me a thief in front of the nation. But I will not offend you. Eagles don't hunt flies, deputy. It is regrettable that you took the word only to call the president of the republic a thief. Very well, thank you, deputy."

The room buzzes with discontented mumbles. Then Chávez supporters begin to boo and display their displeasure over María Corina's remark. Chávez implores calm, then turns to Machado again:

"You fall short. Maybe next time when you have some more political experience ... I would suggest that you come here as deputy and debate with the other deputies and maybe study a little bit of politics. You are young. You are a woman. With all due respect, but the least one can ..."

His voice dies off and he never finishes the sentence. Instead, he says: "Believe me, I am tolerant," and goes on to tell an anecdote from 1999 when he was last insulted in this building. It was back in the days when Acción Democrática and Copei still held the majority of seats, shortly before he dissolved the Congress. He takes out a little book, *El oráculo del guerrero* (The oracle of the warrior), and asks the camera to zoom in on a few words of encouragement that he scribbled to himself in the margin of the text that very same day. It is dated July 5, 1999, and reads: "Come what may, you will always end up victorious."

II

María Corina stops before entering the living room. She catches the tone of gravity in her father's voice and decides not to interrupt. Enrique Machado Zuloaga is talking to his four grandsons—her own two boys and her sister's two boys.

"They are going to take everything away," he tells them. "Of course it's my life and it's your patrimony. But you have a duty now. You have to study and prepare as best as you can because you will be able to build something even bigger and better than I did. And you will be able to do that because your mother and her generation are risking their lives so that you will have a democratic and open society in which to do that."

María Corina leans against the wall, relieved. They have not taken away what matters most, she reflects: hope and our love for our country. On the contrary, they have made it stronger. As for their property, she is convinced the family will get that back some day. The important thing now is not to let it break them.

On Monday, October 29, 2012, the Venezuelan Ministry of Industries seizes the property of the steel company Sidetur. All in all, they take six industrial plants and fifteen scrap collection centers owned by Sidetur and its subsidiaries. Then the company accounts are cleaned out, all funds transferred into the account of the National Steelmaking Complex. The Machado family and other owners receive no compensation.[1]

III

It is June 1, 2012. Thousands of red-clad Chavistas have gathered around a central square in Petare, Caracas. A recording of President Chávez singing the national anthem is streaming from the loudspeakers. A massive puppet of the Comandante dances on stage. Chávez's face stares back from banners, murals, placards, T-shirts, and screens across the nation. It's at the height of Chávez's presidential campaign against Henrique Capriles. But while the Comandante's face is everywhere, Chávez himself is nowhere to be seen.

On February 12, 2012, Capriles won an expected victory in the opposition primaries with more than 60 percent of the votes. Second-runner up was Pablo Pérez Álvarez, governor of Zulia state, with 30.3 percent. María Corina Machado came in third with 3.7 percent of the vote (110,420 votes).[2]

The election had been a peaceful and respectful affair, about ideas rather than people—something the voters hadn't experienced in a long time. Ahead of the results, the candidates sent each other greetings of respect and admiration and promised to remain united regardless of the outcome. So far, they had kept that promise. And Capriles would need all the support he could get. Chávez was a politically astute adversary, but for him, the battle would take place on two fronts.

In June 2011, Chávez was diagnosed with cancer. He traveled to Havana to have a tumor removed from his pelvic area. He returned vigorous. He was undergoing treatment and would recover fully, he announced.

Salvador Navarette, Chávez's former family doctor, told the media that the cancer was terminal and that Chávez had no more than two years to live. Members of the Bolivarian intelligence service, SEBIN, cracked down on his clinic and Navarette was forced to flee to Spain. The government called the doctor a liar and a traitor. Other doctors in white coats appeared on television to tell the nation that, although they could not disclose any details regarding the type of cancer or its location, the public could rest assured that the prognosis was excellent.[3]

But it wasn't long until Chávez was rushed back to Havana for more surgery followed by chemotherapy. When Chávez reappeared bloated and bald, some supporters shaved their heads in support.

Chávez insisted he was recovering but refused to give details, creating a nation of speculators. The president would disappear for weeks, giving rise to all kinds of rumors, only to suddenly resurface again. He changed the official slogan "Fatherland, socialism or death" to "We will live and we will win," removing all references to death from the official communication.[4]

Then, ten months before the 2012 election, Chávez interrupted all programming to broadcast a *cadena* so that the nation could witness him give thanks to God and to the Virgin Mary for curing him. He was fully recovered, he assured. The cancer was gone. Chávez was resurrected, just in time for the election campaign.

"I came here to keep a promise I made in Cuba six months ago. You know that I was in a difficult situation and I put my life in the hands of the holy God, Christ the redeemer, and the Virgin Mary of Coromoto. I prayed a great deal to God and the Virgin to give me life. Because the truth is my life is no longer mine. My life is dedicated to the struggle for the humble, for the poor, for the people. That is my life."

The audience erupted in wild cheers.

"And when I, a humble soldier, knelt before God, knelt before Christ, and the Virgin, and the spirits of the savanna, ... I made this promise. Give me life! Because my life will every day be dedicated to struggle for the ideals of Christ, and of his mother the Virgin Mary. Justice! Justice! Social justice! Equality! And for this I will live all the days I have left on this earth."

But the Comandante was by no means "fully recovered." The truth was that he was dying and only his closest confidants knew just how fast.

Having masked his condition, Chávez now had to mask the declining economy. For this, he turned to China who granted him development loans in return for access to the oil reserves. Chávez used the money to order big pay raises for state workers, especially the army. The mission "Mi Casa Bien Equipada" (My well-equipped home) distributed 1.3 million subsidized washing machines, dishwashers, stoves, and flat-screen TVs made in China with Chávez's name and face printed on the boxes. Through the Great Housing Mission, he handed out keys to new government homes. But a more significant and ingenious move was the creation of a waiting list. Chávez went on television urging people to sign-up for a home. Millions flocked to register. They received stamped receipts with their name, the date, and a registration number. For many, that little piece of paper came to represent their ticket to a new life, a ticket they knew would only remain valid for as long as Chávez remained in power.[5]

As before, the president would disappear, without explanation, for weeks on end. But it didn't seem to matter. His relationship with the people had transitioned from physical to virtual. Live appearances were simply substituted for Twitter campaigns, radio, and TV appearances. To keep followers motivated, the 3 millionth person to sign up to follow the president's Twitter feed was awarded a free house.

His ministers took the stage in his place, invoking the Comandante's words. Campaign managers did their best to thwart any rumors that the president was severely ill.

"Es sano, es sano, levantame la mano!" (He's healthy, he's healthy, lift your hand!), rappers sang to warm up the crowds at government rallies.

* * *

On October 4, 2012, at the closing of the electoral campaign, Chávez is due to address a huge crowd in downtown Caracas. It's in the midst of a vicious rainstorm, and people assume the Comandante will cancel. He doesn't. Dressed in black, jogging and punching the air, he appears on stage to put on one last show.

"We are playing for life. In our hands we will not lose the fatherland, we will not lose the future of the fatherland," he proclaims through the thunder and rain.[6]

He is drenched, but the rain, he says, is a blessing from God. To deafening roars and blasting music, he defies his sick, cancer-ridden body and forces it to dance, one last time, in the downpour before the sea of red.

Three days later, on October 7, Chávez wins his last election: 55 percent versus Capriles' 44 percent. More than 80 percent of the electorate votes—a historic turnout.

Capriles accepts defeat and congratulates the Comandante: "To know how to win, you have to know how to lose. For me, what the people say is sacred."[7]

The country is a mess. Crime rates soar, basic food items such as milk, sugar, and flour are scarce, and the currency has lost a third of its value in the fifth devaluation in a decade. The only countries in a similar or worse situation are Iraq, Myanmar, Congo, and Uzbekistan. But he has pulled it off. Days after the election, Chávez promotes Nicolás Maduro, then foreign minister, to vice-president.

He has done all he can to clear a path for his most loyal disciple.[8]

IV

It is August 25, 2012. An explosion at the Amuay oil refinery in Punto Fijo sends fire and smoke towering so high into the sky that it can be seen from miles away. The mechanical seal on one or more of the pumps collapsed, causing a gas leak. It is the most devastating accident for the global oil industry in over fifteen years. Forty-seven people are dead, 135 seriously injured, and 1.7 billion dollars' worth of damage has been incurred.[9]

* * *

Once regarded as one of the best-run oil companies in the Americas, in the past decade, PDVSA has suffered 392 serious accidents, resulting in a total of 124 deaths.[10] PDVSA's management blames the string of accidents on "sabotage by factors external to our refinery, our industry." Critics and industry experts, on the other hand, blame mismanagement and lack of maintenance, saying that parts aren't replaced until they're broken and that rust is simply covered with fresh coatings of red paint.[11]

In September 2012, María Corina Machado and nine other opposition members of the National Assembly launch the "Truth over Amuay Commission." Their report, published a year later, alleges underinvestment and delays in major maintenance as the root causes for the vapor cloud explosion.

"It is a tragedy that could have been avoided. And a tragedy that continues," Machado says in an interview with *Últimas Noticias*. "The only thing one accomplishes by covering up, burying the truth, are more risks and more losses—human and material. ... Justice has not been done. There has been no indemnity. The flaws and those responsible have not been officially identified, and above all, no corrective action has been taken ... Yesterday, a worker told us that people working in PDVSA cross themselves before entering. A mother of an operator said that while her son worked his shift, she couldn't sleep. That's unacceptable. It can't occur! It doesn't occur in other countries of the world because there is maintenance, investments, adequate training of personnel. When you remove the technical training of the staff and replace it with ideological and political training, tragedies occur."

PDVSA refuses to acknowledge the commission's findings. Meanwhile, the government increases pressure on the nine lawmakers carrying out the investigation.

Stella Lugo, the governor of Falcón, calls for Machado's parliamentary immunity to be removed and for the Attorney General's Office to investigate her for handing out pamphlets "falsely" warning of continued risks in PDVSA facilities.[12]

Before the mass dismissals of strikers in 2003, 3,100,000 barrels of oil were produced each day at PDVSA. In 2013, it is down to 2,800,000, according to OPEC, even though the number of employees has more than doubled, from 69,000 to 145,000. Critics claim this decrease in efficiency is due to employees being hired on the basis of their loyalty to the revolution, while proper training and qualifications are only secondary considerations.[13]

* * *

PDVSA's main office in Puerto de la Cruz, the oil capital of Anzoátegui, is a Soviet-style, massive box made out of gray concrete with tiny windows. Two huge billboards hang by the entrance. Both of them portray Chávez with his fist in the air behind a sea of jubilant PDVSA workers dressed in red and waving their red helmets. One billboard displays the famous Che Guevara quote: "¡Hasta la Victoria Siempre!", while the other reads: "Workers with the revolution!"

The entrance hall houses a photography exhibition portraying the role of oil in the revolution since the 1990s and onwards. An entire wall is dedicated to a massive photo of Chávez, smiling in the rain, water streaming down his face. The exhibition then stretches around the walls of the hall, with Chávez as the constant protagonist. Chávez at his desk, Chávez riding a horse, Chávez hugging his daughters, Chávez playing baseball, Chávez playing the harp, Chávez holding a baby, Chávez visiting a school, Chávez painting, Chávez driving a car, Chávez reading a book, Chávez holding a crucifix, Chávez at the beach, Chávez in his youth. And of course, Chávez drilling for oil and shaking the hands of OPEC tycoons.

Even though the constitution explicitly forbids the use of public institutions for political propaganda, bright red is the dominant color and Chávez and Che Guevara are everywhere. Just beyond the security control there is a massive mural portraying

Che Guevara, followed by Simón Bolívar, and then, last in the line of *libertadores*, is Chávez, immortalized against the backdrop of the Venezuelan flag, donned with his red beret and frozen in a proud salute.

Guarding the entrance is Astudillo Arquimides, fifty-nine years old. He has worked for PDVSA since three days before his eighteenth birthday and can't imagine working anywhere else.

"PDVSA is one. We are all PDVSA. And where there is a functionary of PDVSA there is also a representative proud to be Venezuelan. It is important to have that sense of belonging. PDVSA is everything and does everything," he says.

Since the strike, it could be argued that PDVSA does, in fact, do everything. The company has increasingly shifted its focus from oil and gas to a myriad of social and cultural projects, which have nothing to do with oil. Among other things, the company manages a chain of state grocery stores, builds houses, and sponsors Formula 1 racecar drivers.

More than a third of oil exports are sold at subsidized rates to like-minded regimes, especially Cuba, and most of the funds are used to boost the revolution. This is mainly done through the funding and administration of the missions.

By 2010, PDVSA had spent an estimated US$23 billion on social programs. While social spending was certainly needed, lack of transparency led to charges of corruption and manipulation. Instead of integrating the missions into conventional public service, they remained separate and thereby exempt from public scrutiny.

When budgeting, the government would deliberately underestimate the price of oil. If a barrel of oil sold for US$100, they would calculate with an income of less than half of that. The difference would be channeled into special funds. This gave the president access to billions of dollars—more than half of the government's total revenue—which he spent outside the official, national budget.[14]

Pressured by an opposition legislator, the Ministry of Finance showed how it had spent US$40 billion, which had been channeled into Fonden, the biggest of the special funds. But the fund had received US$69 billion. Where the remaining US$29 billion had ended up, no one could explain. According to NGO Global Financial Integrity, around US$17 billion disappeared into overseas accounts each year.[15]

V

It is December 2012, and Supreme Court Justice Blanca Rosa Mármol de León is about to retire. She is an attractive older lady, with an affable air about her. Her blue eyes usually shine with a humorous glint, but today they are dim. Her twelve-year term has ended, but she wishes she could stay a little longer. Not because she enjoys her work much anymore, but because she was the last judge the opposition had left in the Supreme Court. Now there will be no one to object, even if it rarely makes a difference.

As she hangs up her robe for the last time, she remembers the day, a few years ago, when Chávez came to visit the court.

All the judges lined up to greet him. The Comandante made his way down the line.

"How are you, judge so-and-so? It's been so long. You have my utmost confidence!"

When he got to Blanca, there was nothing to say. No confidence to speak of, nothing in common. They exchanged a few pleasantries.

"How are you, *doctora*? How nice to see you! And how's the family?"

"Fine, thank you, mister president. And how are you?"

"How long have you been here at the tribunal, *doctora*?"

Blanca hesitated a split second before answering. To this day, she still doesn't know where she got the courage to reply in the way that she did:

"Well, in 2012 you and I are both leaving."

Chávez's face lost its color. He took a deep breath, and for an instant Blanca thought he would erupt in a fit of rage. But he simply replied: "I intend to stay longer."

Then he moved on as though nothing had happened.

* * *

The Venezuelan justice system was plagued by corruption and bribes since long before Chávez. After coming to power, Chávez promised to clean it up. But instead of cleaning out dishonest judges, he cleaned out disloyal ones. Loyalty to Chávez and the revolution became the key selection criteria.

Chávez raised the number of judges in the Supreme Court from twenty to thirty-two in order to ensure a clear majority. The new Supreme Court judges were then filmed in their robes chanting pro-Chávez slogans.[16]

In the beginning, there were ten judges sympathetic to the opposition in the Supreme Court, but one by one, as their twelve-year terms expired, they were replaced with loyalists. By 2004, the president had completed most of his spring-cleaning.

In March 2012, Chavista Supreme Court Justice Eladio Aponte Aponte was dismissed because of his ties to suspected drug lord Walid Makled. Before he was due to be questioned by the National Assembly, the judge fled to Costa Rica and from there to the United States. Once in exile, he confessed to manipulating rulings based on requests from Chávez and other top officials.

"They just asked for favors that I complied with. And woe be the judge that refused to cooperate. ... They were dismissed," Aponte Aponte said in a televised interview shortly after leaving the country.

Aponte Aponte claimed he formed part of the Judicial Committee who dismissed judges who refused to cooperate. He also claimed some prosecutors used extortion and threats to influence judges. He said he was routinely telephoned by officials to manipulate cases or look for the right judge to do whatever had to be done.

"The judiciary system is not an autonomous entity. It's not a separate power. That's a fallacy," he told SOiTV and described how "justice" was determined at weekly meetings where participants included the vice-president, the attorney general, the president of the Supreme Court, and other key officials.

"That's where the directives of the justice system come from. They decide what guidelines to follow depending on the political climate," he said.

During the forty-minute long interview on SoiTV, the former judge gave countless examples of cases he had manipulated on orders from the president or other top officials who directed him to charge and convict certain individuals.

Aponte Aponte admitted to having put his loyalty to the president and the revolution ahead of his loyalty to the constitution, but said he was prepared to accept his punishment: "I take the blame for my mistakes and should pay for them, but I will not pay for a crime I did not commit," he said, referring to his alleged dealings with suspected drug trafficker Walid Makled.

Aponte Aponte announced that he had no intention of returning to Venezuela to stand trial: "Knowing the system from the inside, how it works, and how it's handled. I don't think I'd have any rights at all."

Blanca was amazed at the internal reaction, or lack thereof, after Aponte Aponte's revelations. During the next meeting of the tribunal, Luisa Estella Morales, then president of the Supreme Court, didn't comment on it at all. It was as though it had never happened.

Nicolás Maduro, foreign minister at the time, dismissed Aponte Aponte's confessions as lies.

* * *

By the time she retired, Blanca Rosa Mármol had served as a judge for thirty-seven years, including twelve years on the Supreme Court.

She mourned the loss of judicial independence. There were only two types of judges left, she felt: judges who were scared and judges who were grateful to have a position they were not qualified for. Meritocracy was long dead. Any judge, of whom the president did not approve, could simply be substituted or incarcerated.

The most obvious example in recent years was Judge María Lourdes Afiuni. On December 10, 2009, Afiuni ordered the conditional release on bail of businessman Eligio Cedeño, who then fled the country. Cedeño was awaiting trial for evading currency controls. It remained unclear exactly what he had done to cross Chávez, but rumor had it that he had broken the heart of one of Chávez's daughters. Others said he had funded opposition politicians. Either way, the expectation was that he would be put behind bars for a long time. When Cedeño appeared before Judge Afiuni he had been held in pre-trial detention in the basement cell of the Bolivarian Intelligence Services for almost three years. According to Venezuelan law, a prisoner cannot be held without a trial for more than two years. The prosecutors failed to show up for the hearing, as they had on multiple previous occasions. Instead of scheduling a new time, Afiuni decided to follow the letter of the law and release Cedeño on bail. When the prosecutors realized what had happened, they ordered the arrest of Afiuni, assuming she had been bribed. Chávez was furious and immediately went on live television announcing that Afiuni would get the maximum penalty: "This is worse than murder! That judge has to pay for what she has done," he shouted, adding that in the days of Simón Bolívar she would have been shot.[17]

"We have to give this judge and the people who did this the maximum sentence, thirty years in prison!" Chávez roared.

Prosecutors charged Afiuni with corruption and abuse of power. After finding no evidence of any payment, they accused her of "spiritual corruption."[18]

Awaiting a trial that was continuously postponed, Judge Afiuni was sent to jail with many of the prisoners she had herself convicted. According to her lawyer, she was raped and threatened with decapitation and burning.[19]

In February 2011, she had to undergo emergency surgery for cancer and was granted house arrest during her recuperation,[20] before finally being released two years later.[21]

* * *

Blanca picks up the last of her items off the desk and makes her way to her office door. While Judge Afiuni's ordeal frightened Blanca and her colleagues, she is proud that she pressed on. While her influence was limited, her movements tracked, and her trash ransacked, there were still those times where her dissenting opinions made a difference. And now, she can at least serve future generations as a witness to the extent of the corruption of Venezuelan justice, Blanca reflects as she turns off the lights and leaves the room.

8

THE ASCENSION

"It's harder to release a nation from servitude than to enslave a free nation."

Simón Bolívar

I

December 2012. The faces of history flash past on the television screen: Albert Einstein, John Lennon, Abraham Lincoln, Che Guevara, Mahatma Gandhi, Nelson Mandela.

A poetic male voice pours from the speakers:

"Utopia is on the horizon. I know very well that I will never reach it, that if I move ten steps closer; it moves ten steps further away. The more I search for it, the less of it I'll find, because it moves away as I approach. So what then is the point of utopia? The point is this: to keep walking."

A lone keyboard starts to play gently. An animated version of young Hugo Chávez walks among the Venezuelan plains, selling his grandmother's sweets in Barinas.

"One day I'd like to hold the reigns of Bolívar's country," his voice proclaims.

He is still a young boy, sitting alone on a rock, reading beneath a red flag blowing in the wind. The music pauses a moment, then thunders in as the Comandante appears as a grown man—the president, firmly grasping the outstretched hands of his people, kissing them, hugging them, holding their babies, beholding his infinite sea of supporters. Now he roars: "I demand absolute loyalty because I am not me ... I am not an individual, I am a people, damn it!"

Then a flood of photos rush by. People across the world are holding up signs saying: "I am Chávez."

"Yo Soy Chávez" in every province of Venezuela. "Yo Soy Chávez" in front of the Eiffel Tower, "Yo Soy Chávez" in the midst of a snowy Scandinavian landscape. "Yo Soy Chávez" on the Great Wall of China. In Spain, Scotland, Azerbaijan, Turkey, Bolivia, Uruguay, Colombia, Egypt, the Netherlands, Germany, El Salvador, Jamaica, Brazil, the United States, Chile, Finland, Argentina, Ecuador—the whole world is Chávez.

"Even beyond this life we will be loyal to Hugo Chávez," a voice rumbles in the background.

"God bless my Comandante!" shouts another.

Then, the voice of Chávez, to the backdrop of a photograph where he stands in the pouring rain, his face lifted towards the sky: "¡Venezuela! ¡Viva Venezuela!"

It has been a month since Venezuelans last heard from their Comandante. Having flown to Cuba shortly after the election for his fourth cancer surgery, it soon becomes apparent he won't be able to attend his own inauguration. While the opposition questions whether the missing president is even alive, the National Assembly authorizes Chávez to remain in Havana indefinitely, and the Supreme Court agrees to swear him in upon his return.

The question of his presence legally addressed, Chávez's supporters shift their focus to addressing the spiritual implications of his absence with the "I am Chávez" campaign, elevating their incapacitated leader to an icon, and preparing the people for an increasingly inevitable transition. Chávez is no longer just a man, and his ideology—*Chavismo*—is no longer dependent on his physical presence.

II

"I swear ... on this constitution ... of the Bolivarian Republic of Venezuela ... absolute loyalty ... to the values of the fatherland."

It is January 10, 2013. The voice of Nicolás Maduro addresses hundreds of thousands of red-clad supporters outside the presidential palace in Caracas. Their right hands raised, some clutch a copy of the constitution or the Bible in their left hand, as they repeat each line. Many wear T-shirts reading "Yo Soy Chávez." Some even wear masks with the face of the Comandante, making it look like he is everywhere. They, the people of Venezuela, have come to take the presidential oath of inauguration on behalf of their absent president.

On Twitter, the government summoned supporters to the inauguration. Now, the streets are packed.

"We are militant soldiers of our Commander Hugo Chávez," Maduro shouts.

"I am Chávez!" the massive crowd roars back.

The presidents of Uruguay, Bolivia, and Nicaragua, as well as representatives from twenty-seven Latin American and Caribbean countries, attend the ceremony in solidarity.

Bolivian president Evo Morales gives a speech reminiscing about how eating *arepas* makes him feel like he is with Chávez who will "soon be back with us to continue the fight to liberate the people of the world."

"¡Viva Venezuela!" he shouts.

"¡Viva!" the crowd replies.

"Viva brother Chávez!"

"¡Viva!"

"Viva brother Maduro!"

"¡Viva!"

III

It is March 5, 2013.

"Dear compatriots who are listening to us and who can see us throughout the homeland's territories ..."

The familiar fanfare signaling the start of a *cadena* sounds, and the figure of Nicolás Maduro appears on every TV across the nation. He is dressed in all whites, flanked by his wife, and a group of key ministers. "We came here to the military hospital to enquire about our Comandante Presidente's health. Accompanied by his daughters, his brothers, his family members, we received the hardest and most tragic news that we can ever transmit to our people ..."

Maduro's voice breaks and tears well up: "... at 4:25 in the afternoon, today, the 5th of March, the Comandante Presidente, Hugo Chávez Frías, passed away after struggling hard against his illness for almost two years."

IV

It is March 8, 2013. More than two million people have filed past Chávez's coffin to bid farewell to their Comandante. Dressed in uniform with a red beret, he lays in an open casket at the chapel of the Military Academy. After the state funeral, attended by leaders from all over the world, his remains are transferred to the museum El Cuartel de la Montaña in 23 de Enero where Chávez directed his failed 1992 coup and delivered his famous "por ahora" speech.

"We are all Chávez" announce the murals leading the way to the entrance of the museum. Over the gate, towers a giant red

"4," followed by a massive "F." A burning fire symbolizes the flame of the revolution and beneath it a sign announces: "The Dawn of Hope—February 4, 1992."

Young sergeants give guided tours about the life of their *Comandante Supremo* or supreme commander. Over the years, Chávez's nicknames have become increasingly grandiloquent. He has gone from *Comandante* to *Presidente*, to *Comandante Presidente*, to *Comandante Supremo* or *Comandante Eterno*, meaning eternal commander. To emphasize a personal bond, many of Chávez's followers also add the "my" in front of whichever epithet they choose for the occasion.

Inside the sand-colored building with its pinkish-red roof and window frames are photo exhibitions from Chávez's life—or as the sign announces: "The life of a giant." There is Chávez hugging his daughters, Chávez and Fidel Castro, Chávez as a young boy in Barinas, and endless quotes by Chávez.

At the center of it all is his corpse, enclosed in a massive marble sarcophagus. Visitors must keep their distance. Four presidential honor guards stand at attention around the tomb in two-hour shifts between 6 a.m. and 6 p.m. year round. Donned in Venezuela's finest military attire, with sables and feathered bearskin hats, they remain perfectly still.

To celebrate the Comandante's love of nature, wild flowers grow in the garden outside. In honor of his memory, a cannon is fired every afternoon at the exact time of his death: twenty-five minutes past four. That was when, the sergeants explain, the supreme commander united his spirit with those of other great leaders, such as Guaicaipuro, Miranda, Bolívar, Martí, Rodríguez, Zamora, and Che Guevara.

9

NO MAN'S LAND

"To understand revolutions and their participants, we must observe them at close range and judge them at great distance."

Simón Bolívar

I

"Anyone who votes against Nicolás Maduro, votes against himself. The curse of Maracapana will befall him," exclaims Maduro at an election rally in Amazon state.

It is April 6, 2013, and the presidential election is eight days away. As part of his presidential campaign, Maduro casts a centuries-old Indian curse on any supporter of his opponent Capriles, whom he compares to the enslaving Spanish occupiers of past centuries.

Wearing feathered headgear, he attempts to bond with the largely indigenous population of this jungle region.

"I'm not a hypocritical and phony bourgeoisie. I feel these symbols in my soul! I feel the spirit of Guaicaipuro." Maduro lifts both hands to touch the feathers on his head as he invokes Guaicaipuro, one of the most well-known indigenous Venezuelan tribal leaders of the sixteenth century. "I am the Indian Nicolás Maduro, heir of Guaicaipuro."[1]

Dancing and moving his arms like a gangster, he then goes on to perform a self-composed rap about Capriles:[2]

"*Caprichito*, *caprichito*, petty bourgeois, petty bourgeois, little copycat, little copycat. We will give you a beating on April 14 ... *Caprichito*, *caprichito*, tiny congressman, tiny congressman. Don't think you are Chávez ... *Caprichito*, *caprichito*, petty bourgeois, petty bourgeois, here is Madurito, Madurito, the honest one, the honest one."

It is Governor Capriles pitted against acting President Maduro. The campaign is characterized by an abundance of personal attacks on both sides and a dearth of any real political debate. Maduro implies that the single Capriles is gay. Capriles counters by calling Maduro "Satan" and "Birdbrain," adding that Maduro's wife is so ugly he can't understand how anyone could be with her.[3] Maduro claims Chávez has been assassinated, the cancer somehow induced by Venezuela's "historic enemies"—the United States and the CIA.

Although imitating Chávez's showmanship is a near impossible feat, Maduro tries hard. He lacks charisma, but every chance he gets he reminds everyone he is the successor the Comandante chose. He refers to Chávez as "the redeemer Christ of the Americas" and to himself as his "apostle" and "son." He even claims reincarnations of Chávez visit him while he prays.[4]

On April 2, at the start of the campaign, Maduro told television audiences how he was praying at the birthplace of Chávez in Barinas, before a large photograph of the Comandante, when "all of a sudden a little birdie flew in." The little bird was Chávez coming to bless him.

"He flew around my head three times." Maduro illustrated with his hand spinning his head three times while making helicopter-like sounds "chuck, chuck, chuck ... chuck chuck,

chuck ... chuck, chuck, chuck ... It stopped on a wooden beam and began to whistle beautifully. I stayed listening and then I began to whistle back to him. If you whistle, I whistle."

Maduro whistled into the microphone, then continued: "The little bird looked at me in a strange way. It sang for a while, then span around me and went away and I felt his spirit giving us a blessing. He was telling us: Today the battle begins. Go to victory!"

* * *

Maduro mentions Chávez some 7,000 times during the short campaign. The message is clear: a vote against Maduro is a betrayal of Chávez. At rallies, he often erects giant screens playing video recordings of Chávez calling on voters to support Maduro or singing the national anthem. "I never wanted to be president," he says during a rally in Chávez's home state of Barinas. "If I am running it is because I am following the orders of the Supreme Commander Hugo Chávez."[5]

Billboards, graffiti, and T-shirts with the promise "Chávez te lo juro, mi voto es para Maduro" (Chávez, I swear to you, my vote is for Maduro) are everywhere.

In several municipalities, the government organizes events where paid tattoo artists perform free tattoos on anyone wishing to immortalize the Comandante by tattooing his signature or portrait on their body. Thousands line up, and some even go so far as to tattoo Chávez's signature on their face.[6]

* * *

On April 14, the election takes place. Maduro wins by a mere 200,000 votes, or 50.78 percent against Capriles' 48.95 percent. Capriles objects to the results, claiming fraud. He calls supporters of the opposition to the streets to demand that Maduro not be officially declared the winner until a full audit has been conducted.

For years, the opposition has accused the government of committing electoral fraud, but so far they have been unable to prove any foul play beyond the obvious misuse of state resources as though they were party campaign resources. Chavista candidates would appear in televised broadcasts giving away homes or household appliances financed with government resources to faithful supporters. And thanks to the government-imposed *cadena*-broadcasts, there was no lack of free airtime and exposure.

Over the years, the infamous Tascón list of everyone who signed to have Chávez removed from office had also been expanded and turned into a software program called Maisanta. Holding data of all registered voters, it enabled officials to check things like political allegiance, voting participation, and access to social benefits. Besides determining whether or not someone was fit for government employment, critics claimed the system enabled the government to use the ID-numbers of non-voters for their own purposes.

"If there is a person who hasn't voted in the past two elections, and resides for example in Spain, someone else can have an ID card made and use that identity to vote, maybe in a different part of Caracas or even in a different city," says Roberto Abdul, president of election monitoring NGO Súmate.

In the past, international election observers have found elections to be mathematically correct, but in recent years proper international monitoring has not been possible, as Venezuela's National Electoral Council no longer wishes to cooperate.

II

It is April 15, 2013. Antonio Rivero is on his way home, but the streets of downtown Caracas are clogged with demonstrators protesting the election results. Passing through Altamira Square on his motorbike, Rivero spots some opposition students he knows. Spontaneous protests with no leadership carry a heightened risk of ending in violence. A large organized demonstration is planned for tomorrow and he wishes they would just wait.

"Who is in charge of organizing this march?" he asks them.

"Nobody."

A few days before, *colectivos* had interfered with a student protest, throwing rocks and bottles at the students. Rivero doesn't want to see that happen again.

"Be careful," Rivero tells them. "Don't do anything crazy! And watch out so you don't get attacked. Stay together and protect yourselves."

"Protect ourselves how?"

"Use the lids of big pots for protection. With them you can ward off rocks, ward off bottles, and ward off blows, like the ancient shields. Always stay together, okay? Don't disperse! ... It's important that you keep everything you do in line with the directives issued by Capriles."

One of the students films as Rivero is talking. This film is later given to Timothy Tracy, an American journalist making a documentary about the political divisions gripping Venezuela.

As predicted by Rivero, clashes between the students and Chavistas turn violent later that day. Property is damaged, and within a few hours at least half a dozen people have been killed and many more injured. The government blames Capriles for having instigated violence by calling people to the streets. After the incident, graffiti calling Capriles a murderer spring up all over the country. Maduro announces that members of the opposition are "coup-plotting fascists," and threatens to jail Capriles. Fearing that the government will infiltrate the opposition's planned march to the headquarters of the National Electoral Council (CNE), Capriles decides to cancel it.[7] Instead, he submits a complaint to the CNE, listing more than 3,000 election irregularities, or "questionable events," including intimidation of voters at polling stations.

The opposition demands a recount and full audit of the votes. The CNE, made up of loyal Chavistas, agrees to audit the remaining boxes of voting machine receipts that have not yet been verified (54 percent of the boxes had been previously verified in the presence of witnesses from both parties). But the opposition wants the complete electoral registry audited, verifying the authenticity of every signature and fingerprint in the voting record books. The purpose is to make sure there are no cases of double voting, stolen identities, or dead people voting. The CNE denies the request, saying that the opposition has already audited and signed off on the electoral rolls, and that verifying 15 million signatures and fingerprints would be impossible.

"It is important to note that the political parties already audited the electoral process at each stage, certifying the integrity and correct functioning of the system," Tibisay Lucena, president of the CNE, tells the media. She claims the complaint is nothing but an attempt by the opposition to discredit the electoral process.

According to Lucena, the opposition's complaint is too generic, lacking enough detail to make an investigation possible.

"The documents submitted by Capriles do not state clearly and precisely the incidents in which the rules were broken. They do not give the specific voting centers, who was involved, nor what possible damage could have occurred as a result," she says.

Capriles later appeals to the Supreme Court where his request is turned down for lack of evidence.[8]

III

"You can ward off rocks. Ward off bottles. Ward off rocks. Ward off bottles. Ward off rocks. Ward off bottles. Ward off blows, like the ancient shields ..."

Rivero flinches when he sees his own face stare back at him from the television. There he is, like a broken record, repeating the same thing over and over. The heavily edited video clip ends as abruptly as it began. All the context has been cut out.

It is April 24, 2013, and Miguel Rodríguez Torres, minister of the interior and justice, as well as head of the Bolivarian intelligence service, is giving a televised press conference where he informs the public that Antonio Rivero is wanted for instigating the violence that erupted after the April 15 demonstrations. He has him on tape, talking to students about rocks, bottles, and blows. What more could one ask for?

Unable to pin the violence on Capriles, the government has decided to use the video recordings of American filmmaker Timothy Tracy to shift their accusations. Tracy has been arrested, accused of espionage, instigating unrest, and financing violent groups.[9] And now they are after Rivero, using this heavily edited video sequence as evidence that he is instigating violence and training students to fight.

Rivero is in shock. Miguel Rodríguez Torres is an old friend of his from the Military Academy. Although Torres has advanced far within the Chavista ranks, the two have kept in touch and remained friends throughout it all. During Rivero's time as head of Civil Protection, Torres would always provide him with helicopters whenever an emergency arose. Every so often, they would get together. Rivero can't believe Torres would do this without even talking to him first. But here he is, wanted on national television. He should probably leave the office now. They might come looking for him. But where should he go? Best not to go home. His elderly godparents live a few blocks away. He decides to head there.

* * *

Two days later, on April 26, Rivero is invited to give his version of events on the TV show *Buenas Noches*. During the show, Rivero takes the opportunity to reach out to Rodríguez Torres directly:

"Miguel, think about what you are doing. You know that nothing of what you are claiming is true. Think it over, brother. ...You know me and you know that I would never do what you say I've done. Act without letting anyone influence you. I am not afraid. When I resigned I made a brave denunciation without having anyone to pave my way. You know that I am not violent, but I am not going away. Here I'll stay insisting on change and progress in Venezuela."[10]

* * *

The following morning, the phone rings, waking Rivero. The sound startles him. Usually, he keeps it off and removes the battery whenever he is stationary to avoid being tracked. It's 10 a.m. He answers, but remains silent.

"General Antonio Rivero?" asks the voice on the other end.

"Yes."

"This is Superintendent Martinez, calling on behalf of Minister General Rodríquez Torres. The minister would like to speak to you. Can you come to El Helicoide right away? He is leaving by helicopter at noon."

Rivero hesitates. "Okay, tell him I'll be there at 11."

Rivero remains seated with the phone in his hand long after the call with Martinez is over. He should be pleased. This request for a meeting must mean that Torres saw him on television last night and that he is prepared to listen. Still, he can't help but feel somewhat uneasy. He gets up, puts on a pair of beige pants, a white T-shirt, and a red shirt on top. Then he walks to the kitchen to talk to his godmother.

"That was Torres' office."

"Go see him Antonio! So that this persecution comes to an end. You can't keep hiding. You need to have a normal life. Go sort things out!" she advises.

Rivero is not entirely convinced. Wasn't Torres supposed to be in Maracaibo now? He must have returned during the night.

The previous day, Rivero spoke to Leopoldo López, the leader of his political party Voluntad Popular. López too stressed the importance of clarifying the situation. He'd better go.

* * *

From the window of the taxi, Rivero spots the massive building from about a kilometer away. El Helicoide is the headquarters of the Bolivarian intelligence service: a twelve-story architectural achievement erected under Jiménez. Built around a massive rock in the heart of Caracas, it is reminiscent of a space-age pyramid. Though he has visited the building many times before, its unique spiral design still fills Rivero with awe. At the top floor, a white cupola-like shield prevents outside surveillance. Pretty on the outside, but ugly on the inside, Rivero reflects.

"Antonio Rivero to see the director," he tells the guards by the gate. They nod and gesture for him to proceed to a vehicle where two armed men in civilian attire are already waiting for him. Rivero jumps into the backseat and they drive him up the winding highway spiraling around the building to the entrance of the department for strategic investigation.

The men escort him inside to the duty officer.

"The director is on his way. Please, come inside," he says.

Rivero takes a seat by the reception. A few minutes later, the officer returns with a colleague and asks Rivero to follow them. They make their way toward the area where the prison cells and accompanying offices are located. They reach a small office, and the duty officer asks Rivero to take a seat by the entrance.

"Wait here, general. The director is on his way. He will see you in this office shortly."

By now, Rivero is becoming apprehensive. Why would they take him down this way toward the cells? Why would Torres ask to meet him in this dark, damp, and scruffy part of the building? The tiny office in this out-of-the-way location does not seem worthy of a minister. It doesn't make sense.

As the duty officer leaves, the second guard who accompanied them stays behind. Rivero notices that he is armed. Soon, the duty officer returns holding an opened, yellow envelop in his hand. He takes a seat in the chair opposite Rivero.

"I'm sorry, general. I just received this."

He holds up the yellow envelope and continues: "I didn't know what it was. I called the director and he told me to open it, show it to you, and proceed."

The duty officer pulls out a white piece of paper and hands it to Rivero. It is an arrest warrant.

"My apologies. I didn't know."

Rivero looks at the paper.

"What is this? What kind of a joke is this? They invited me here to speak to the minister. How can it be that I now have an arrest warrant in my hand?"

"I'm sorry, general. I didn't know anything about this. I just received the envelope. You are under arrest and there is nothing I can do. This is an order. The director will be here shortly."

"I want to speak to the director! I want to speak to the minister! That's what they called me here for!"

"I'm sorry general. There is nothing I can do. You'll have to give me your phone now."

"But I didn't come here for this. I have things to do. I have a plane to catch. I have to go!"

Rivero gets up to leave, but the guard blocks his way and grabs hold of the cellphone Rivero is holding in his hand.

"Please cooperate, general."

"What do you mean cooperate? This is illegal. Arbitrary! Where is Miguel? I want to speak to the director."

"It's not my fault. I'm merely following orders."

"But what order? If this is an arbitrary decision."

"Let me go call the director. I'll be right back," says the duty officer and leaves Rivero with the guard. About ten minutes later, he comes back with the director of strategic investigations.

"Where is Miguel? I want to speak to Miguel!"

"Miguel's not here. You'll have to speak to me first."

"How can you put me in this position? Trick me like this?

"Please calm down!"

"Calm down?! How do you expect me to calm down under these conditions when my liberty is being taken away from me? What is my crime? You should be ashamed of yourselves!"

"Please calm down, general!"

"No, I will not calm down. I want to speak to Miguel! Where is Miguel?"

Rivero feels trapped. He has to get out before it's too late. He starts punching the table. As he grows increasingly agitated, he begins to feel dizzy. He struggles with high blood pressure and can feel that he is approaching the danger zone.

"I'm not feeling well. I need a medic!" he exclaims.

When the medic arrives, Rivero's blood pressure is high—200/120. While this troubles him, he also senses an opportunity. If they put him in an ambulance with an officer or two, he might be able to escape. And if not there, then at the military hospital he might get a second opportunity. There must be someone there who knows him, who would help him if he caused a scene. They wouldn't shoot him. Not in public anyway. And if all else fails, he might be able to launch himself from the ambulance on the way back. This might be his only chance.

Rivero begins to hyperventilate in an attempt to worsen his condition and appears pale and affected.

"I need a doctor. I need an ambulance to take me to a hospital," he cries.

While the officers call for an ambulance to remain on standby outside, they say they can't authorize Rivero's departure without consulting a doctor. Rivero realizes he won't be able to fool a doctor so he has to make the most of the moment. His whole body shaking, Rivero collapses onto the white tile floor of the office, hoping this will prompt a transfer to the ambulance. Instead, the officers proceed to film him as he lies shaking on the floor. The film is later posted on YouTube under the headline "The crybaby calls for violence but faints like a baby when he is detained."

When the doctor arrives, he helps Rivero to take a seat in a chair. He then takes his blood pressure, and after confirming that it is is still high, he asks Rivero to stop hyperventilating.

"That affects it you know," he comments. "What medicine do you take?"

"Olmetec 20 mg."

"Do you have it on you?"

"No, at home."

The medic turns to one of the officers and says: "Have the Cuban send one over."

"The Cuban?!"

Rivero freaks out again. To have a Cuban come attend him here, at the headquarters of the national intelligence service, that would be the last straw.

"I don't want any Cubans here. I will not be responsible for what I might do if a Cuban doctor comes to attend me here!" Rivero shouts.

He scrutinizes the doctor.

"Are you Cuban?"

"No."

"Show me your ID!"

The doctor obliges and Rivero calms down a little.

"Take me to a hospital," Rivero pleads.

"First, we're going to try to calm you down here. If you calm down, your blood pressure will go down. We don't have authorization to take you anywhere yet," the doctor replies.

Twenty minutes later, the assistant arrives with Rivero's medicine and his pressure begins to stabilize.

The head of the division returns to try to talk to Rivero. With him is an old friend of Rivero's, a colonel who happened to be in the building. Seeing him there makes Rivero even more upset.

"Look what Miguel is doing to me! Watch the infamy, the betrayal! Please speak to Miguel. Tell him to come show his face. How can he do this to me? Trick me into coming and now here I am, sick and not even allowed to go to the hospital. I won't be held responsible for my actions if I'm kept like this."

"Please calm down! I had no idea," the colonel replies. "I'll speak to Miguel."

"How am I supposed to calm down?" Rivero punches the walls. "Enough of the abuse! Enough arbitrariness! You are responsible for his. You are immoral! I have not committed any crime."

He is furious and wants the colonel to convey that fury to the minister. After the colonel leaves, he feels a little more at peace. It seems to him that the guards treat him with more respect now. Some even seem a little embarrassed. They offer him a hamburger that he refuses to eat. But the offer alone makes him feel better. Soon, another superintendent stops by.

"Tomorrow we'll take you to court and I'm sure you'll be set free," he says. "Don't worry. We'll put you up well. You won't be in a bad cell. We'll treat you with all due respect. Do you want to call a lawyer or your brother?"

Rivero calls both. Then he is put through booking procedures, fingerprinted, and photographed.

Politicians from the opposition denounce Rivero's detention. The case quickly garners a great deal of media attention and with it a public outcry. Leopoldo López immediately calls a press conference in which he refers to Rivero as the first political prisoner of Nicolás Maduro.

"We want to remind the people of Venezuela that this is not an isolated event, it is a policy of the state that the government has escalated in the last few days in order to divert the attention from our just, democratic, and peaceful efforts to unveil the truth about what happened on April 14. ... They will not divert us from our path of peaceful, democratic struggle, the struggle in which millions of Venezuelans hope their votes will turn into a positive change for the country," López tells the media.[11]

* * *

Rivero is placed in a cell with seven bunk beds, which he shares with six officers from the national intelligence service, who are detained, awaiting charges.

Later that evening, when Rivero's lawyer and brother arrive to see him, they are told the same thing: There is nothing to worry about; tomorrow the court hearing will take place and the judge will likely release Rivero. Anything else seems far-fetched. Reluctantly, Rivero settles in to try to get some rest. But when supper comes he won't touch it.

"I won't eat again until I'm out of here," he says.

"That may take a while," comments one of the officers. "I've been here forty-five days waiting for my court hearing. It's always tomorrow. This justice is not for us."

The following morning, Rivero is offered *arepa*, scrambled eggs, juice, and coffee, but he refuses to touch it. Around lunch-time, the superintendent shows up to let him know the hearing has been cancelled.

"The judge is tired. He needs to rest today. You'll go to court tomorrow," he says and hands over a plate of rice and chicken. Still, Rivero refuses to eat.

"I will not eat until I've regained my freedom," he tells the superintendent.

"But general, you have to eat. You have to look after yourself."

But Rivero is determined. This will be his front in the battle, one of the few things he can control. They can take his freedom, but he will not let them humiliate him.

"I will not accept any food from you," he reiterates.

* * *

The following day, the hearing takes place. Three cars and ten motorbikes escort the vehicle transporting Rivero to court.

At the courthouse, Rivero is overcome by the sensation that he is watching a play, with the prosecutor and judge delivering a series of well-rehearsed lines. That feeling is further enhanced when he and his lawyer are asked to review the protocol to sign off on their statements. Their testimonies are full of errors, some factual, but most grammatical. The statements by the prosecutor and judge, on the other hand, are flawless. How could the same secretary have written this when the quality of writing is so uneven? It must have been prepared ahead of the hearing, a sort of script for the prosecutor and judge to read, Rivero figures.

As expected, the judge follows the recommendation of the prosecutor and charges Rivero with "inciting hatred" and "conspiracy to commit a crime." The only evidence upon which the prosecutor bases the accusations is the video where Antonio Rivero is speaking to students demonstrating against the results of the recent presidential elections.[12]

The judge orders that Rivero be sent to the military prison Ramo Verde. Rivero asks to remain in El Helicoide. That way he will still be in Caracas where people can easily demonstrate against his detention.

When the hearing is over, the judge steps down and walks over to greet Rivero. He holds out his hand, and as he takes it, Rivero says: "From this moment on, and after not eating for more than forty-eight hours, I am officially on hunger strike. I want my freedom, as I want the freedom of Venezuela!"

The judge squeezes his hand and says: "Best of luck, general. You are in the right." Rivero later learns that the judge has gone on sick leave.

"There is no justice left in this country," Rivero reflects as he writes a message to the press about his decision to go on hunger strike, to be read by his brother outside the court.

* * *

When Rivero returns to his cell, two of his fellow detainees have left. Four police officers remain, awaiting their trial. The cell they share is approximately 8 by 4 meters, with seven bunk beds. The walls are made of concrete and there is a small toilet, sink, and shower. As it is located underground, surrounded by rock, the cell is very humid. Wastewater flows past in channels just outside the entrance, adding to the humidity and unpleasant smell.

The first five days on hunger strike are the worst. Rivero is constantly hungry and suffers from abdominal pains and headaches. Every meal placed before him looks delicious. There is rice and chicken, *arepa*, pasta, different stews, meats and omelets. The guards photograph each plate they offer. If Rivero starves to death, they will not be held accountable.

On the third day, Rivero begins to experience chills. Then the body starts to adapt to not having food. The weaker he becomes, the less pain he feels. After ten days, he begins to experience frequent dizziness. After twelve days, it is a challenge to stay upright. Then, he decides to stop drinking as well. Soon, Rivero spends most of his time sitting or lying down as he is now too weak to move much. By now, his fellow cellmates all agree that a great injustice is being committed. They pity Rivero, taking pictures of his untouched food and his poor physical state. One of the inmates even lends him his phone so that Rivero can text his family at night.

It's a surreal experience to witness the rapid deterioration of one's own body. Rivero watches as his skin dries out, practically before his eyes. When he runs his fingers over his arms or face, it feels like he is stroking sandpaper. The taste in his mouth is bitter. He develops pneumonia and after fifteen days, he is very ill. His blood pressure drops dramatically and his respiratory infection worsens.

On Mother's Day, Rivero's mother visits him in prison, pleading with him to end the strike. She has brought him some vegetable soup and begs him to eat it as his Mother's Day gift to her.

But Rivero won't touch it. At this point he has gone fifteen days without food. The following day, he is hospitalized. His eighty-one-year-old mother then launches her own hunger strike and threatens to chain herself to the doors of the prison. Finally, after seventeen days, Rivero gives up his strike to avoid causing his family any more pain.

The first few days of eating again are almost worse than the first few days of not eating. His first meal is fruit compote and a protein drink, which turns out to have a laxative effect. Rivero experiences terrible abdominal pains and has to rush to the toilet where his feces are mixed with blood. The pain and his low blood pressure cause him to faint.

* * *

Five days later, Rivero is finally released pending trial. He spends thirteen days in a hospital recovering from his ordeal. No definite reason for his release is given. It is as arbitrary as his detention. But Rivero believes it must have been the pressure from the public that finally began to have effect. Various nations, as well as the public and many of his former military colleagues, had condemned his arbitrary incarceration. Amnesty International and the United Nations had also protested his imprisonment. He is conditionally released, but his travel restrictions remain. Every week, he has to appear before the court in Caracas and once a month before the military tribunal in Bolívar. He is prohibited from leaving Venezuela, entering military installations, and making public statements. Revealing classified information is the most severe of all the accusations against him, as this, in a military context, is equivalent to treason.

IV

It is April 30, 2013. Parliament is in chaos. Amid the benches, an imposing, obese man wearing a flag-striped jacket throws punch after punch into a dark-suited man who has bent over in a fruitless effort to protect himself. A few steps behind, another battle is underway. Almost immediately, a circle of men forms and it becomes impossible to discern who is rushing to join the fight and who has come to break it up. The House of Parliament has turned into a free-for-all.

Through it all, a government deputy drones on over the microphone about recent budgetary changes as though nothing is happening.

* * *

The brawl was precipitated by María Corina Machado's fiery speech at the previous session, where she said the opposition would not recognize Nicolás Maduro as president unless the government kept its word of counting all the ballots, a commitment Maduro made after the elections.

"Open the ballot boxes and count the votes! You are so attached to power, ready to do anything, that you prefer to bring Venezuela to violence before opening the boxes. But if President Maduro himself agreed to count the votes, why aren't you counting them now? Why did he retract it? The answer is clear. He said he had to discuss it. That's why I say: Señor Raúl Castro, give Nicolás Maduro permission to count the votes. It is what all Venezuelans want. Count the votes! Why won't they do it? Because they know they lost."

Diosdado Cabello (whose name literally means "God-Given Hair") was furious and demanded that each opposition MP accept Nicolás Maduro as the legitimate president before being allowed to speak again.

"I will never do that unless he counts the ballots," Machado insisted.

* * *

Next time they enter parliament, opposition deputies come prepared. Asserting their right to speak, they carry a banner: *Golpe al Parlamento* (parliamentary coup). As the proceedings begin, they blow whistles and vuvuzelas frustrating the Chavistas in their efforts to conduct business as usual. Eventually, violence erupts.

María Corina watches as opposition MP Julio Borges is punched in the face. As she rushes over to check on him, she hears a woman call her name.

"María Corina!"

When Machado turns, a punch in the face knocks her to the floor. Dazed, she stands back up and looks at her attacker, a Chavista deputy. Blood streams down María Corina's face, but the adrenaline keeps her from feeling the pain. She makes her way over to Diosdado Cabello.

"End the session! Unlock the doors! Get these people out of here!" she urges him.

As Machado appeals for Cabello to intervene, her assailant returns, grabs her by the hair, pulls her to the floor and kicks her.

By the end of the session, twenty-two members of parliament have been injured, and seventeen of them are from the opposition.[13] Machado's nose is broken in five places.

V

It is May 14, 2013, and Bolívar's new, personal mausoleum is finally ready for inauguration. Ever since the exhumation of the Liberator's remains in 2010, Chavistas have been busy preparing a grander resting place for the Liberator.

The 54-meter tall, white-tiled, modern building has set the government back some 140 million dollars. It is shaped like a giant, ascending curve. Supporters liken it to the snow-covered Andean peaks Bolívar traversed in pursuit of his Spanish foes, while critics say it bears more resemblance to a skateboard ramp. Situated in the heart of old Caracas, it stands in sharp contrast to its neighbors: an eighteenth-century military fortress and the National Pantheon—the church where Bolívar used to be interred among Venezuela's other national heroes.

Presiding over the celebrations is President Nicólas Maduro.

"Bolívar was always present in the heart of the people," he tells the audience, consisting of government officials and dignitaries from neighboring countries.

"The Indian Bolívar, the black Bolívar, the mixed-race Bolívar, the Bolívar of people, the Bolívar of struggle, the Bolívar of future, was always there, latent, in the nineteenth and twentieth century, in all the generations of men and women who rose up in this fatherland in search of equality, justice, democracy, and liberty. They always wore Bolívar as their banner, their reason, their symbol."

A crystal sarcophagus has replaced the leaden one that used to hold Bolívar's remains. Surrounding it is an elaborate casket of the finest wood, decorated with eight gold stars, forty-seven gold spear tips—one for each year of life and struggle—and numerous precious pearls. A new flag has been handcrafted by a group of indigenous women to include the extra star that Bolívar had decreed but never lived to see added to the Venezuelan banner.

Maduro continues his speech to the audience, and the nation:

"Bolívar was always there. He was in Zamora in 1848; only six years after his remains arrived here in Caracas. The oligarchy couldn't withstand the popular pressure from the people who loved Bolívar, so they had to bring his remains here to convert him into marble and bronze. And they tried to keep deceiving the people in the name of Bolívar. But in 1848, a fair, mustachioed youngster emerged in Cúa and took up arms with the peasants, the Indians, the poor of the land, the barefoot, our grandfathers and grandmothers. They rose up against the oligarchic republic. Only eighteen years had passed since the death of Bolívar and this young man, Ezequiel Zamora, carried the banner of Bolívar. His father, Alejandro, had been a captain in Bolívar's army and fought at Carabobo. Throughout the nineteenth and twentieth century all the just causes always had Bolívar as their banner, their inspiration, their strength."

And, as if just remembering that Bolívar also served as inspiration for his opponents, Maduro adds: "The oligarchy and the bourgeoisie didn't merely convert Bolívar into marble and bronze. They also began to distort history in an attempt to smother the independence struggle, to distort it so that people would forget. It wasn't until the Bolívarian revolution, the patriotic insurgency of February 4, 1992, that Bolívar began the long process of resurrection and history was brought back to life. History became about the people, about the struggle for justice in our time. To speak of the twenty-first century and Bolívar, is and always will be, to speak of a historic figure who knew how to incarnate the Liberator's cause and carry it to the greatest results. To speak of Bolívar in the twenty-first century is to speak of Húgo Chávez Frías, his great defender ... Húgo Chávez, the Bolívar of the twenty-first century, the Liberator of the twenty-first century."

VI

Narrow paths snake their way up the steep hill. Red cinderblock houses topped with corrugated tin are perched haphazardly along the slope. This is Petare, home to 500,000 poor, and one of Latin America's largest, most populous slums.

It's November 22, 2013, and members of the opposition party Primero Justicia (Justice first) are rallying supporters as they campaign for reelection.

A jeep donned with giant speakers blasts dance songs and election mantras delivered to music. Behind it, the candidates walk or jog up and down the narrow streets, calling at different houses where residents can greet the candidates, tell them about their problems, or boo from a balcony if they are not in favor. It's known as a "caminata casa por casa," literally a "walk house by house." Every so often, the candidates stop to dance. Party members with megaphones shout: "Quien commanda? Sucre es lo que manda!" (Who commands? Sucre is in charge!) The volume is alarming. No one escapes.

In a doorway stands an old, balding man. He is bare-chested, wearing nothing but gray shorts pulled up high over his belly button. His body is splattered with white paint. The crowd jogs past his house, arms raised, music blaring, like a touring circus act. He watches with a blank expression, but when the entourage stops, his poker face vanishes and gives way to a bright smile.

"I'm with the opposition," he says and sneaks into his house only to return with a gigantic poster of Henrique Capriles. It's so big it covers his entire body. Only his head sticks up behind it. "Vota por tu futuro" (Vote for your future) it reads.

Contrary to popular belief, Petare is no longer a Chavista stronghold. In 2008, after having lost two consecutive elections, the opposition's mayoral candidate Carlos Ocariz unexpectedly won. The residents of Petare had rejected the Bolivarian revolution, thereby challenging the notion that the political divide in Venezuela is based on class.

The electoral fiesta continues amid streets so steep it's hard to keep control over dancing legs and feet. Street vendors, *buhoneros*, shout out their offerings. Idle residents enjoy a few beers in the sunshine. Kids run playfully through the winding alleys. On the surface, it has a pleasant, friendly neighborhood feel to it, but Petare is one of the most violent slums in Latin America. Between thirty and sixty deaths are registered each week. Most families have lost someone to violence.[14] Since the opposition came to power in the municipality, they have devoted a lot of effort to keep youth away from delinquency, mainly through academic scholarships and sports. On vacant land, they have built gyms and sports facilities. Once finished, the local community is left to run and maintain the facilities, encouraging a sense of local ownership and participation. While the measures have gained popularity for the opposition, it has done little to affect the appalling murder rates, which keep rising.

Around a concession-style kiosk near the main square, a group of neighbors watch the spectacle from afar. A middle-aged man in a red jacket leans on the counter with his motorcycle helmet under his arm.

"A todo el mundo le gusta patchanga" (Everybody likes a party) he comments dryly. He claims he doesn't bother to vote, as "both sides are just as bad."

He is the exception. Most people in Petare know exactly for whom to vote. They are either die-hard Chavistas or vehemently against the government. Nearly every other wall or window is adorned with posters of Chávez or Maduro. On the other half is the face of Capriles or one of the opposition's local candidates.

Political allegiance seems more emotional than rational for most.

"I am Chavista," an older lady in the crowd comments proudly. "Chavista from the heart," she adds and places a closed fist on her chest.

"Chávez is the devil," exclaims Elia Osorio, a woman with few teeth but a beautiful smile.

Like many others, she still speaks of Chávez as though he were still alive.

"But Maduro is even worse," she adds.

Elia is out admiring the new stretch of asphalted road running past her house. It gleams in the sun, making her squint, which further deepens the wrinkles in her prematurely aged face.

"The opposition told me they would fix this road and they did," she says triumphantly.

In return, she says she has persuaded ten of her family members to vote for Ocariz in the upcoming election.

But her neighbor Jorge Luis Pérez is not convinced:

"The opposition never did anything for the people. Why would they start now?"

* * *

One of the local candidates is Vicente Paez. He was born and raised in Petare by parents who are loyal Chavistas. So is the rest of his family. Yet, Vicente always supported the opposition. Today is his sister's birthday. Vicente has bought a beautiful birthday cake for her. It's wrapped in a fragile paper box, constantly at risk as the procession makes its way through the crowds. So when the group is relatively near her house, Vicente sneaks off to drop off the cake and congratulate her. He jogs down a winding alley and enters a little tinderbox home on the slope. A young girl at the entrance eyes passersby with a mixture of curiosity and suspicion, but lights up when she sees Vicente.

This is the home of Vicente's parents, which they share with several of their children and grandchildren. In the living room, a window has been barred and converted into an altar devoted to Chávez. A portrait of the Comandante wearing a uniform and a red beret rests against a background of the Venezuelan Andes. Several other, smaller photos of deceased family members surround it, as well as countless amulets, crucifixes, candles, flowers, and finally a statue of the Virgin Mary. Numerous photos of the late president adorn the walls. In one enlarged and carefully framed photo, Vicente's father is standing slightly behind, to the left of Chávez in what appears to be an official ceremony of some kind. Chávez is giving a speech and one can't quite make out his face, but the distant profile, combined with the proud look on the face of Vicente's father as he beams at the camera, leaves little doubt that the speaker is in fact the Comandante.

Vicente's sister Johanna is also a Chavista. She is in her thirties, but when she speaks of the Comandante her face takes on the look of an enamored teenager. Nobody has done more for the people, she says. Not for her family per se, but she has a friend who received government housing and another one who received a life-transforming eye operation. But her allegiance does not get in the way of her affection for her brother.

"Sure, there are disputes, but family comes first," she says and reaches out to hug Vicente.

VII

It is November 28, 2013. Local elections are due to take place in just over a week. All over the country, election campaigns are competing for the attention of the fatigued electorate who have lived through twenty-four elections and referendums in the past fifteen years.

María Corina Machado and members of her liberal political movement Vente Venezuela are driving the 120-kilometer route west of Caracas to Maracay, capital of Aragua province. The traffic is so bad that, after four hours, they are still only halfway there.

Green, rolling hills and sugar cane plantations line the road. This is where the sugar used in Venezuela's exquisite Rum is produced. On the left-hand side of the road, they pass the facilities of car manufacturer Venirauto, a joint venture between Venezuela and Iran. The factory wall is decorated by a massive heart with the text "Hecho en socialismo" (Made in socialism). Outside Caracas, the signs of *Chavismo* are everywhere. Chávez points from massive billboards on the side of the road: "Chávez vive, la lucha sigue!" (Chávez is alive, the struggle continues!) and "Pa'lante Comandante" (Forward commander!).

In Maracay, María Corina is scheduled to do a neighborhood walk, together with Delson Guárate, the opposition's candidate for mayor in El Limón. But traffic is making her unacceptably late. A motorbike comes to pick her up and she arrives, perched on its back, smiling and waving at her supporters as it zigzags through traffic. It makes for a dramatic entrance. Once off the bike, supporters and television cameras from opposition media outlets surround her. Because of her late arrival, the walk becomes more of a run. There are many hands to shake, cheeks to kiss, and babies to hug in a short period of time. "Segiumos votando! Seguimos contando!" (We'll continue voting! We'll continue counting!) the participants shout as they jog along the narrow streets past the homes of potential voters.

"Mas ánimo!" (More spirit!) shouts Delson Guárate when he feels the group is too subdued or quiet.

* * *

"My dear citizens. Brothers of this cause for democracy and freedom."

Machado's voice echoes in the sport's arena of the small town Cagua, the delegation's next stop in the Aragua province.

"We understand the nature of the regime we face. We know what they want for Venezuela. They want Venezuela to be like Cuba ... A broken country."

Dressed in the turquoise color of Vente, María Corina speaks in support of the opposition's candidates running for mayor and councilors in Cagua. It is nearing the end of a very long day, but if she is tired, it doesn't show. Her charisma lights up the venue.

"They destroy everything they touch. Companies have been turned to cemeteries. And it's not because something went wrong, because they made a mistake, because they are inefficient. They are very efficient! What they wanted was destruction so that they can force us to submit, to bring us to our knees. They don't want citizens. They want slaves. They want to turn people against people, one against the other, so as to divide us."

She gestures with her arms to draw attention to the local politicians sitting beside her at the center of the arena.

"On December 8, we will not only elect these men and women as mayors and councilors. On December 8, the voice of every Venezuelan has to be raised, strong and clear, delivering a message to those who are illegitimately in Miraflores and to those who control us from Havana that this nightmare is over!"

VIII

It is December 3, 2013. Juan Carlos drives like a mad man, zigzagging through traffic at terrifying speed. He wears an ill-fitting helmet. In the event of an accident it would be useless, but it serves the purpose of avoiding fines.

While an average of three bikers are killed each day in Caracas, this is not on Juan Carlos's mind as he swerves to avoid another collision. His handlebars clip another car as he rushes between the lanes. Suddenly, a truck pulls out in front of him. His breaks squeal as he slides to a stop. Witnesses shout, raising their fists at the reckless truck driver. In Caracas, bikers rule.

Juan Carlos has already been involved in one serious accident, which left him unconscious and hospitalized. It hasn't deterred him. Driving a car means spending countless hours stuck in traffic jams. Biking may be hazardous, but it's efficient. The only option for a man as busy as he is.

Juan Carlos parks outside the restaurant where he has agreed to meet C, his only friend among *los colectivos*.

As he steps inside, the buzz of lively conversation dies as all eyes turn to him. At the table immediately to his right, a man with dark hair and a prominent moustache locks Juan Carlos in a hostile glare. He is from a *colectivo* that the students often clash with. Juan Carlos holds his gaze just long enough to not lose face. Then he looks away and keeps walking. As he reaches the back of the restaurant, he continues out the back door. He'll need to find another place. He gets back on his bike and rides until he spots a Chinese restaurant. He enters and picks a corner table, giving him overview of the entrance as well as the other tables. Juan Carlos texts C to let him know that the rendezvous point has changed.

A few minutes later, C shows up. He is attractive in a bad boy way. His dark brown eyes are defiant, unwavering, quick to judge. A long scar stretches diagonally across his left cheek. He was twelve when a rival gang cut up his face. Since then, he has developed the habit of gently tracing the scar whenever his hands are idle. It serves as a reminder to those around him that he is not to be crossed. The one who gave it to him is long dead.

Before Chávez, when he was seventeen, C did time for murder. He claims he was innocent, that the police had him confused with someone else from his barrio. Either way, he spent three months in an adult penitentiary, despite being a minor. These days, police steer clear of the *colectivos*. If C falls, it will not be at the hands of law enforcement.

At seventeen, C took his first bullet, in the shoulder. At twenty-two, he was shot in the head. At twenty-four, he got a bullet in his back, and at thirty, one in the leg. Along the inside of his left thigh an ugly scar stretches, all the way up to his crotch and down again along the inside of his other thigh.

The leg injury was the worst, not only because it just missed his artery, but because the guy who shot him was a friend from another *colectivo*.

Today, C is reserved and cautious as he takes a seat across from Juan Carlos. He wears a black, leather jacket which he leaves on, keeping one hand inside its opening at all times, as though ready to pull out a gun or a knife or whatever he keeps in there.

Juan Carlos buys a round of beers in an attempt to ease the atmosphere. They start small talking. C's Spanish is thick and filled with colloquialisms.

C was thirteen when he joined the revolutionary movement Tupamaro, named after Túpac Amaru, the last Incan leader of

Peru who was executed by Spanish authorities in 1572 for opposing colonial rule. Based on Marxism, the movement was born in 1992 to fight injustices perpetrated by previous governments. With the rise of Chávez, the movement, like other *colectivos*, joined his support base. But they were always controversial allies, as their members were often accused of attacking students, carrying out drug trafficking activities, and operating death squads.

Like everything else in Venezuela, opinions about the *colectivos* vary. Opposition sympathizers generally regard them as violent thugs, while Chavistas insist they are committed defenders of the community.

C turns thirty-six on December 17, 2013, or the day the Liberator died, as he likes to refer to his birthday. If he can keep tricking death, his future looks bright. He's a third-year law student, with social work as his minor, and with his connections he's likely to have some interesting career opportunities.

He chose law school because he is passionate about justice. In 1999, massive flooding killed tens of thousands of people in Vargas state. Members of the *colectivos* pitched in to provide disaster relief to the victims. They did so by robbing delivery trucks, like Coca-Cola or chicken deliveries, and bringing their contents to the victims. C doesn't like the epithet thief. He prefers to think of himself as a sort of Robin Hood. Thieves, drug dealers, or other unwanted individuals run the risk of being executed by Tupamaros patrolling on motorcycles if they dare enter their turf.

Gang members also intimidate members of the opposition, and C does not deny that a well-known opposition member like Juan Carlos would be very unwise to venture into their infamous neighborhood, 23 de Enero in Western Caracas.

When something is about to go down, C usually tries to warn Juan Carlos. They get together every now and then to talk or share a meal. In here, they are friends, but on the outside, sworn enemies.

"It's not that we want violence, but left-wing politicians like us understand that violence is sometimes necessary. The end justifies the means," says Juan Carlos.

C nods in agreement.

"You're sounding like more of a Chavista than me," he laughs.

Juan Carlos is a Marxist, but he despises Chavismo.

"The Bourgeoisie never give up power voluntarily," he says.

* * *

There are about a hundred *colectivos* in Caracas, out of which close to half are based in 23 de Enero. Each *colectivo* is autonomous with its own leader and has between fifty and 100 members, marking their territory with murals, slogans, and dress codes. Most *colectivos* cooperate with the state in administering social programs and promoting political participation. They organize afterschool programs to keep children out of trouble, childcare centers, puppet shows, drug rehabilitation, and sports programs.

C is adamant that members of the *colectivos* are not criminals. Yet he does not deny that they commit crimes. They have a vision for the country and like any political project it requires resources. The most gruesome way of obtaining such resources is through ordered killings.

Having someone killed used to be expensive, C says, but during the economic crisis prices sank as low as 1,000 bolívares (roughly US$17 at the time of writing), for an unimportant person. Recently, prices have increased again due to the rising price of ammunition.

C stayed with the Tupamaros for two and a half years. After leaving, he joined the movement of Lina Ron, the most famous leader of the civilian militias. With her platinum-bleached hair and bright red lips, she was Chávez's most colorful sidekick at official events.

Ron became famous when she burnt the US flag after the September 11 attacks, saying the Yankees had received a taste of their own medicine. Her motto was "Con Chávez todo, sin Chávez plomo" (With Chávez everything, without Chávez lead), referring to the lead of her bullets. With her crew, she rode around Caracas on her motorbike, stirring up mayhem, attacking any institution that opposed the revolution.

In March 2011, she died of a heart attack, at the age of fifty-one. At her televised funeral, Chávez likened her to Jesus on the cross: "Seeing her here reminds me of the crucified Christ. Like Christ she gave her life for the people ... Women like Lina don't die, nor will they die. Today, Lina became eternal."

Ron's death left a void in her movement, Unidad Popular Venezolana (UPV), causing people like C to leave.

These days, C claims he doesn't belong to any particular *colectivo*, though he still participates in activities. He fears that if the opposition wins the upcoming election, the pressure on the *colectivos* would increase again.

"Then things will get worse. What used to happen to us will happen again. They will pour hot water on us or take minors prisoners. We were persecuted before Chávez. I had friends disappear and if the opposition were in power that would happen again. That would create a civil war because now we are prepared. It's no longer like it used to be. We are not kids anymore; we're all grown up now," he says, looking intently at Juan Carlos.

"Look," Juan Carlos leans in. "It's because of the current circumstances that we support Capriles ..."

C eyes him expectantly, his hand still firmly in his jacket.

"Because we don't like Maduro and we want him gone. But once the opposition is in power ..." Juan Carlos leans back in his chair, "it's probable that we'll join forces with the Chavistas and become the new opposition."

C raises his eyebrows instinctively. The two men size each other up for a moment in silence. As if responding to an unasked question, Juan Carlos adds: "The neoliberal politics of some members of the opposition will not work for the people."

IX

It is December 8, 2013, or the "Day of Loyalty and Love for Supreme Commander Hugo Chávez and the Fatherland," as it is now officially known. Exactly one year ago, Chávez gave his last speech to the nation. Today, new elections are underway.

Deep in the neighborhood of 23 de Enero, twenty members from a *colectivo* have gathered. They are dressed in black trousers, black army boots, blue shirts, and the scarf that betrays their allegiance—Alexis Vive. Outside the voting station where Chávez used to vote, the group awaits the arrival of Vice President Jorge Arreaza.

At the center of the group stands the only woman. Her dark hair is pulled back in a ponytail, exposing a confident, naked face. No make-up and no pretense. She looks very young, like the little sister or daughter of the men around her. Far from it, she is the spokesperson of the movement and an important leader. Her name is Ana Marín, she is twenty-four years old, and ever since she was fifteen she has been a so-called militant of the *colectivo* Alexis Vive, one of the most prominent groups in 23 de Enero. A militant is someone who devotes their life to the struggle and who is at the service of the revolution 24/7, 365 days a year.

According to Marín, being in a *colectivo* means thinking and acting collectively.

Alexis Vive is a Marxist–Leninist organization founded in 1993, long before Chávez came to power. It used to be called La coordinadora Simón Bolívar, but in 2002 it changed its name to Alexis Vive (Alexis lives), in honor of Alexis González, a devoted member who was killed trying to defend Chávez during the coup on April 11.

That year, the influence of armed civilian groups like the *colectivos* increased. After the coup, Chávez no longer trusted the armed forces. It was the people, not the generals who had rescued the revolution when they took to the streets, chanting his name. Recognizing the shift in his power base, Chávez began to arm his supporters to defend against future coup attempts. He encouraged *los colectivos* and created other armed civilian forces such as the militia and El Frente Francisco de Miranda, a socialist youth organization founded in 2003 by Chávez and Fidel Castro in Havana. In 2013, it had over 20,000 members, many of whom had received revolutionary training in Cuba.

By 2011, the militia supposedly totaled 125,000 volunteers from all walks of life: students, civil servants, housewives, and pensioners. Commanded directly by the president, their job was to defend and consolidate Venezuela's socialist revolution.

"If I fall, unleash a whirlwind," Chávez told them. "You know what you would have to do: Simply take all power in Venezuela, absolutely all! Sweep away the bourgeoisie from all political and economic spaces. Deepen the revolution!"[15]

The army initially protested against this arrangement, but Chávez insisted that the militia was a "complementary," not a parallel, force, and put an end to the discussion.[16]

Many of the Cuban guest workers also joined the militia. In 2007, Juan José Rabilero, then head of the Committees for the Defense of the Revolution (CDR), proudly announced that there were more than 30,000 Cuban members, known as *cederristas*, in Venezuela. Many of them had military training. Would they take up arms to protect the Venezuelan revolution if need be?[17]

* * *

In 23 de Enero, Alexis Vive controls an area of about 12,000 inhabitants. They refer to their community as a *panal*, Spanish for honeycomb, because unlike ants who disperse when attacked, bees join forces to defend their honeycomb.

As one of the biggest *colectivos*, Alexis Vive manages a wide range of projects and activities. They don't believe in paternalism. The community has to generate its own goods and services in order to be sustainable. The *colectivo* owns and runs a sugar factory, a bakery, a butcher's shop, a sewing workshop, a cinderblock factory, and a TV and radio station—Radio Arsenal 98.1 FM.

For Alexis Vive, ensuring the people control the means of production is crucial to the revolution. It is a horizontal organization where the idea is that any member can fill any function. No one is irreplaceable.

Members of Alexis Vive claim that efforts to brand all *colectivos* as "terrorists" or "violent thugs" are false and only aim to discredit their movement and the concept of communes. They insist that managing the security of their area does not depend on weapons, but on prevention and surveillance. There are hidden security cameras throughout the community, and youth at risk of turning to crime are provided with other means to make a living. Marín claims it works so well that in four years there has not been a single violent incident on their turf.

For those who share the vision, there is work and community. But stray from the revolutionary principles, and you're expelled from the *panal* like a male drone by the female bees.

* * *

After a long wait, Vice President Jorge Arreaza finally arrives, donning the same kind of colorful sport's jacket that Chávez used to wear. With him are his wife Rosa Virginia, who is Chávez's eldest daughter, their children, and Chávez's second daughter María Gabriela.

Like soldiers, Marín and her companions from Alexis Vive line up to greet them. They stand against the wall of the voting station, which has been completely covered with a mural to mark their territory.

"Welcome to the Alexis Vive foundation," it reads in big colorful letters as though welcoming visitors to a pre-school. A subtle reminder that any non-Chavista aspirant to the throne will have to get through the *colectivos* first. Or, as Ana Marín tells anyone who will listen: "We are the ones who will fulfill Chávez's legacy, or we will die like he did."

X

"Social and political movements can take place in days—it's a matter of leadership," says María Corina Machado. "183 years after the death of the Liberator, our generation will defend his legacy: independence, liberty and the republic."

It is December 18, 2013, and ten days have passed since the local elections. Vente's Caracas office is bustling with activity as people dressed in the movement's characteristic turquoise shirts welcome partners and friends to a Christmas lunch and end-of-year wrap-up.

The disappointment from the recent election is still fresh. The local elections had been the opposition's chance to prove that they were in fact the majority and that the presidential election had been fraudulent. But the effort failed.

While the opposition won in a number of large cities, their share of the overall vote was less than 40 percent, compared with the 49 percent Capriles had obtained as presidential candidate in April. The next presidential election is not due until 2018.

Machado, like her colleagues, has always been a vocal supporter of the democratic process, but the prospect of five more years under Maduro is too much for her. Addressing her colleagues, she calls for regime change ahead of elections.

"When you have a regime that takes control of all institutions and public powers, that progressively destroys every possibility of autonomy and independence in the media, in the private sector, and the unions, and that creates a system in which they can stay in power forever, not respecting popular sovereignty, you cannot keep calling that a democracy, because it is not. Even though it calls for elections. You have elections in Cuba and in Russia, but nobody believes they are democracies. In Venezuela we've had to fight against a system that understands that legitimacy is one of their fundamental pillars and that has used elections in a very effective way. It's not true that the only possibility of a change of the regime is to wait for the next presidential election," she says.

What Venezuela needs now is strong leadership: "A leadership that tells the truth about what we are facing. It's much easier to say we will overcome this effortlessly without risking, just voting. I would love to believe that's enough, but we've proven that it's not."

Machado is convinced that the country can't afford to wait much longer: "In that time, the forces of the regime will destroy all those who are unwilling to submit."

XI

It is February 2, 2014, and thousands of people have gathered at Plaza Brión de Chacaíto in Caracas. Standing at the edge of the stage to address them all is María Corina Machado: "Dear Venezuelans, today the people of Venezuela make themselves heard in every corner of our homeland. We, who were born in democracy, are gathered here, as a genuine expression of men and women who will not permit them to destroy our land."

She is dressed in jeans and a white blouse. The sea of people before her is so vast it seems infinite. "We want to live in liberty, like those men and women of previous generations who gave their lives for the independent and democratic republic that we inherited. Now we will show that we can defend that legacy."

She glows. This is what she was born to do: "There is no democracy here today. This is a regime without scruples that is crushing us. But we are united in the knowledge that democracy is more alive than ever because it lives in us, in every Venezuelan!"

Machado is surrounded by the powerhouses of opposition politics. To her right stands Leopoldo López, his blue shirt darkened by sweat in the baking sun. To her left, in a checkered blue-white shirt and a baseball cap, the mayor of metropolitan Caracas, Antonio Ledezma.

Just over a week ago, the three leaders launched this movement to advocate a change of government. They call it La Salida, Spanish for both "the way out" and "the departure" of Maduro. The president has to resign, they argue. The situation is too serious to await another election, and the institutions are in any case too compromised by the government. Urgent action is needed. Under the motto: "The street is the way out," they summon people to the streets to protest against raising inflation, crime, and the lack of staple foods.

Today, thousands of people have shown up to this first assembly to air their frustrations and agree on solutions for how to move forward.

Many are keen to share their stories of ordeals ranging from violent crime to economic hardships and lack of basic necessities such as milk, rice, and toilet paper.

Rufino Carmona, a middle-aged man in a black jacket and thinning hair, steps up to the microphone:

"Sunday, January 26, I was kidnapped in my home. A truck followed my truck and four heavily armed individuals entered my residence. They beat me and put a pistol in my mouth. They threw me on the floor and grabbed my three-year-old daughter. As she was crying, they slapped her. It was three and a half hours of agony."

Carmona's voice breaks and he begins to cry: "I don't know how to go on."

Luisa Mayorca, a young woman wearing Vente's turquoise T-shirt, recounts how both her parents were killed in a car robbery. "It is not about isolated events, but about what keeps occurring before the blind and completely apathetic authorities. I am not scared of appearing here with my name and face, of appearing in photographs. No, I am afraid to keep living like this," she concludes.

But it is the leadership the crowd has been waiting for, someone to guide them in their search for solutions. Machado returns to the microphone. "Today, the regime tells us they have a plan for peace. I ask you, this plan of peace, is it to subdue the delinquent gangs called *colectivos*?" she asks.

"No," the crowd replies.

"Is it to subdue the gang leaders who are running the mafias of crime, kidnappings and extortion from our prisons? Is it to subdue them?"

"No!"

"Who do they want to subdue?"

"The people!"

"Who do they want to subdue?"

"THE PEOPLE!"

"And will we let them?"

"NO!"

"They want to subdue the brave students of Merida and other Venezuelan cities who took to the streets to defend the lives of their friends. They want to subdue the tenacious workers and their union leaders in Guayana, in Caracas, in Maturín ... persecuted for defending the workers and unions. They want to subdue the public employees ... They want to subdue we the citizens who don't recognize a regime that has disregarded popular sovereignty in perverted, dirty, and manipulated elections. But faced with this tyranny's pretense of pacifying us, the people of Venezuela have one response—rebellion—RE-BEL-LION!

"RE-BEL-LION! RE-BEL-LION!" the crowd echoes.

"We will not rest until we conquer a free, sovereign, and democratic Venezuela!"

The crowd roars in approval.

"There are some who say we should wait," says María Corina, referring to the fact that moderate MUD leaders like Capriles have distanced themselves from La Salida, saying that such a stance will only further polarize an already divided society. The best way forward, they argue, is for the opposition to focus on governing well in the municipalities they won.

"No!" the crowd shouts.

"Wait for some elections in some years ..."

"No!"

"I ask you, can the political prisoners wait? Can the mothers who can't find food for their children wait? Can the public employees wait? The farmers? The merchants whose rights to work and property they have taken away?"

"No!"

"At this time, the only one waiting is Venezuela. And she is waiting for us, her sons and daughters!"

"Yes, we can! Yes, we can!" shouts the crowd.

María Corina waits for her supporters to settle down. Then, in a softer, almost lamenting tone of voice, she pronounces the verdict the crowd has already arrived at:

"Venezuela cannot wait any longer."

It's nearing the end of the assembly, and it's time to wrap up and agree on resolutions. Visibly moved by the crowd's overwhelming response to her discourse, María Corina turns to her sea of supporters once more: "I ask you, are we committed to building a great movement of citizens' assemblies, covering every corner of Venezuela, to debate and to bring an end to this horrible regime?" she shouts.

"Si!" the crowd roars, raising their right hand in a vote of approval.

To her right, López raises his hand. To her left, Ledezma does the same. Behind her, Juan Carlos Requesens. All around her on stage, the other student leaders and activists do the same. Standing before her supporters, María Corina radiates.

"Do you agree?" she shouts.

"Si!" the roar is deafening.

"Approved!"

The crowd cheers and blows vuvuzelas.

"I propose that we declare February 2 as Venezuelan Citizens' Day."

Machado turns to López, Ledezma, and the student leaders on stage and continues: "I propose that we accept the invitation from the student leadership, Mayor Ledezma, and Leopoldo López for a mass demonstration across Venezuela, at 10 a.m., on February 12, when we will assert the unyielding force of our youth and claim the day of victory."

The crowd roars in approval.

"Today, this historic day, we do not only feel deeply Venezuelan, but also proud to have been born to this land and to this generation—the generation that will rescue the dignity, sovereignty, prosperity, love, and liberty of our land. ¡Viva Venezuela!"

The crowd echoes: ¡Viva!

"Viva freedom!"

¡Viva!

"God bless you all! Now let's sing our national anthem to mark this historic moment."

XII

It is February 12, 2014, the Day of Youth in Venezuela. A group of students are posing for a photo outside a classroom. They smile and give thumbs up. Dressed in jeans, T-shirts, and sneakers, with their school bags thrown over the shoulder or resting on the ground, they look as though they are about to go on a field trip. Ten girls and four boys hold up a large, handwritten banner. Carefully printed letters in the colors of the Venezuelan flag read: "Mother, I went to fight for Venezuela. If I don't come back, I've left with her."

One of them, smiling broadly, is twenty-three-year-old student Bassil da Costa.

* * *

Soon after the picture is taken, the students join 10,000 others at Plaza Venezuela in Caracas to protest recent police violence against demonstrating students.

Carrying Venezuelan flags or homemade signs saying: "Demonstrating is a right. Free the students," the protesters march to the offices of Attorney General Luisa Ortega Díaz to demand the release of those imprisoned and a solution to the crime problem. Ortega refuses to receive the protestors, and the leaders of the march call for the participants to disperse. Defying the instructions, a group of students stay behind and clashes erupt between the students and the security forces. Rocks and petrol bombs are hurled at the building, and several police vehicles set alight.

Juan Carlos is in the midst of the multitude when he feels his phone vibrate in his pocket. "Bassil is dead!"

The young student has taken a bullet to the head. His face lies covered in blood on the concrete. His eyes are rolled back in their sockets. His friends pick him up to rush him to the sidelines. Tears and pain smear their dirt-covered faces as they realize there is no need to rush. It is already too late.

One of the men carrying Bassil da Costa is twenty-eight-year-old Roberto Redman.

"I saw the shooter! I saw who did it," he cries as they hand over the body.

A few hours later, Redman is also gunned down, shot to the head by what witnesses describe as civilian gunmen.

Forty-year-old Juan "Juancho" Montoya, a key leader of the Alexis Vive *colectivo*, is also killed. Montoya recently made national news for participating in a disarmament campaign aimed at persuading *colectivos* to hand in their weapons.

By the end of the day, three people have been killed, twenty-three people injured, and twenty-five arrested; four police vehicles burned and some government offices vandalized.[18] The government initially blames the opposition, but footage later reveals that the gunmen in the streets near the Attorney General's Office are uniformed members of the Bolivarian intelligence service SEBIN and armed members of the *colectivos*.[19]

President Maduro claims that individual SEBIN members have defied his instructions to stay off the streets. He removes the head of the SEBIN and those identified in the videos are placed under arrest. On April 11, José Ramón Perdomo, an SEBIN officer, is formally charged with the murder of Bassil da Costa. The two other murders, however, remain unsolved.[20]

XIII

It is March 5, 2014, in El Carrizal, southwest of Caracas. Moisés Guánchez, a nineteen-year-old student, is at work in a fast food restaurant in La Cascada mall. On the highway that passes in front of the mall, a demonstration has been underway since early that morning. At 10 a.m., the restaurant staff begin to hear yelling and sporadic gunshots. At lunchtime, the boss decides to close the restaurant. There won't be any customers today. Moisés and his co-workers clean up and get ready to leave. But as they attempt to exit the mall, they discover that the main entrance has been locked, likely in an effort to keep it shielded from the demonstration. Moisés makes his way to the mall's open-air parking lot, located between the mall and the street. There are about forty people in the lot, watching as members of the national guard fire teargas canisters toward protesters on the highway.[21]

Then, four national guard motorcycles, with two guardsmen on each, break into the parking lot, firing rubber bullets as they drive toward the group. Moisés and the others begin to run back toward the mall. But a motorcycle blocks his path. He turns and begins to run in the other direction, toward a parking lot exit.

"There! There! Shoot him!" Yells one of the guardsmen.

He hears them fire, but none of the shots hit him. Then, another motorcycle in front of him stops. The soldier on the back aims at his head. Instinctively, Moisés raises his arm to protect his face. He feels the impact of the shots on his arm. He continues to run. Then he feels several impacts on his backside and falls down on the pavement.

By this point, there are more motorcycles in the parking lot. Two guardsmen grab Moisés and pull him up. Holding on to an arm each, they start punching him repeatedly in the ribs. Then, a third guardsman approaches. He points his rifle at Moisés' genitals and fires. Moisés manages to cover most of his testicles with his leg, causing the leg to absorb the bulk of the impact. The guardsmen force Moisés, who is now soaked in blood and in excruciating pain, to walk across the parking lot and board a motorcycle in-between two guardsmen. The soldier sitting behind him points a pistol at his head and threatens to kill him if he moves. Moisés is later handcuffed and loaded onto a black pick-up truck with no license plates. The soldiers say that if he bleeds to death they will dump his body in a canal. They then threaten to rape him with a broomstick.[22]

Upon realizing that they are not going to kill him, but take him to a hospital, Moisés passes out. As they enter the emergency room, the attending doctor asks the soldiers to help lift his body onto a stretcher, but they refuse. They also refuse to remove his handcuffs. Not until the doctor threatens to have them cut off do they produce the key to unlock them.[23]

Moisés is given three blood transfusions and operated on immediately to remove five rubber bullets from his leg. Doctors also locate rubber bullet wounds in his arm and his rear, and he is operated on for damage to one of his testicles. All of his personal possessions, including his wallet, cellphone, and a gold chain, have disappeared.

Two days later, while still hospitalized, Moisés is charged with public incitement to commit crimes and attacks undermining security on public roads. The judge, however, rules there is no evidence to charge him with any crime and the case is dismissed.[24]

* * *

Violence reigns in the streets of Caracas and other major cities throughout the country. What started as protests against insecurity and rising inflation soon transforms into larger protests against the repressive reaction of the government.

Human rights organizations like Amnesty International and the UN High Commissioner for Human Rights are troubled. The victims of abuse are often unarmed individuals who are not violent or engaged in criminal activity.[25]

By the end of April, the Venezuelan Penal Forum (FPV), a group of lawyers who provide free legal assistance to victims of alleged human rights abuses, has received over 500 complaints of torture with detainees testifying to abuses ranging from beatings and electric shocks, to sodomy with a rifle barrel.[26]

10

ENDGAME

"God grants victory to perseverance."

Simón Bolívar

I

On February 17, 2014, four armed men wearing civilian clothes and black helmets force their way into the offices of opposition party Voluntad Popular in Caracas. They point their pistols through the glass doors that mark the entrance to the reception. The receptionist opens the door, and the handful of people present in the area put their hands in the air as the men barge in. Holding them at gunpoint, the men search those seated in the small waiting area. They then proceed to kick in the doors leading to the offices.

It is 15:50 in the afternoon, and national coordinator Antonio Rivero is in the office. Since February 14, there has been a warrant out for his arrest, as well as the arrest of national coordinator Carlos Vecchio and party leader Leopoldo López. President Maduro holds them responsible for the deaths at the Youth Day demonstrations, claiming they have been organizing and training youth street fighters.

The armed men take a quick look around, but leave when pressed for a search warrant by members of Voluntad Popular. Certain that they will be back with reinforcements, staff quickly spread the word on social media.

At nearby Plaza Altamira, a demonstration with about 500 participants is underway. When the protestors get word of the raid, they run towards the offices of Voluntad Popular. From a window on the seventeenth floor, Rivero and Vecchio watch them approach.

"I'm going down to talk to them. We'll be a lot safer with the support of the crowd," Rivero says.

As he exits the building, a lieutenant and an armed civilian approach.

"Come with us. We're here to help you," one of the strangers says.

"Are you crazy? Get out of here," shouts Rivero. But as he turns around to head back into the building, the national guard arrives. Their commander, General Antonio Benavides Torres, immediately recognizes Rivero and orders his men to detain him.

Rivero tries to get away, but five guardsmen jump him. They push him into a column made of concrete by the entrance of the building. When he manages to break free, they pin him to the opposite wall. As they drag him toward the hallways of the building, away from all the people, Rivero calls for help. The protestors react almost immediately, jumping the national guardsmen. More guardsmen come running, but there are only about thirty of them, and by now hundreds of protestors are rushing toward them. In response, the guardsmen launch tear-gas. But the space by the entrance is tight, and as the guards are not wearing masks, the gas affects them as much as the protestors. In the confusion that follows, Rivero manages to break free from the waist grip of the last guardsman clinging onto him, and he escapes into the fog of gas.

Not knowing how many more guards or intelligence officers are in the crowd, he flees into the building. Back on the seventeenth floor, with ripped shirt and scratches across his body, his party colleagues help Rivero and Vecchio hide in an empty office on a different floor of the massive building. Just then, twelve uniformed officers of the General Directorate of Military Counterintelligence, DGCIM, force their way back in to the offices of Voluntad Popular. Better prepared this time, the entire reception area is packed with supporters, making it nearly impossible to pass.

"Where is the warrant? They won't get past without a warrant!" people shout.

The uniformed men push their way through, each side filming the other.

"Dictatorship! Dictatorship!" people scream.

With so many people present, it is hard for them to conduct a thorough search.

With all lights turned off, Rivero and Vecchio watch from the window of their hiding place as reinforcements from the national guard arrive. They seize the building and secure the exits. The crowd outside has already been dispersed with teargas, though many remain in the offices of Voluntad Popular. About thirty guardsmen enter and spend the following three hours meticulously searching the entire floor of the building occupied by Voluntad Popular before finally giving up. As they leave, they seize countless documents, cameras, security camera recordings, and computers.

Hours later, under the cover of night, Rivero and Vecchio slip out of the building undetected.

II

It is February 18, 2014. Antonio Rivero is standing by the bathroom mirror, holding a razor to his chin, when he realizes he won't be shaving today. Instead, he should be growing something. What will it be? A moustache? A beard? He studies his reflection: the short dark hair, the pouting lips, the birthmark just below his left eye in the shape of a teardrop. Time has sketched fine lines around his eyes and on his forehead. More than twenty years have passed since he last had to modify his appearance and go underground. Then it was for his allegiance with Chávez, jailed after the failed coup. This time it is for his association with Leopoldo López, who is about to hand himself in.

It should make for some interesting reflections. But now is not the time. Rivero has a march to attend. But first he must disguise his face.

* * *

In the morning hours of February 18, henceforth referred to as 18F, thousands of people stream to Plaza Brión de Chacaíto in Caracas. Dressed in white, the color of peace, they have come to show their support for Leopoldo López.

After coloring his beard gray, Rivero also heads out. He is wearing a white shirt, with a Venezuelan flag tied over his shoulders, and a blue, red, and yellow baseball cap on his head.

Avenida Francisco de Miranda is packed with people. Rivero relaxes a bit. When everyone is dressed the same, blending in with the crowd is easy. He arrives at Plaza Brión de Chacaíto just in time for López's speech.

With a Venezuelan flag draped around him like a cape, López climbs a statue of Cuban liberation hero José Martí and addresses his supporters:

"One of the options I had was to leave the country, but I will never leave Venezuela! The other option was to stay in hiding, in the shadows; but that choice may have made some people question—even some of those present here today—whether we had something to hide. But we have nothing to hide! I have not committed any crime! I am not a criminal! I simply have no reason to hide! So the only option left for me is to show my face."

Rivero watches from a distance. He hopes that López will change his mind. Or that the crowd will ask him not to turn himself in. Maybe he'll put his fate in their hands, Rivero speculates. Ask them, "Do you want me to turn myself in?" Then everyone would shout "NO" and this whole nightmare could be avoided. With this many people present, there is no way for the police to reach López unless he wants them to. Rivero can help him stay hidden. Though a life in hiding is not easy, it is certainly better than life behind bars. López doesn't know what he is in for. Rivero does. He has been there.

But López is determined. He jumps down from the statue and with one armed raised, clutching a Venezuelan flag and a handful of white oxeye daisies, he makes his way to the national guardsmen across the square.

"If my imprisonment helps awaken our people, it will have been worth it!" he shouts to the jubilant crowd.

The guardsmen usher him to an armored vehicle, but with a megaphone López keeps addressing his supporters, urging them to remain calm, until the moment the doors shut.

Rivero heads towards a Voluntad Popular truck near the armored vehicle holding López. He climbs onto the truck, takes off his hat and glasses and begins to address the crowd alongside other Voluntad Popular politicians:

"You have to stay strong. Leopoldo's surrender stems from a bravery that we cannot weaken. We have to continue the struggle, stay in the streets. This regime is a dictatorship. We have to fight for the liberty, not only of Leopoldo, but of the whole country. We have to continue to pressure the government to make way for a transitional government that can call for clean, fair elections."

Rivero stays all afternoon. The armored vehicle holding López is not going anywhere. There are so many people surrounding it that it is unable to advance. Every now and then, the doors open and López resurfaces, asking the crowd to calm down. The hours go by. Finally, the guardsmen transfer him to a truck, and after López has pleaded with the crowd it is able to make slow progress. Shouting "Liberty!" and "Leopoldo, amigo, el pueblo está contigo!" (Leopoldo, friend, the people are with you!), the crowd accompanies him all the way to La Carlota Air Base, where López is transferred to a helicopter and taken away.

The images spread around the world. Leopoldo kissing his wife Lilian Tintori goodbye. His parents dressed in all-whites, eyes filled with tears. María Corina Machado by his side until the end. The sea of supporters.

It is likened to Chávez's famous "*por ahora*" speech and surrender after the failed coup. A new Liberator had crowned himself. But would the support for him be strong enough to carry him on that same journey from prison to the throne in Miraflores?

López is sent to a military prison outside Caracas. Shortly thereafter, Maduro announces that Daniel Ceballos, mayor of San Cristobal, and key member of the opposition, would soon join López.

"It's a matter of time until we have him in the same cold cell," he says.[1]

In March, the Bolivarian National Intelligence Service detains Ceballos without an arrest warrant.[2] On March 25, the Supreme Court sentences him to twelve months in prison for inciting violence.[3]

On September 10, 2015, López is sentenced to thirteen years and nine months in prison after being convicted of the same offense. The court refused to hear all but one of sixty-five witnesses for the defense, while allowing the testimony of 108 witnesses for the government.[4]

III

It is March 18, 2014. In the National Assembly of Venezuela, Chavista deputy Tania Díaz stands at the speaker's podium, wearing an army-green, military-style jacket, and a burgundy baseball cap with matching lipstick. "It is not enough to be the majority and to win elections to obtain a change of power ..."

The session is being broadcast live to the nation, and the camera zooms in on Diosdado Cabello, head of the National Assembly, as he lets out a little laugh of amusement.

Díaz continues: "It is time that our political generation stakes out a route and assumes leadership, although it might not be that easy. The objective is not to strengthen our position as a political alternative. The objective is to obtain power."

She is quoting María Corina Machado, building evidence in the hopes that the assembly agrees to impeach her. Triumphantly, Díaz looks up from her notes and out at the assembly: "Did she say it or not? Is it true or is it a lie?" she asks.

María Corina Machado nods in her seat, seemingly unaffected by all the commotion. She doesn't have a microphone, but her mouth shapes the words: "Yes, I said it. Absolutely!"

Then Díaz launches her next piece of evidence, a video recording from a televised speech by Machado who is standing behind a podium marked "La Salida."

"Let us turn off the lights of our houses for ten minutes because it's time to light up the streets ..." Díaz pauses the recording before Machado has completed her sentence which ends "with responsible civic struggle," and says: "At this moment, the state of Tachira was on fire, responding to the instruction that these irresponsible politicians were giving," she exclaims.

"What does La Salida consist of? What is this soft *coup d'état* looking for? It's after one thing and one thing only. It is not to demonstrate in the streets. It is not to fight against shortages.

No, sir! It's not even the resignation of the president per se. What they are after is a civil war. What they are after is that we Venezuelans kill one another. They are looking to generate confusion, generate chaos, and infiltrate paramilitary elements to plant terrorist actions in this country, and you know it! You keep cowardly quiet, but you know it! They hide behinds these kids, but they know it! They organize student protests, then they hide, and then they come out and say: 'They are violating the human rights of these kids.' That's what this faction does. That's what the international media does."

Machado and the opposition request an opportunity to reply to the accusations before the matter is put to the vote, but Diosdado Cabello takes out the white book of parliamentary rules. He reads out loud a lengthy passage from Article 79 and then goes on to say: "Nowhere in the rules does it call for a debate."

The television camera remains zoomed in on Cabello's face, but on the assembly floor there seems to be commotion because Cabello urges calm.

"I ask you please. This is the bench of the president ..." He motions to the podium behind which he sits. "Where I am seated because of life's circumstances. Because of life's circumstances! Not because I want to. Not because I want to! I ask you please, return to your seats. Not because I want to. Not because I want to, but because of life's circumstances. You decide how you want it. You decide. I always say: as you wish."

He pauses, then resumes: "This comrade deputy has made a proposal in front of the nation, for the peace and justice of this country. For it seems that they have sold, through the big media outlets, how democratic it is that a president, elected by the majority of the people, should have to renounce because four whimsical bourgeoisie want him to renounce."

Cabello begins to shout: "No! President Nicolás Maduro will not renounce!"

The assembly erupts in cheers. The Chavista deputies rise to their feet, clapping their hands. Then the camera shifts to Machado's face as Cabello continues his rant.

"This deputy is an accomplice, instigator of murders in this country. Murders! One has to call things by their correct name—MURDER! Twenty-nine deaths in this country. And the democratic process would be for Nicolás to renounce because she wants to be president? You will never be president of this country, did you hear? NEVER! Put that in here!" He points to his head. "Now, she has been saying things lately that call for attention ..." Cabello puts both hands on his heart and continues in a soft voice: "that she was elected by a people and that the people should be the ones to decide whether she should continue. Ah, and Nicolás was not elected by a people? See how they are, the Venezuelan bourgeoisie? She has rights! But not Nicolás! Fascist! Terrorist!"

Cabello is shouting again and waving his finger agitatedly: "All deputies in favor of suspending this session and going immediately to the prosecutor's office to request the lifting of the parliamentary immunity of this deputy so that she pays for the crimes committed in this country since February 12 ..."

He doesn't even have to finish. The deputies are already standing, arms raised in approval.

"The revolutionary majority approves! Let's go straight to the general prosecutor's office to submit this document requesting an investigation. There will be no impunity. If there is no justice there will not be peace in this country!"

IV

"I will be congresswoman until the people decide otherwise," Machado shouts to a rally of supporters in Chacaíto. "Now the whole world recognizes that Venezuela has a regime that represses and oppresses."[5]

It is March 26, 2014, and Machado has recently returned to Venezuela from Washington, DC, where she addressed the Organization of American States as a guest of Panama. In a session that took place behind closed doors, Machado testified to the human rights abuses that occurred in the wake of recent demonstrations.

In Venezuela, the National Assembly immediately voted to strip Machado of her seat in parliament. By agreeing to join Panama's delegation without assembly approval, authorities claimed she had violated the Venezuelan constitution and acted as a Panamanian official.

On national television, Diosdado Cabello justified the decision by quoting Article 149 from the Venezuelan constitution: "Public officials cannot accept posts, honors, or compensation from foreign governments without the authorization of the National Assembly," he exclaimed, holding up a small paper copy of the constitution before the camera.

As a result, Machado lost her parliamentary immunity and could now be prosecuted for her alleged responsibility in the violent demonstrations of the past few months.[6]

Many interpreted this as the first step toward detaining Machado, who still chose to return home to Venezuela two days later.

* * *

On March 31, Venezuela's Supreme Court backs Machado's ouster from parliament. But Machado vows to defy them. She intends to participate in the upcoming weekly session.

Dressed in white and draped in a Venezuelan flag, she marches to the congressional palace. She carries a bouquet of roses to symbolize peace. With her are twenty-two opposition deputies, as well as thousands of protestors.[7]

"You will not break us! You will make us stronger! You will give us more reasons to fight!" she shouts.[8]

One street away from parliament, riot police block her path. She waves her parliamentary ID card. The police respond by hurling teargas to break up the crowd. With eyes swollen shut from the gas and cheeks wet with tears, Machado and her supporters turn away.[9]

Some protestors wearing gasmasks throw the canisters back. Then, seizing the momentum, they rush the Housing Ministry and set it on fire.[10] The following day, state media show photos of a little girl, about three years old, wearing an oxygen mask and holding on to a firefighter as he rescues her from the burning building. According to the government, there were eighty-nine children in the building, some of whom had to be treated with oxygen.[11]

V

It is April 2014. Daytime opposition rallies attract hundreds of thousands of people. The government responds by dispersing them, frequently with teargas, water cannons, or plastic bullets. At night, radical students erect *guarimbas*, street barricades defended by masked youth. They are meant to stop security forces from entering opposition-held areas. Nightly battles between members of the opposition, mainly students, and the security forces ensue in opposition strongholds like Altamira and Chacao.[12]

Though they represent only a fraction of the movement, media soon turn the masked *guarimberos* into the face of the opposition. Capriles and moderate MUD leaders argue against the barricades, saying the violence only plays into the hands of the government. If Maduro can't fix the racing inflation, rampant crime, and lack of staple goods, he can at least avoid taking responsibility for it by pointing the blame away from himself. Images of radicals throwing rocks or burning down their neighborhoods make for great government propaganda.[13] But despite the appeals of the moderates, the *guarimbas* grow in both number and impact.

At the height of the protests, Juan Carlos visits a *guarimba* in Merida, the center of the student protests. Suddenly, the barricade is swarmed by hundreds of bikers wearing the red stars of the Tupamaro *colectivo* on their shirts and caps. Juan Carlos is used to clashes with *colectivos* at the university. They typically fire some shots in the air to intimidate. The students, for their part, know to hold their ground and show no fear. Then both sides back down.

But this time it's different. The bikers level their guns and, without warning, they unleash a hail of bullets on the crowd. About 5 meters to the right of Juan Carlos, a student crumples to the ground. An artery in his arm has been hit. Blood gushes out with every beat, blackening the ground beneath him. Oblivious to the ongoing battle, Juan Carlos watches as the student's friends try to triage his wounds, pile him onto a motorbike, and rush off to a hospital. But the boy is already dead. The students and *colectivo*s disperse.

Juan Carlos finishes his visit to Merida, though later he'll be able to recall little of it, and travels home. It's not until he is back in his bedroom in Caracas, paralyzed by shock, staring blankly at a wall, that he realizes the game has changed.

By May 8, the death toll has reached forty-one people; 813 people have been injured and thousands detained, according to Attorney General Luisa Ortega Díaz.[14]

Of the forty-one official deaths, thirty-two are civilians and the remainder police and military personnel. Most have been shot, often to the head. In the first quarter of 2014, the *colectivos* carry out at least 437 violent attacks on demonstrators.[15]

There is no doubt that some protesters also use violence, including throwing rocks and Molotov cocktails at security forces. According to the government, more than 200 security force members and government officials are injured in the protests, and at least nine die.[16] Accidents caused by barbed wire or other obstacles forming part of the barricades also claim several lives.[17]

VI

It is Saturday, December 14, 2013. In his one-bedroom apartment in the hills of Bello Monte in southern Caracas, Folco eats his breakfast. While his coffee is brewing, he goes online to read *El Sol de Margarita*, Isla de Margarita's daily newspaper. One of the headlines catches his eye: "New Resolution for Sardines Approved." The Socialist Institute of Fisheries and Aquaculture has announced a three-month ban on sardine fishing. They fear the complete extinction of the sardines.

Not knowing whether to laugh or cry, Folco gets up and goes to the kitchen to fetch his coffee.

Ever since Puerto de La Mar was expropriated, the sardine population around the island has declined rapidly. While marine biologists attested that the cruise ships would not affect the sardines, they warned that overfishing would. The fishermen, it appears, did not heed the warning.

In 2004, 120,000 tons of sardines were caught in the state of Nueva Esparta. In 2013, that number fell to 7,000 tons—a 95 per cent decline. Around the island it was even worse. In La Isleta, catches fell by more than 99 percent, from 4,000 tons to 30 tons annually. So now, in a last effort to avoid extinction, the Socialist Institute of Fisheries and Aquaculture has declared a fishing ban.[18]

As he sits back down with his coffee cup in hand, Folco realizes he is neither surprised, nor upset. He knows his opponents were determined to find an excuse; if not the sardines, then it would have been something else.

He calls his brother Giampiero, who now lives in Miami, to share the story. Folco tries to laugh about it, but soon turns serious: "Giampiero, all of Venezuela has become Puerto de La Mar. Everything the government touches turns to shit. Anyone who has anything to offer is leaving. The government has fueled so much resentment toward people who want to be successful that they've made it impossible to stay."

"So why do you?" his brother replies.

On February 19, 2014, Folco and his mother visit Giampiero in Miami to celebrate her birthday. It's at the height of the protests in Venezuela, and at first the family follows the news with great concern. But with all the political propaganda and conflicting information circulating in the media, not to mention Twitter, separating facts from fiction becomes increasingly difficult. Folco can't tell if it was radical Chavistas or radical *guarimberos* who started it this time. Nor does he care. Neither side will bring a positive end to Venezuela's challenges. To change what is wrong in the country he agrees that the opposition must be firm and persistent, but above all they must be peaceful, or they will lose the moral high ground and escalate the cycle of violence again.

As he wanders the streets of Miami, Folco is reminded of all that Venezuela lacks. Peace. Security. Abundance. Freedom.

After just three days, he decides to stay, leaving everything, including personal belongings, behind.

VII

It is May 28, 2014. The "Political High Command of the Bolivarian Revolution" is giving a televised press conference:

"I will present a series of emails which are part of a penal and criminal investigation brought forward by the Venezuelan justice system," says Caracas Mayor Jorge Rodríguez.

Seated beside him at a long table are Diosdado Cabello, first lady Cilia Flores, and Vice President Jorge Arreaza, among others.

"Here is an email from Señora María Corina Machado," Rodríguez continues.

He holds up a sheet of cardboard onto which the printout of an email has been glued. Big, red, construction paper arrows point from an email address to Machado's name, and then on to a photo of the supposed recipient of her email: Gustavo Tarre.

"Here is the account of María Corina Machado." Rodríguez points to an email address pasted on the cardboard: 77galla@gmail.com, and circles it with his blue pen.

"This lady, María Corina Machado, writes an email on March 23, 2014, at 6:19 p.m. to Señor Gustavo Tarre, a supposed constitutional lawyer, a supposed professor of constitutional law at the Universidad Central de Venezuela, a supposed democrat, and a supposed Christian, because he is or has been a militant member of the Venezuelan Christian Democracy and the Christian democratic parties for years. What democrat, what Christian supports a blood bath?"

Rodríguez takes a rhetorical pause, then adds: "He does!" while pointing agitatedly to the photo of Gustavo Tarre.

"What democrat, what Christian supports a presidential assassination? She does and he does." He points to Machado's name on the cardboard and again to Tarre.

"What Venezuelan, what human being, supports violence, assassinations of brothers and sisters against brothers and sisters? She does and he does!" he exclaims.

"Listen to what Señora Machado writes: While Leopoldo is isolated and humiliated by the regime, and I'm risking my peace of mind, exposing myself to the lout Diosdado ..."

Rodríguez looks up from the cardboard sheet and adds, in case the audience doesn't know to whom she is referring: "Our brother Diosdado Cabello, president of the National Assembly, who has put immense effort into defending the democracy, the constitution, the laws, and the institutions of the republic."

The camera zooms in on the face of Diosdado Cabello, staring furiously into space. Then Rodríguez continues reading: "... and his band attacking me in the National Assembly, there are those who all they do is send formal declarations and tweets."

Rodríguez looks up again: "Here we notice the role play of good cop, bad cop. They ..." He points to the name of Machado and the photo of Tarre, "presidential assassins, coup plotters, and thugs, while there are others playing the role of good cop."

He continues to read the email: "No, I have already decided. This struggle is until the regime is gone, writes María Corina Machado to Señor Gustavo Tarre who has an email address which is also under criminal and penal investigation by the Venezuelan justice system."

The camera zooms in as Rodríguez circles it with his blue pen and triumphantly exclaims: "gtarre@gmail.com"

He continues to read: "Yes, I went to San Cristobal and expressed myself before the OAS."

He looks up at the camera and adds: "Here she recognizes what is already public and notorious, that she was named ambassador of a foreign country—Panama—and as a consequence of being named ambassador, voluntarily and spontaneously, she resigned from her position as deputy of the Venezuelan parliament."

He continues to read: "I am not afraid of anything."

"Drumroll, please," he says as he has now arrived at the part of the email that has been highlighted in yellow. "And please, in a certain country to the north of this continent, translate what I am about to read to the English language."

He reads: "Kevin Whitaker has already confirmed support and indicated the next steps. We are counting on a stronger check-book than the regime's to break the international security zone that the regime has created with taxpayer money."

"Let's make a small parenthesis," Rodríguez continues. "Who is this Mister Kevin Whitaker?"

He takes out another piece of cardboard with a photograph and the CV of Kevin Whitaker glued to it. He then goes on to explain that Whitaker is the current US ambassador to "our sister republic Colombia," with a background in Latin America, El Salvador, and France.

"It is fit to ask oneself, did the State Department of the United States of America know that when the Venezuelan rightwing extremists engage in their criminal activities, in violation of the constitution, peace, and democracy, they ask for instructions and authorization from an official of the North American state department? Did President Barack Obama know? Did the Secretary of State John Kerry know? Did Assistant Secretary of State for Western Hemisphere Affairs Roberta Jacobson know? Or is this Mister Kevin Whitaker acting on his own? Because there is other evidence that incriminates him. We have loads of emails. What we are showing you is just the tip of the iceberg."

VIII

It is September 2014. Juan Carlos is at home in the Caracas apartment where he lives with his parents. He is studying; forcing himself to focus. After all, he has to graduate at some point. He is still president of the student movement. With all the turbulence of the past few months, organizing new student elections has not been possible.

During the first six months of 2014, 6,369 protests occurred, according to the Venezuelan Observatory of Social Conflict. That makes for an average of thirty-five protests per day, with the bulk taking place in February and March.

Then, in June, the number of protests decreased dramatically. People blamed the start of the soccer World Cup in Brazil. It was part joke, part truth. The students were exhausted by the daily marches and the constant drama. Watching the games became a welcomed break and an excuse for those whose youthful invincibility had been replaced by fear.

As for Juan Carlos, he finally had time to reflect on what had been achieved. The photos of lost ones were everywhere. When he asked himself if it had been worth it, "Yes" was the only possible answer. It was inconceivable to look at the faces of the dead and accept that their sacrifice had no worth. If nothing else, they had unmasked the government.

IX

It is December 4, 2014. María Corina Machado arrives outside the National Prosecutor's Office in Caracas. She has come to be indicted as an alleged conspirator in a plot to assassinate President Maduro.

Dressed in riot gear, an imposing contingent of national guardsmen use their shields to create a wall around María Corina. The police have blocked off all surrounding roads, and succeeded in shutting out the vast majority of supporters hoping to accompany Machado all the way to the entrance.

"I have not come to turn myself in. I have come to face the infamy. I am a responsible citizen who defends her rights and duties. And so today I confront the lie with the truth," Machado tells the media before embracing her mother and entering the building with her lawyers.

Her speech is marked by sadness. She looks weary. The general consensus is that she is not likely to come out again. And even if she does, it will only be a temporary respite. In the past few years, Machado has been accused of terrorism, treason, and murder. She has been accused of ordering buses burned, of instigating lawlessness, of "plotting a silent coup," of seeking to generate chaos and panic, of infiltrating provocateurs into queues for scarce basic goods, of killing six guards, of "seeking a civil war," and much more. On various occasions, Machado has had her personal email correspondence read aloud on national television, and personal phone calls and conversations broadcast. She has been called a "whore of the empire," "the worst the homeland has borne," and "the face of fascism." She has been kicked and punched in the face in parliament. Stripped of her parliamentary seat for denouncing human rights violations. Prevented from leaving the country for the past six months. She has been threatened with the death penalty—in a country that doesn't even have the death penalty. And now she is charged with conspiring to assassinate the president.[19]

Shortly after the press conference in May 2014, where Machado was publicly accused by the "High Command of the Bolivarian Revolution," Google certified the emails as forgeries. Machado was subpoenaed and subjected to an eight-hour long interrogation at the prosecutor's office. But nothing more came of it. She was released and the whole event soon forgotten.

Then, suddenly, on November 26, agents of SEBIN came to Machado's home to summon her to the National Prosecutor's Office once more. That morning, Machado had demanded the resignation of the openly loyal Chavista directors of the National Electoral Council.[20]

"They charge me for telling the truth, for calling things by their names, for demanding the resignation of Maduro, and for promoting the struggle and organization of the citizens. Everybody knows there is no crime, but in Venezuela, with its *oficialista* justice system, there doesn't have to be neither crime nor proof to pressure the citizens," Machado tells Colombian television.

* * *

At 1 p.m. on December 4, María Corina Machado leaves the prosecutor's office. The charges against her have changed from plotting to kill the president to conspiracy. There is no word when the trial might start, but she will not go to jail. Not yet. Not today.

The following day, Machado is back at work, organizing civil society in its attempt to put pressure on the government and search for a constitutional solution. Her spark is back. As the motto of the opposition goes: "El que se cansa, pierde" (He who tires loses).

When people ask her how she does it, her standard reply is: "What are my options? Run away? Keep quiet? Give up? Our only option is to fight! ... We were the first nation to dream of independence for South America. I believe that just like 200 years ago, the future of freedom in Latin America is being fought on Venezuelan soil and I'm absolutely convinced that we will triumph as we did 200 years ago."

X

It is an early September morning in 2014. Antonio Rivero stands on the deck of a boat leaving the Venezuelan coast headed for the open sea. Now in his early fifties, Rivero remains fit and strong. His perfectly straight posture gives him an air of military discipline even though he no longer wears a uniform.

His face is turned toward the blue sky, tense with anticipation. Two Sukhoi fighter jets blast by. He sees them before he hears them. His perceptive brown eyes follow them until they disappear on the horizon. He smiles. He could not have asked for a better parting salute.

Since February, he has couch-hopped across the country, hiding in the homes of friends and supporters, never staying more than twenty days in any one place. Virtual communication with other members of the opposition has been difficult, and physical meetings nearly impossible. At times, he disguised himself to participate clandestinely in a protest march, give a few hurried statements to the press, and quickly disappear again. He enjoyed being the chameleon, breaking the isolation, if only temporarily, but he knew it was dangerous.

Eventually, the routine became unsustainable and Rivero decided to go into exile, just as he did twenty years previously. His role was similar then, as were his motives—a democratic Venezuela; a free and progressive country living up to its potential.

It makes him sad to think that, in a way, he contributed to the current disaster. He feels responsible. And now the situation in Venezuela has escalated to a point where he no longer believes democratic and peaceful measures will be enough. Not without a transparent electoral system. Not without an independent justice system. Not when all state employees are political prisoners. Not when a foreign military force has infiltrated the ranks. Not with tens of thousands of Cuban militia ready to defend the revolution. With these obstacles to democratic resolution, Rivero believes forceful action against the regime is justified, that the system is so broken that it couldn't even be called a *coup d'état* anymore. It should happen. It will happen. But he cannot be the one to initiate it. Militaries launch coups, not civilians. He is no longer part of the armed forces. He no longer has command of troops. But if someone who did were to call him and ask him to participate, he would no longer hesitate.

On Venezuela's independence day, July 5, Rivero published nine of the confidential military agreements in his possession. These were documents outlining the secret military agreements between Venezuela and Cuba; documents he had previously referred to, but never disclosed. In doing so, Rivero knowingly gave the government legitimate grounds to try him for treason. Yet, he did it out of loyalty to Venezuela, its sovereignty, and its constitution.

As the boat heads out to sea, gray clouds amass on the horizon. Soon, Venezuela's coastline disappears in the distance and Rivero finds himself already fantasizing about his return.

XI

"Our Chávez, who art in heaven, in the earth, in the sea, and in we the delegates, hallowed be thy name." The words of PSUV delegate María Estrella Uribe resonate before an audience of loyal Chavistas.

It is September 1, 2014, and the party congress of Venezuela's socialist party, PSUV, is coming to an end. And what better way to finish than by reciting the new rendition of "The Lord's Prayer," featuring Venezuela's new deity, Hugo Chávez Frías.

A chapel in Caracas has declared him a saint; one church even tried unsuccessfully to make him bishop posthumously.[21] Frequently depicted with a Christian cross, many followers have come to believe Chávez was on a divine mission.

Few would argue that Chávez wasn't good-intentioned and genuine about his dream to erase poverty. Toward that end, he poured billions of dollars of oil money and expropriated assets. He helped the poor develop self-esteem, taught them that their needs were important, and that they deserved a place at the table. According to government statistics, poverty was reduced from 44 percent in 1998 to 27 percent in 2011 under his rule. But considering the colossal amount of social spending, that is still a humble outcome. According to the UN, poverty in Venezuela fell by 40 percent between 2002 and 2011. In Brazil, poverty fell by 44 percent, in Chile by 46 percent, and in Peru by 50 percent in that same period. Unlike Venezuela, they also managed to diversify their economies and invest in infrastructure to create sustainable growth. And they did it without the oil wealth or the incendiary revolutionary rhetoric of Chávez.

Chávez passed away before losing a presidential election. Perhaps that saved him from moving into the pantheon of dictators. When he lost the referendum in 2007, he ignored the will of the people, pushing through most of his proposed changes anyway and putting the issue of term limits to a new vote the following year. Had he lost an election, his record suggests a reluctant handover of power.

Supporters say Chávez lives in the rain, in the wind, in each of them. He is magical realism embodied. Those who don't believe still can't escape him. His face stares back from the sides of buildings, murals, posters, and paintings across the nation. His quotes and recordings are everywhere. Chavistas invoke him on a daily basis. Like Bolívar, Chávez is no longer here, but his voice endures. And his ghost remains the main challenge to the opposition.

"Thy legacy come, so we can spread it to people here and elsewhere. Give us this day your light and guide us. Lead us not into the temptation of capitalism; but deliver us from the evil of oligarchy, like the crime of contraband, because ours is the homeland, the peace, and the life. Forever and ever. Amen."

With her fist clenched, María Estrella Uribe beholds her fellow party delegates, raises her left arm straight up in the air and shouts: "¡Viva Chávez!"

EPILOGUE

It is November 2013. On the beautiful Spanish archway that marks the entrance to Puerto de La Mar, a massive UBV sign has been stapled. It reads Universidad Bolivariana de Venezuela. The gate is plastered with election posters of past and future candidates—"Dante Rivas for Mayor" and "Vote for Maduro." The beams of the archway, once painted white, have turned gray from dirt and neglect.

When the government took over, the goal was to accommodate 5,000 students. But, since Puerto de La Mar was designed as a port, there were no classrooms. In the five years that have passed since expropriation, there has been no maintenance, never mind the necessary renovations needed to support any more than a few hundred students.

The receptionist claims the campus has 400 students, but on this Monday morning, no more than a couple of dozen are scattered in small groups amid the rubble. They sit on red plastic chairs around plastic cafeteria tables, under the open sky, or, when it rains, under the archways.

Many of the cobblestones leading up to the entrance are gone, leaving water to collect in massive puddles in their place. The paint is peeling and plaster is crumbling off the walls of the buildings. Wall lights hang from their cables. Across the terracotta colored stones that make up the plaza, someone has written VIVA CHÁVEZ in big block letters. The beautiful fountain on Plaza La Sirena sits dry. Strings of dried mud hang from the mouths of the decorative fish heads that once sprayed water into the surrounding pool.

* * *

On Playa Guaraguao, a short walk from the ruins of Puerto de La Mar, sits fifty-nine-year-old Oscar Lozada, gazing out at the sea. The sun reflects in the waves, making his warm brown eyes sparkle. Oscar is one of the fishermen who opposed the development of Puerto de La Mar. Wilmer González, as well as most of the other fishermen, are out at sea, but Oscar has taken the day off to participate in a rally for the local candidate of the socialist party in the upcoming elections. He is dressed in a red shirt and a PSUV baseball cap.

Even on a day off, like today, he comes down to the beach to watch the others bring in the daily catch. Born and raised a fisherman here on Margarita, he finds it hard to stay away.

A few customers have started to gather. The fishermen don't have any equipment to keep their catch cool, so everything must be sold immediately. The fish is often so fresh that it is still alive when they carry it ashore.

Playa Guaraguao is the base of about two dozen traditional fishermen as well as boat-builder Rafael, whom everybody calls Tonnton. He makes beautiful wooden fishing boats entirely by hand.

Even now, with most of the sardines gone, Oscar Lozada is happy that nothing ever came of Puerto de La Mar. Life would have been very different had things proceeded according to plan. Wealth promised to the people never trickles down. Oscar is convinced any profit would have stayed with the owners of the port and its businesses.

"We should just be grateful to have the richness of the sea," he reflects as he looks out at the turquoise waters where there is still no sign of the returning boats.

* * *

Sheets of plywood painted by students block some of the openings and arches at Puerto de La Mar. One painting depicts the great Liberator Simón Bolívar waving a sword that has the word *Patria*—homeland—written in big, blood red letters across its blade. The other depicts a contemplative Comandante sitting alone on a fence against a backdrop of blue ocean and blue skies. Two of the vendor carts, missing their wheels and canvas roofs, remain standing. The others lay collapsed in ruin.

The grooves in the steps of the non-functional escalator to the second floor of the port building are filled with little pebbles. Plastic bags and cups are jammed between the steps. Garbage punctuates the floors. Armies of weeds are moving in. Socialist graffiti mocking the logos of the world's most recognizable brands adorn the walls. Instead of Adidas—*Adiccion* (addiction). Retailer and Puerto de La Mar investor Rattan has been converted to *Ratas* (rats). The logo of the other investor—Conferry—has been transformed to *Sinferry* (without ferry). Burger King is rehashed as *Burdel* (brothel) King and McDonald's as *McLandro's* (McDelinquent).

The white walls have tie-dye-like patterns of gray, brown, and black from exposure to the weather and lack of maintenance. Decaying palm leaves litter the plazas like fallen soldiers.

Toppled from his pedestal and placed upright upon the ground among a scattering of red plastic chairs, stands the pale, white bust of Simón Bolívar. Limbless but dressed in his finest general's coat, he surveys the battlefield from the sidelines, staring down at the advancing army of weeds, coming for him in their tireless effort to liberate the land.

NOTES

PROLOGUE

1. King, Kiki, "24,000 Murders Last Year Confirm Venezuela as One of the World's Most Dangerous Countries," *The Guardian*, January 12, 2014; http://www.theguardian.com/world/2014/jan/12/violent-crime-makes-venezuela-dangerous.

1. ORIGINS

1. Arana, Marie, *Bolívar: American Liberator*, London: Simon & Schuster, 2013, p. 66.
2. Blanco, Eduardo, *Venezuela heroica: Historical Vignettes*, trans. Götz, Ignacio, L., New York: Peter Lang, 2016, p. 2.
3. Arana, *Bolívar*, p. 100.
4. Ibid., pp. 129–33.
5. Ibid., pp. 134–5.
6. Ibid., pp. 337–8.
7. Ibid., pp. 339–42.
8. Ibid., p. 351.
9. *Caudillos*, a type of warlord or authoritarian strongmen.
10. Bolivar, Simon, *El Libertador: Writings of Simon Bolivar*, trans. Fornoff, Frederick, Oxford: Oxford University Press, 2003, p. 144.
11. Arana, *Bolívar*, p. 450.
12. Speech delivered by Páez at Government House, at the conclusion of the public ceremonies, December 23, 1842, in *Autobiografía, II*, p. 356,

quoted in Lynch, John, *Simon Bolívar: A Life*, New Haven: Yale University Press, 2007, chapter 12.

13. Arana, *Bolívar*, p. 460.
14. Ibid., p. 461.
15. Ibid.
16. Ibid.
17. Gobierno Bolivariano de Venezuela, Comisión Presidencial para la Conmemoración del Bicentenario de la Independencia de la República Bolivariana de Venezuela, "Venezuela celebró el Centenario del natalicio del Padre de la Patria, Independencia 200," 2010; i200.cnh.gob.ve/pdfs/1883.pdf (accessed April 20, 2016).
18. Gobierno Bolivariano de Venezuela, Comisión Presidencial para la Conmemoración del Bicentenario de la Independencia de la República Bolivariana de Venezuela, "Inaugurado ferrocarril Caracas-La Guaira, Independencia 200," 2010; i200.cnh.gob.ve/pdfs/1883.pdf (accessed April 20, 2016).
19. Castillo Herrera, Luis Fernando, "La exposición nacional de 1883: Memoria, identidad y nación," *Tzintzun*, 56 (2012), pp. 228–32; http://www.scielo.org.mx/scielo.php?script=sci_arttext&pid=S0188–28722012000200008 (accessed April 20, 2016).
20. Calzadilla, Pedro Enrique. "La exposición nacional de 1883: Balance simbólico y exhibición identitaria," *Tierra Firme*, 21, 81 (2003), pp. 77–95; http://www2.scielo.org.ve/scielo.php?script=sci_arttext&pid=S0798–29682003000100007 (accessed April 20, 2016).
21. Arana, *Bolívar*, p. 461.
22. Burbach, Roger, Michael Fox, and Federico Fuentes, *Latin America's Turbulent Transitions: The Future of Twenty-First-Century Socialism*, Kindle edn, London: Zed Books, 2013, loc. 1075.
23. Archivo del Libertador, "Larga travesía de un archivo," Bolivarium, Instituto de Investigaciones Históricas, Universidad Simón Bolívar; http://libertador.bolivarium.usb.ve/presentacion1.html (accessed April 28, 2016).
24. Bercovitch, Alexander Philip, "The Bolivar Archive: Politicizing the Past in Venezuela 1962–2010," BA thesis, Department of History, Harvard University, Cambridge, MA, 2014, p. 44.

25. Ibid.
26. Ibid.
27. Ibid., p. 45.
28. Ibid., p. 48.
29. Ibid., p. 52.
30. Ibid., pp. 26–7.
31. Ibid.
32. Ibid., p. 28.
33. Ibid., pp. 27–31.
34. Tarver, Michael, and Julia C. Frederick, *The History of Venezuela*, Kindle edn, Westport, CT: Greenwood Press, 2005, loc. 1400.
35. Ottawa, Marina, *Democracy Challenged: The Rise of Semi-authoritarianism*, Washington, DC: Carnegie Endowment for Peace, 2003, p. 78.
36. Ibid.
37. Bercovitch, "Bolivar Archive," p. 31.
38. Tarver and Frederick, location 1400.
39. Bercovitch, "Bolivar Archive," pp. 34–5.
40. Ibid, p. 35.
41. Tarver and Frederick, *History of Venezuela*, loc. 1500.
42. Ibid.
43. Bercovitch, "Bolivar Archive," pp. 36–41.
44. Ibid., p. 32.
45. Ibid., pp. 32–3.
46. Tarver and Frederick, *History of Venezuela*, loc. 1508.
47. Ibid., loc. 1516–69.
48. Ibid., loc. 1647.
49. Ibid., loc. 1686–865.
50. Toro, Francisco, and Juan Cristobal Nagel, *Blogging the Revolution: Caracas Chronicles and the Hugo Chávez Era*, ebook edn, Key Biscayne: Cognitio Books, 2013, loc. 314.
51. Bercovitch, "Bolivar Archive."
52. Nation Master, "Economy: GDP Per Capita in 1950; Countries Compared"; http://www.nationmaster.com/country-info/stats/Economy/GDP-per-capita-in-1950 (accessed February 2015).
53. Tarver, Michael H., with Alfredo Angulo, Rathnam Indurthy, and

Luis Loaiza Rincón, *Venezuelan Insurgency, 1960–1968*, Bloomington: Xlibris, 2001, pp. 84–5.

54. Carroll, Rory, *Comandante: The Life and Legacy of Hugo Chávez*, ebook edn, Edinburgh: Canongate, 2013, loc. 1141.
55. Ibid., loc. 1159–90.
56. Bercovitch, "Bolivar Archive," pp. 85–6.
57. Carroll, *Comandante*, loc. 1159–90.
58. Gott, Richard, *In the Shadow of the Liberator: Hugo Chávez and the Transformation of Venezuela*, London: Verso, 2000, pp. 40–1.
59. A *llanero* (literally meaning plainsman) is a Venezuelan or Colombian herder. The name comes from the Llanos grasslands in Western Venezuela and Eastern Colombia. The *llaneros* have a mixture of Spanish and Indian heritage, and a distinctive culture known for its music and storytelling.

2. THE CALL TO PURPOSE

1. Gott, Richard, *Hugo Chávez and the Bolivarian Revolution*, London: Verso, 2005, pp. 64–6.
2. Ibid., p. 66.

3. TESTS, ALLIES, AND ENEMIES

1. Radio Caracas Television, RCTV, *¿Quien es quien en el gobierno de Hugo Chávez?* Golpe de estado Venezuela, November 27, 1992, broadcast November 27, 2012.
2. Ibid.
3. *Tapaditos* are small boats that go back and forth to the mainland transporting low-income travelers and workers.
4. Caldera, Rafael, speech to the Venezuelan Congress on February 4, 1992; http://www.soberania.org/Articulos/articulo_6025.htm
5. Bercovitch, Alexander Philip, "The Bolivar Archive: Politicizing the Past in Venezuela 1962–2010," BA thesis, Department of History, Harvard University, Cambridge, MA, 2014, p. 62.
6. Carroll, Rory, *Comandante: The Life and Legacy of Hugo Chávez*, ebook edn, Edinburgh: Canongate, 2013, loc. 1335.
7. McCaughan, Michael, *The Battle of Venezuela*, London: Latin America Bureau, 2004, p. 32.

8. Wilpert, Gregory, "Venezuela's Mission to Fight Poverty," Venezuela Analysis, November 11, 2003; http://venezuelanalysis.com/analysis/213#_ftn7
9. Kelly, Janet, and Pedro Palma, "The Syndrome of Economic Decline and the Quest for Change," in McCoy, Jennifer, and David Myers (eds), *The Unraveling of Representative Democracy in Venezuela*, Baltimore: Johns Hopkins University Press, 2006, p. 207.
10. Bercovitch, "Bolivar Archive," pp. 66–7.
11. McDermott, Jeremy, "Hugo Chávez Invents New Half-Hour Time Zone," *The Telegraph*, December 9, 2007, http://www.telegraph.co.uk/news/worldnews/1572014/Hugo-Chavez-invents-new-half-hour-time-zone.html
12. Nolan, Rachel, "The Realest Reality Show in the World," *The New York Times*, May 4, 2012; http://www.nytimes.com/2012/05/06/magazine/hugo-chavezs-totally-bizarre-talk-show.html?pagewanted=all&_r=0

4. THE ORDEAL

1. Morrison, David, "Hugo Chávez: The Man Who Raised Oil Prices," Labour & Trade Union Review, November 2000.
2. Conway, Christopher, "Afterword: Bolivarian Self-fashioning into the Twenty-First Century," in Conway, *The Cult of Bolívar in Latin American Literature*, Gainesville: University Press of Florida, 2003, p. 158.
3. Marcano, Cristina, "Las relaciones desmedidas," *El País*, March 30, 2014.
4. "MARN otorga permiso al Puerto de La Mar," *El Sol de Margarita*, July 23, 2006.

5. THE PUNISHMENT

1. Frontline, PBS, *The Hugo Chávez Show*, broadcast November 19, 2008; http://www.pbs.org/wgbh/pages/frontline/hugochavez/view/
2. Ibid.
3. Mander, Benedict, "Venezuela: Up in Smoke," *Financial Times*, September 16, 2012.
4. Carroll, Rory, *Comandante: The Life and Legacy of Hugo Chávez*, ebook-edn, Edinburgh: Canongate, 2013, loc. 1389.

5. Carroll, *Comandante*, loc. 1389.
6. Ibid., loc. 1376.
7. "Chávez Defeats Recall Attempt," *Washington Post*, August 17, 2004; http://www.washingtonpost.com/wp-dyn/articles/A4208–2004Aug16.html
8. BBC News, "Rallies as Venezuelan TV Closes," May 28, 2007; http://news.bbc.co.uk/1/hi/6696699.stm
9. Carroll, *Comandante*, loc. 1460.
10. BBC News, "Students Stage Anti-Chávez Rally," 30 November, 2007; http://news.bbc.co.uk/1/hi/world/americas/7120133.stm
11. Carroll, Comandante, loc. 1092 and 1491.
12. Carroll, *Comandante*, loc. 1601.
13. Ibid., loc. 3496.

6. DEATH, RESURRECTION, AND DELUSION

1. Marcano, Cristina, "Las relaciones desmedidas," *El País*, March, 30, 2014.
2. Ibid.
3. Ibid.
4. Delgado, Antonio María, "Deserciones masivas de médicos cubanos en Venezuela," *El Nuevo Herald*, May 5, 2014.
5. Marcano, "Las relaciones desmedidas."
6. NTN24, "María Corina Machado asegura haber dado un paso para conseguir la democracia en Vzla," July 2, 2014; http://www.ntn24.com/noticia/María-corina-machado-asegura-haber-dado-un-paso-para-conseguir-la-democracia-en-vzla-17322
7. Voice of America News, "Venezuelan Steel Company Vows to Fight Expropriation," October 31, 2010; http://www.voanews.com/a/venezuelan-steel-company-vows-to-fight-expropriation—106480878/164137.html
8. Reportero 24, "Sidetur: Impiden protestar a los trabajadores", November 2, 2010, http://www.reportero24.com/2010/11/sidetur-impiden-protestar-a-trabajadores/
9. Márquez, Humberto, "Brazil's Capitalist Invasion Builds Socialism 'a la Venezuela,'" IPS News, November 20, 2010; www.ipsnews.net

10. Rodríguez, Dulce María, "13,4 millardos de dólares debe el Gobierno a empresas expropiadas," *El Nacional*, January 12, 2013.
11. Carroll, location 2039.
12. Carroll, Rory, *Comandante: The Life and Legacy of Hugo Chávez*, ebook edn, Edinburgh: Canongate, 2013, loc. 2044.
13. *Colectivos* (collectives, literally translated), is a term that covers revolutionary pro-government community movements of various kinds, most of them non-violent. The term has come to be associated in particular with the armed groups of the extreme left that have gained influence since the rise of Chávez.
14. Ibid., loc. 2050.
15. Márquez, Humberto, "Venezuela: Reviving the Debate on Presidential Reelection," IPS News, December 1, 2008; http://www.ipsnews.net/2008/12/venezuela-reviving-the-debate-on-presidential-reelection/
16. Carroll, *Comandante*, loc. 2050.
17. Ibid., loc. 2065.
18. "Diez razones para amar a Chávez," *El País*, January 30, 2009; http://internacional.elpais.com/internacional/2009/01/30/actualidad/1233270004_850215.html
19. Carroll, *Comandante*, loc. 3588.
20. "Cubanos en Venezuela," *El Universal*, May 5, 2013; http://www.eluniversal.com/nacional-y-politica/130505/cubanos-en-venezuela.

7. GOLIATH WINS

1. Marcano, Ender, "Sidetur denuncia ocupación ilegal de todas sus instalaciones," *El Universal*, October 30, 2012.
2. "A Total of 3,040,449 Votes Were Cast in Opposition Primary Election," *El Universal*, February 14, 2012.
3. Carroll, Rory, *Comandante: The Life and Legacy of Hugo Chávez*, ebook edn, Edinburgh: Canongate, 2013, loc. 3580.
4. Ibid., loc. 3644.
5. Ibid., loc. 3730.
6. Watts, Jonathan, "Venezuela Election: Chávez Holds Mass Rally on Final Day of Campaigning," *The Guardian*, October 5, 2012; http://

www.theguardian.com/world/2012/oct/05/venezuela-election-Chávez-rally

7. Carroll, *Comandante*, loc. 3771.
8. Ibid., loc. 3792.
9. Sosa, Charlette, "New Venezuelan Report Preaches Sabotage at Amuay Tragedy," Pan Am Post, September 12, 2013; http://panampost.com/charlette-sosa/2013/09/12/new-venezuelan-report-preaches-sabotage-at-amuay-tragedy/; Rosati, Andrew, "What Was behind Venezuela's Deadly Oil Refinery Explosion?," *The Christian Science Monitor*, September 16, 2013; http://www.csmonitor.com/World/Americas/2013/0916/What-was-behind-Venezuela-s-deadly-oil-refinery-explosion
10. Author interview with Ramírez, Eddie, head of the Gente del Petróleo NGO, November 2013.
11. Rosati, "What Was behind Venezuela's Deadly Oil Refinery Explosion?"
12. Sosa, "New Venezuelan Report Preaches Sabotage at Amuay Tragedy."
13. Author interview with Ramírez, Eddie, November 2013.
14. Carroll, *Comandante*, loc. 2202.
15. Ibid., loc. 2204.
16. Ibid., loc. 3186.
17. Carroll, location 3193–3220.
18. Carroll, location 3257.
19. Ibid., loc. 3264.
20. BBC News, "Venezuela Judge Maria Afiuni Moved to House Arrest," February 3, 2011; http://www.bbc.co.uk/news/world-latin-america-12350814
21. Neuman, William, and María Eugenia, "Court in Venezuela Orders Release of a Judge Once Scorned and Jailed by Chávez," *The New York Times*, June 14, 2013; http://www.nytimes.com/2013/06/15/world/americas/court-in-venezuela-orders-release-of-a-judge-once-scorned-and-jailed-by-chavez.html?_r=0

9. NO MAN'S LAND

1. Cawthorne, Andrew, and Deisy Buitrago, "Chávez Protégé Invokes Venezuelan Curse on Opposition Voters," Reuters, April 7, 2013; http://

in.reuters.com/article/2013/04/07/venezuela-election-Chávez-macarapana-idINDEE93600B20130407

2. "Maduro se burla de Capriles a ritmo de rap," *Republica*, April 4, 2013; http://www.republica.com/2013/04/07/maduro-se-burla-de-capriles-a-ritmo-de-rap/
3. Robertson, Ewan, "Venezuela's Snap Presidential Election: A Campaign without Issues?," Venezuela Analysis, April 8, 2013; www.venezuela-analysis.com; Palmgren, Lars, "Starka känslor i Venezuelas valkampanj," Ekot, Swedish Radio, April 9, 2013; http://sverigesradio.se/sida/artikel.aspx?programid=83&artikel=5498779
4. Carroll, *Comandante*, loc. 3816.
5. Rueda, Manuel, "Chávez Tattoos Express Love for Socialism and Possible Cult of Personality," ABC News, April 12, 2013; http://abc-news.go.com/ABC_Univision/News/Chávez-tattoos-express-love-socialism-cult-personality/story?id=18939466
6. Calviño, Frank, "Tattooing Chávez: The Art of Suppressing the Individual," PanAm Post, August 4, 2014; http://blog.panampost.com/frank-calvino/2014/08/04/tattooing-Chávez-the-art-of-suppressing-the-individual/
7. Neuman, William, "*Post-election Tensions Escalate in Venezuela as Demonstrations Turn Deadly*," *The New York Times*, April 16, 2013.
8. Carlson, Chris, "Venezuela's Electoral Council Says Capriles Lacks Proof of Fraud," Venezuela Analysis, April 28, 2013; http://venezuel-analysis.com/news/8905.
9. CNN, "Venezuela Accuses American Filmmaker of Instigating Unrest," April 27, 2013; http://edition.cnn.com/2013/04/26/world/americas/venezuela-american-arrested/
10. "Detuvieron al general Antonio Rivero," *La Nación*, April 28, 2013; http://www.lanacion.com.ve/nacional/detuvieron-al-general-antonio-rivero/
11. López, Leopoldo, "Leopoldo López a Maduro: 'Hagan lo que hagan no vamos a retroceder en nuestra lucha pacífica,'" April 27, 2013; http://www.leopoldolopez.com/leopoldo-lopez-a-maduro-hagan-lo-que-hagan-no-vamos-a-retroceder-en-nuestra-lucha-pacifica/
12. Amnesty International, "Document: Venezuela; Opposition Politician

Arbitrarily Detained; Antonio Rivero," UA: 115/13 Index: AMR 53/006/2013 Venezuela, May 8, 2013.

13. Bacchi, Umberto, "Venezuela MPs Brawl in Parliament: Politicians Trade Punches over Opposition Speaking Ban," International Business Times, May 1, 2013; http://www.ibtimes.co.uk/venezuela-parliament-fight-video-463260
14. Bernal, Pilar, "Petare, el barrio más peligroso de Caracas," Informativos Telecinco, October 12, 2012; http://www.telecinco.es/informativos/internacional/Venezuela-Petare-Caracas-barrio_2_1488930040.html
15. Carroll, *Comandante*, loc. 2035.
16. "Venezuela's Militia, A Caribbean Tripoli?," *The Economist*, April 7, 2011.
17. Naím, Moisés, "¿Cómo conquistó Cuba a Venezuela?," *El País*, April 19, 2014.
18. Wallis, Daniel, and Diego Ore, "At Least Two Killed by Gunfire at Venezuela Protests," Reuters, February 12, 2014.
19. Crisis Group Latin America Briefing, "Venezuela: Tipping Point," no. 30, May 21, 2014, p. 7.
20. Ibid.
21. Human Rights Watch, "Punished for Protesting: Rights Violations in Venezuela's Streets, Detention Centers, and Justice System," May 2014, pp. 49–53.
22. Ibid.
23. Ibid.
24. Ibid.
25. Ibid.
26. Crisis Group Latin America Briefing, "Venezuela: Tipping Point," p. 13.

10. ENDGAME

1. "Venezuela Jails 2 More Opposition Leaders," Associated Press, March 20, 2014; http://www.cbc.ca/news/world/venezuela-jails-2-more-opposition-leaders-1.2580726
2. Kurmanaev, Anatoly, and Corina Pons, "Venezuela Arrests Mayor of City Where Nationwide Unrest Began," Bloomberg Business Week, March 20, 2014; www.businessweek.com/news/2014–03–20/venezuela-arrests-mayor-of-city-where-nationwide-unrest-began

3. Vyas, Kejal, and Minaya Ezequiel, "Venezuela Opposition Lawmaker Returns in Challenge to Government," *Wall Street Journal*, March 27, 2014.
4. Vyas, Kejal, and Sara Schaefer Muñoz, "Venezuela Court Sentences Leopoldo Lopez to More Than 13 Years in Prison," *Wall Street Journal*, September 11, 2015.
5. Vyas and Ezequiel, "Venezuela Opposition Lawmaker Returns."
6. BBC News, "Venezuela Opposition Congresswoman's Mandate Revoked,"March26,2014;http://www.bbc.co.uk/news/world-latin-america-26726282
7. Sky News, "Venezuela Ministry Torched by Protesters," April 2, 2014; https://uk.news.yahoo.com/venezuela-ministry-torched-protesters-094601485.html#GVn5BMs
8. Ibid.
9. Ibid.
10. Ibid.
11. Trujillo, Manuel Rubén, "Maduro revela que hay un detenido por ataques a ministerio de Vivienda," *El Universal*, April 3, 2014.
12. Crisis Group Latin America Briefing, "Venezuela: Tipping Point," pp. 7–8.
13. Ibid., p. 8.
14. Ibid., p. 12.
15. Ibid.
16. Human Rights Watch, "Punished for Protesting," p. 2.
17. Crisis Group Latin America Briefing, "Venezuela: Tipping Point," p. 12.
18. Escalona, Yanet, "Aprueban nueva resolución para sardina," *El Sol de Margarita*, December 14, 2013; http://www.elsoldemargarita.com.ve/posts/post/id:125563/Aprueban-nueva-resolución-para-sardina
19. Toro, Francisco, "The A-to-Z of Violating María Corina Machado's Rights," Caracas Chronicles, December 3, 2014; http://caracaschronicles.com/2014/12/03/the-a-z-of-violations-of-María-corina-machados-rights/
20. Duarte, Emiliana, "María Corina, and a Unified Theory of Rationed Repression," Caracas Chronicles, December 2, 2014; http://caracas-

chronicles.com/2014/12/02/María-corina-and-why-rationed-repression-is-the-worst-kind/

21. Rueda, "Chávez Tattoos Express Love for Socialism."

BIBLIOGRAPHY

Books and reports

Amnesty International, "Document: Venezuela; Opposition Politician Arbitrarily Detained; Antonio Rivero," UA: 115/13 Index: AMR 53/006/2013 Venezuela, May 8, 2013; http://www.amnesty.org/en/library/asset/AMR53/006/2013/en/81a64cc1-b660-41e4-9e16-ad-85cb5ae58a/amr530062013en.html

Arana, Marie, *Bolívar: American Liberator*, London: Simon & Schuster, 2013.

Archivo del Libertador, "Larga travesía de un archivo," Bolivarium, Instituto de Investigaciones Históricas, Universidad Simón Bolívar, Caracas, Venezuela; http://libertador.bolivarium.usb.ve/presentacion1.html, (accessed April 28, 2016).

Bercovitch, Alexander Philip, "The Bolivar Archive: Politicizing the Past in Venezuela 1962–2010," BA thesis, Department of History, Harvard University, Cambridge, MA, 2014.

Blanco, Eduardo, *Venezuela heroica: Historical Vignettes*, trans. Götz, Ignacio, L., New York: Peter Lang, 2016.

Bolivar, Simón, *El Libertador: Writings of Simón Bolivar*, trans. Fornoff, Frederick, Oxford: Oxford University Press, 2003.

Carroll, Rory, *Comandante: The Life and Legacy of Hugo Chávez*, Edinburgh: Canongate Books, 2013.

Crisis Group Latin America Briefing, "Venezuela: Tipping Point," no. 30, May 21, 2014.

Gobierno Bolivariano de Venezuela, Comisión Presidencial para la Conmemoración del Bicentenario de la Independencia de la República Bolivariana de Venezuela, "Inaugurado ferrocarril Caracas-La Guaira, Independencia 200," 2010; i200.cnh.gob.ve/pdfs/1883.pdf (accessed April 20, 2016).

——— "Venezuela celebró el Centenario del natalicio del Padre de la Patria, Independencia 200," 2010; i200.cnh.gob.ve/pdfs/1883.pdf (accessed April 20, 2016).

Gott, Richard, *Hugo Chávez and the Bolivarian Revolution*, London: Verso, 2005.

——— *In the Shadow of the Liberator: Hugo Chávez and the Transformation of Venezuela*, London: Verso, 2000.

Human Rights Watch, "Punished for Protesting: Rights Violations in Venezuela's Streets, Detention Centers, and Justice System," May 2014.

Kelly, Janet, and Pedro Palma, "The Syndrome of Economic Decline and the Quest for Change", in McCoy, Jennifer, and David Myers (eds), *The Unraveling of Representative Democracy in Venezuela*, Baltimore: Johns Hopkins University Press, 2006.

Lynch, John, *Simón Bolívar: A Life*, New Haven: Yale University Press, 2007.

McCaughan, Michael, *The Battle of Venezuela*, London: Latin America Bureau, 2004.

Ottawa, Marina, *Democracy Challenged: The Rise of Semi-authoritarianism*, Washington, DC: Carnegie Endowment for Peace, 2003.

Tarver, H. Michael, *Venezuelan Insurgency, 1960–1968: A Successful Failure*, Bloomington: Xlibris, 2001.

Toro, Francisco, and Juan Cristobal Nagel, *Blogging the Revolution: Caracas Chronicles and the Hugo Chávez Era*, Key Biscayne: Cognitio Books, 2013.

Articles and televised broadcasts

Associated Press, "Venezuela Jails 2 More Opposition Leaders," March 20, 2014; http://www.cbc.ca/news/world/venezuela-jails-2-more-opposition-leaders-1.2580726

Bacchi, Umberto, "Venezuela MPs Brawl in Parliament: Politicians Trade

Punches over Opposition Speaking Ban," International Business Times, May 1, 2013; http://www.ibtimes.co.uk/venezuela-parliament-fight-video-463260

BBC News, "Rallies as Venezuelan TV Closes," May 28, 2007; http://news.bbc.co.uk/1/hi/6696699.stm

——— "Students Stage Anti-Chávez Rally," November 30, 2007; http://news.bbc.co.uk/1/hi/world/americas/7120133.stm

——— "Venezuela Judge Maria Afiuni Moved to House Arrest," February 3, 2011; http://www.bbc.co.uk/news/world-latin-america-12350814.

——— "Venezuela Opposition Congresswoman's Mandate Revoked," March 26, 2014; http://www.bbc.co.uk/news/world-latin-america-267 26282

Bernal, Pilar, "Petare, el barrio más peligroso de Caracas," Informativos Telecinco, October 12, 2012; http://www.telecinco.es/informativos/internacional/Venezuela-Petare-Caracas-barrio_2_1488930040.html

Caldera, Rafael, "Speech to the Venezuelan Congress," February 4, 1992; http://www.soberania.org/Articulos/articulo_6025.htm

Calviño, Frank, "Tattooing Chávez: The Art of Suppressing the Individual," PanAm Post, August 4, 2014; http://blog.panampost.com/frank-calvino/2014/08/04/tattooing-chavez-the-art-of-suppressing-the-individual/

Calzadilla, Pedro Enrique, "La exposición nacional de 1883: balance simbólico y exhibición identitaria," *Tierra Firme*, 21, 81, Caracas (March 2003), pp. 77–95; http://www2.scielo.org.ve/scielo.php?script=sci_arttext&pid=S0798–29682003000100007

Carlson, Chris, "Venezuela's Electoral Council Says Capriles Lacks Proof of Fraud," Venezuela Analysis, April 28, 2013; http://venezuelanalysis.com/news/8905

Castillo Herrera, Luis Fernando, "La exposición nacional de 1883: memoria, identidad y nación," *Tzintzun*, 56 (2012), pp. 228–32; http://www.scielo.org.mx/scielo.php?script=sci_arttext&pid=S0188–28722012000200008 (accessed April 20, 2016).

Cawthorne, Andrew, and Deisy Buitrago, "Chávez Protégé Invokes Venezuelan Curse on Opposition Voters," Reuters, April 7, 2013; http://

in.reuters.com/article/2013/04/07/venezuela-election-chavez-macarapana-idINDEE93600B20130407

"Chávez Defeats Recall Attempt," *Washington Post*, August 17, 2004; http://www.washingtonpost.com/wp-dyn/articles/A4208–2004Aug16.html

CNN, "Venezuela Accuses American Filmmaker of Instigating Unrest," April 27, 2013; http://edition.cnn.com/2013/04/26/world/americas/venezuela-american-arrested/

"Cubanos en Venezuela," *El Universal*, May 5, 2013; http://www.eluniversal.com/nacional-y-politica/130505/cubanos-en-venezuela

Delgado, Antonio Maria, "Deserciones masivas de médicos cubanos en Venezuela," *El Nuevo Herald*, May 5, 2014.

"Detuvieron al general Antonio Rivero," *La Nación*, April 28, 2013; http://www.lanacion.com.ve/nacional/detuvieron-al-general-antonio-rivero/

"Diez razones para amar a Chávez," *El País*, January 30, 2009; http://internacional.elpais.com/internacional/2009/01/30/actualidad/1233270004_850215.html

Duarte, Emiliana, "María Corina, and a Unified Theory of Rationed Repression," Caracas Chronicles, December 2, 2014; http://caracaschronicles.com/2014/12/02/maria-corina-and-why-rationed-repression-is-the-worst-kind/

Escalona, Yanet, "Aprueban nueva resolución para sardina," *El Sol de Margarita*, December 14, 2013; http://www.elsoldemargarita.com.ve/posts/post/id:125563/Aprueban-nueva-resolución-para-sardina

Frontline, PBS, *The Hugo Chávez Show*, broadcast November 19, 2008; http://www.pbs.org/wgbh/pages/frontline/hugochavez/view/

King, Kiki, "24,000 Murders Last Year Confirm Venezuela as One of the World's Most Dangerous Countries," *The Guardian*, January 12, 2014; http://www.theguardian.com/world/2014/jan/12/violent-crime-makes-venezuela-dangerous

Kurmanaev, Anatoly, and Corina Rodríguez Pons, "Venezuela Arrests Mayor of City Where Nationwide Unrest Began," Bloomberg Business Week, March 20, 2014; www.businessweek.com/news/2014–03–20/venezuela-arrests-mayor-of-city-where-nationwide-unrest-began

"Maduro se burla de Capriles a ritmo de rap," *Republica*, April 4, 2013; http://www.republica.com/2013/04/07/maduro-se-burla-de-capriles-a-ritmo-de-rap/

Mander, Benedict, "Venezuela: Up in Smoke," *Financial Times*, September 16, 2012.

Marcano, Cristina, "Las relaciones desmedidas", *El País*, March 30, 2014.

Marcano, Ender, "Sidetur denuncia ocupación ilegal de todas sus instalaciones," *El Universal*, October 30, 2012.

"MARN otorga permiso al Puerto de La Mar," *El Sol de Margarita*, July 23, 2006.

Márquez, Humberto, "Brazil's Capitalist Invasion Builds Socialism 'a la Venezuela,'" IPS News, November 20, 2010; www.ipsnews.net

——— "Venezuela: Reviving the Debate on Presidential Reelection," IPS News, December 1, 2008; http://www.ipsnews.net/2008/12/venezuela-reviving-the-debate-on-presidential-reelection/

McDermott, Jeremy, "Hugo Chávez Invents New Half-Hour Time Zone," *The Telegraph*, December 9, 2007; http://www.telegraph.co.uk/news/worldnews/1572014/Hugo-Chavez-invents-new-half-hour-time-zone.html

Morrison, David, "Hugo Chávez: The Man Who Raised Oil Prices," *Labour & Trade Union Review*, November 2000.

Naím, Moisés, "¿Cómo conquistó Cuba a Venezuela?," *El País*, April 19, 2014.

Nation Master, "Economy: GDP Per Capita in 1950; Countries Compared," http://www.nationmaster.com/country-info/stats/Economy/GDP-per-capita-in-1950 (accessed February 2015).

Neuman, William, "Post-election Tensions Escalate in Venezuela as Demonstrations Turn Deadly," *The New York Times*, April 16, 2013.

Neuman, William, and Maria Eugenia, "Court in Venezuela Orders Release of a Judge Once Scorned and Jailed by Chávez," *The New York Times*, June 14, 2013; http://www.nytimes.com/2013/06/15/world/americas/court-in-venezuela-orders-release-of-a-judge-once-scorned-and-jailed-by-chavez.html?_r=0

NTN24, "María Corina Machado asegura haber dado un paso para conseguir la democracia en Vzla," July 2, 2014; http://www.ntn24.com/noticia/maria-corina-machado-asegura-haber-dado-un-paso-para-conseguir-la-democracia-en-vzla-17322

Nolan, Rachel, "The Realest Reality Show in the World," *The New York Times*, May 4, 2012; http://www.nytimes.com/2012/05/06/magazine/hugo-chavezs-totally-bizarre-talk-show.html?pagewanted=all&_r=0

Palmgren, Lars, "Starka känslor i Venezuelas valkampanj," Ekot, Swedish Radio, April 9, 2013; http://sverigesradio.se/sida/artikel.aspx?programid=83&artikel=5498779

Radio Caracas Televisión, RCTV, *¿Quien es quien en el gobierno de Hugo Chávez?*, broadcast November 27, 2012.

Reportero 24, "Sidetur: Impiden protestar a los trabajadores", November 2, 2010,http://www.reportero24.com/2010/11/sidetur-impiden-protestar-a-trabajadores/

Rodríguez, Dulce María, "13,4 millardos de dólares debe el Gobierno a empresas expropiadas," *El Nacional*, January 12, 2013.

Robertson, Ewan, "Venezuela's Snap Presidential Election: A Campaign without Issues?," Venezuela Analysis, April 8, 2013, venezuelaanalysis.com

Rosati, Andrew, "What Was Behind Venezuela's Deadly Oil Refinery Explosion?," *The Christian Science Monitor*, September 16, 2013; http://www.csmonitor.com/World/Americas/2013/0916/What-was-behind-Venezuela-s-deadly-oil-refinery-explosion

Rueda, Manuel, "Chávez Tattoos Express Love for Socialism and Possible Cult of Personality," ABC News, April 12, 2013; http://abcnews.go.com/ABC_Univision/News/chavez-tattoos-express-love-socialism-cult-personality/story?id=18939466

Sky News, "Venezuela Ministry Torched by Protesters," April 2, 2014; https://uk.news.yahoo.com/venezuela-ministry-torched-protesters-094601485.html#GVn5BMs

Sosa, Charlette, "New Venezuelan Report Preaches Sabotage at Amuay Tragedy," Pan Am Post, September 12, 2013, http://panampost.com/charlette-sosa/2013/09/12/new-venezuelan-report-preaches-sabotage-at-amuay-tragedy/

Toro, Francisco, "The A-to-Z of Violating María Corina Machado's Rights," Caracas Chronicles, December 3, 2014; http://caracaschronicles.com/2014/12/03/the-a-z-of-violations-of-maria-corina-machados-rights/

"A Total of 3,040,449 Votes Were Cast in Opposition Primary Election," *El Universal*, February 14, 2012.

Trujillo, Manuel Rubén, "Maduro revela que hay un detenido por ataques a ministerio de Vivienda," *El Universal*, April 3, 2014.

"Venezuela's Militia, A Caribbean Tripoli?," *The Economist*, April 7, 2011.

Voice of America News, "Venezuelan Steel Company Vows to Fight Expropriation," October 31, 2010; http://www.voanews.com/a/venezuelan-steel-company-vows-to-fight-expropriation—106480878/164137.html

Vyas, Kejal, and Ezequiel Minaya, "Venezuela Opposition Lawmaker Returns in Challenge to Government," *Wall Street Journal*, March 26, 2014.

Wallis, Daniel, and Diego Ore, "At Least Two Killed by Gunfire at Venezuela Protests," Reuters, February 12, 2014.

Wilpert, Gregory, "Venezuela's Mission to Fight Poverty," Venezuela Analysis, November 11, 2003, http://venezuelanalysis.com/analysis/213#_ftn7

INDEX